THE VISUAL ARTS TODAY

THE VISUAL

ARTS TODAY

edited by GYORGY KEPES

WESLEYAN UNIVERSITY PRESS

MIDDLETOWN, CONNECTICUT

Permission to reprint the passages noted has been graciously extended by the follow-ing holders of copyright: The National Institute for Architectural Education for the quotations from Richard Lippold, "Three in one," *Balance* (now the *Bulletin*), 1957, *4*: 6-7; to the Royal Institute of British Architects for the quotations from Reg. Butler and Basil Taylor, *R.I.B.A. Journal*, February 1958, *65*: 118-119, 122; to Farrar, Straus and Cudahy, Inc., for the quotations from Le Corbusier and José Luis Sert, *The Heart of the City*, edited by J. Tyrwhitt, J. L. Sert, and E. N. Rogers (New York: Pellegrini and Cudahy, Inc., 1952, CIAM 8), pp. 14, 16, 48, 52; to John Holroyd-Reece for the passage from Julius Meier-Graefe, *Vincent van Gogh: A Biographical Study*, translated by Mr. Holroyd-Reece (London: The Medici So-ciety, Ltd., 1928, first edn. 1922), pp. 25-26; to Wittenborn and Company for the excerpt from Wassily Kandinsky, *Concerning the Spiritual in Art and Painting in Particular* (Documents of Modern Painting, vol. 5, 1912), p. 73; and for that from Piet Mondrian, *Plastic Art and Pure Plastic Art* (1945), p. 15; to Lund, Humphries & Company, Ltd., for the excerpt from Daniel-Henry Kahnweiler, *Juan Gris: His Life and Work*, translated by Douglas Cooper (1947), pp. 138-139, Section 4, "Notes on My Painting"; also to Lund Humphries & Company, Ltd., and to the Harvard University Press for the quotation of Naum Gabo, "Image," from *Naum Gabo: Construction—Sculpture—Paintings—Drawings—Engravings* (1957), pp. 179 ff.; to Harry N. Abrams, Inc., for the passage from Will Grohmann, *Paul Klee* (1954), pp. 365-366; to the Princeton University Press for the passage from José Ortega y Gasset, *The Dehumanization of Art and Other Writings* (Doubleday Anchor Books, Anchor A72, n.d.; first published in *Revista del Occidente*, Madrid, 1925), p. 27; to Le Corbusier for his essay, "Architecture and the Arts," *Le Corbusier: Architect, Painter, Writer* (New York: Macmillan Company, 1958; translated by Maria Jolas; from a discussion at La Maison de la Culture, Paris, 1936; first published in *Transi-tion*, no. 25, Fall 1936), pp. 141-145; to The Bodley Head, Ltd., for the essay by Fernand Léger, "Painting and Reality," in Myfwany Evans, *The Painter's Object* (London: Howe, 1937; first published in *Transition*, no. 25, 1936), pp. 15-20; to the Harvard University Press for the excerpt from Suzanne K. Langer, *Philosophy in a New Key* (1942), pp. 166-169 passim; to Alfred A. Knopf, Inc., for the excerpt from Albert Camus, *The Rebel: An Essay on Man in Revolt* (New York: Vintage Books, 1956), pp. 257-258; to the Art Institute of Chicago for the excerpt from Theodore Roszak, *In Pursuit of an Image* (1955), pp. 6-11; to Giorgio di San Lazzaro, editor of *XXe Siècle*, for the quotations from Joan Miró, Pierre Soulages, and Jean Dubuffet (*XXe Siècle*, Juin 1957, no. 9), pp. 24-25, 35; to Alfred M. Frankfurter, editor of *Art News* for the essays by Marcel Duchamp and Stuart Davis, from *Art News*, Summer 1957, Fifty-Fifth Anniversary Number; to Ben Shahn and the Spiral Press for the quotation from *Paragraphs on Art* (1952), p. 4.

For their kind permission to reprint the illustrations for Dr. Weiss's article, we are indebted to the following: Henry Holt and Company (Fig. 3, from P. Weiss, *Prin-ciples of Development*, 1939); R. Buchsbaum (Figs. 9, 10, and 12, from R. Buchs-baum, *Animals Without Backbones*, University of Chicago Press, 1938); The Open Court Publishing Company (Figs. 6 and 7, from V. Cornish, *Waves of Sand and Snow and the Eddies Which Make Them*, Chicago, 1914); Giuseppe Levi (Fig. 11, from G. Levi, *Trattato di Istologia*, Torino, 1946); Georg Thieme Verlag (Fig. 14, from E. von Herrath and S. Abramow, *Atlas der normalen Histologie und mikro-skopischen Anatomie des Menschen* (Stuttgart, 1950); Hugh Huxley (Fig. 15); *Biological Bulletin* (Fig. 16, from C. E. Hall, M. A. Jakus, F. O. Schmitt, "An In-vestigation of Cross Striations and Myosin Filaments in Muscle," vol. 90, pp. 32-50); General Biological Supply House, Inc., Chicago, Ill. (Fig. 18, from *Turtox News*); Cambridge University Press (Fig. 20, from D'Arcy W. Thompson, *On Growth and Form*, 1942); the Alien Property Office, Washington, D. C. (Figs. 1, 5, 13, and 19); the American Museum of Natural History (Fig. 4). We are indebted to Indiana University Press for permission to reproduce the page from Theodore Bowie, *The Sketchbook of Villard de Honnecourt* (1959), plate 51; and to the Harvard Univer-sity Press for permission to reproduce Le Corbusier's Modulor from his *The Modulor* (1954), p. 65, Fig. 22.

The design on the cover of this volume is by Jean Arp, and is taken from his illustra-tions for Yvan Goll: *Die siebente Rose* (Paris: Poésie & Co., o. J. (1930?); and was reproduced in Carola Giedion-Welcker: *Jean Arp* (New York: Harry N. Abrams, 1957), Bibl. 78.

Contents

Foreword

WHEN TOWARD the end of his life Galileo came to write the last page of his great work on naturally accelerated motion in the *Discourses Concerning Two New Sciences,* it seemed to him that "the door is now opened, for the first time, to a new method fraught with numerous and wonderful results which, in future years, will command the attention of other minds." As he foresaw, his discoveries were to lead to "many another more remarkable result": the law of free fall carried within it the presage of a Descartes and a Newton. Not only can a scientific discovery summarize the past and illuminate the present states of a field, it can also prophesy—sometimes vaguely, sometimes distinctly—what may await beyond the opened door.

Such a threefold content also resides in the various productions of the arts today: they help define the features of our times, they carry indications of our past, and also of our future. The writers of original articles for this symposium have been empowered to move along any of these three coordinates. Some view the productions of the arts in their documentary aspect, connected with other activities on the map of the present by aesthetic or psychological or sociological lines. Some look back to the origins of our arts. Others read the anticipations to be discerned in the work of sensitive artists, just as the precursors of coming waves can be read from the delicate recordings of a seismograph.

Contemporary art has numerous aspects that reward scrutiny. The compilation in this book has a structure reflecting the varied interests of our authors. After the Introduction by Gyorgy Kepes, there appears a group of seven articles dealing with the background of the visual arts today: their social setting, their historical continuity, their psychological roots, and their physical setting. Then follows a group of selected statements concerned with motivations, goals, and methods by more than a score of artists; these are often drawn from existing sources, but in several cases have been specifically written for this issue. The same section provides a set of visual documents, chiefly from paintings and sculptures by the artists cited. The newer media of the arts are discussed in the next six essays; these are concerned with the moving image and art in advertisement. Then four contributors write on the relations between science and art, while the last group of four deal with the interpretation of artistic values.

GERALD HOLTON

THE VISUAL ARTS TODAY

GYORGY KEPES

Introduction

HERE many minds representing many disciplines are brought to bear on our visual culture. Our justification for an examination of the visual arts of today lies in the key role of vision in our effort to come to terms with our environment.

Vision is above all a cognitive act. The focusing of the welter of optical signals coming from outside to make perceptual images is a basic form of comprehending. We use vision to explore the world, to make ourselves at home in it, and to change it. Even without instruments to aid us, our eyes can establish relations with things as far away as the fixed stars. In our closer environment we depend upon vision to measure and locate things, to identify danger or opportunity.

No less important than the outer vision with which we explore our environment is the inner vision we use to explore ourselves and to find significance and meaning. Our inner world is peopled with sense images—visual, auditory, kinesthetic, tactual —formed from the traces in our systems left by our sensory traffic with the environment. These images inside our heads we use to focus experience, code our sensations, crystallize feelings, build our dreams, and set our goals. Without these images our experience would not cohere and our memories would be disconnected and meaningless.

The created visual image, the visible forms we make with our hands and eyes together, link the outer vision that explores the external world with the inner vision that shapes our felt experience into symbols. These created pictures—graphic images, sculptured forms—are basic to communication, expanding an individual experience into one that is shared. They provide a foundation for the arts and sciences and make social and intellectual growth possible.

The artistic image—the work of visual art—is the created image in its highest form, a significant message delivered simultaneously to our senses, our feelings, and our minds. At every stage of history men have looked for images that would keep them oriented in the world, that would tell them what the world was like, how sweet and rich it was, how good or bad,

3

and what was their own place in it. Artistic images have served to bring their outer and inner worlds into correspondence, providing them with means for inducing inner pictures of the outer environment—pictures shaped with sympathy, with the joys and sorrows, fears and hopes in the heart of man. And above all the work of art has sustained man with visions of a felt order. It has returned understanding to the indispensable eye, the foundation of our thought and feeling, the core of experience.

The common denominator of artistic expression has been the ordering of a vision into a consistent, complete form. The difference between a mere expression, however intense and revealing, and an artistic image of that expression lies in the structure of the form. This structure is specific. The colors, lines, and shapes corresponding to our sense impressions are organized into a balance, a harmony or rhythm that is in an analogous correspondence with feelings, and these in turn are analogues of thoughts and ideas. An artistic image, therefore, is more than a pleasant tickle of the senses and more than a graph of emotions. It has meaning in depth, and at each level there is a corresponding level of human response to the world. In this way, an artistic form is a symbolic form grasped directly by the senses but reaching beyond them and connecting all the strata of our inner world of sense, feeling, and thought. The intensity of the sensory pattern strengthens the emotional and intellectual pattern; conversely, our intellect illuminates such a sensory pattern, investing it with symbolic power. This essential unity of primary sense experience and intellectual evaluation makes the artistic form unique in human experience and therefore in human culture. Our closest human experience is love, where again sensation, feeling, and idea compose a living unity.

The essential unity of first-hand percept and intellectual concept makes artistic images different from scientific cognition or simple animal response to situations. To repeat, it is the unity of the sensory, emotional, and rational that can make the orderly forms of artistic images unique contributions to human culture. The meaning of the artistic experience is impoverished if any one of these areas of experience takes undue preponderance.

Images deriving solely from a rational assessment of the external world, without passion of the eyes, are only topographical records. Images of emotional responses without real roots in the environment are isolated graphs of a person's inner workings: they do not yield symbolic form. And the most beautiful combinations of color and shape, the most exquisitely measured proportions of line, area, and volume, leave us where they find us if they have not grown out of rational and emotional participation in the total environment. Each of these visions is a fragment only.

The visual images of the twentieth century provide a broad spectrum of fragmented artistic vision.

If I may be allowed to speak in a subjective vein, I now see my own evolution as a painter as a succession of partial insights. As a young painter, I was interested in nothing but an exploration of the sensory variety and riches of the visible world, its wealth of color, texture, and light. Soon, however, I had to face my own feelings and emotions. I took to the expressive reporting of my emotional ups and downs, and made explosive gestures in which the image lost all coherence. In consequence, the need of bringing my feelings and responses into order impressed me, and my conscious goals became discipline and precision. I received immense satisfaction from the very notion of building forms that could live independently because of their inner consistency, their spatial clarity, and balance of color. I felt like a creator—shaping, ordering, making forms that came alive.

My next stand was brought about by environmental change: the world came to exhibit primary attributes of mass poverty, depression, and social unrest. I lost confidence in the validity of creating such forms in isolation from the main stream of events, and in my subsequent phase I interested myself in the impact of man-made images on people, in a visual communication of ideas to make life better. Such a communication had to be on a broad basis, I felt, it had to become mass communication. Painting now seemed an anemic medium, and in my search for idioms with breadth and power I turned toward film as the most advanced, dynamic, and accordingly potent social form of visual communication.

But again, the enormous expansion of human conflict in World War II and its consequences made so many ideas seem shallow that I was impelled, like many others, to search for values rather than tools. The social horizon, with its immense and seemingly insoluble problems, did not seem to contain the key to those values. The scientific revolution, with its menaces, benefactions, and promises, did seem to open an emotional window. Basically, I felt, the world made newly visible by science contained the essential symbols for our reconstruction of physical surroundings and for the restructuring of the world of sense, feeling, and thought within us. I was drawn to the converging contributions made by art and science, and to the distillation of the images common to our expanding inner and outer worlds.

I now recognize that the metamorphoses in my approaches to art are a history of changing assumptions. Whatever concealed motivation patterned the road of change, new artistic goals arrived without conscious and systematic decision. These

5

goals arose through my own encounter with concrete realities. Each convincing new image became a kind of deduction from a set of postulates of knowledge and value. Like these artistic images, all purposive human acts are based on such sets of postulates. What we see or feel, how we think or act, depends upon the basic assumptions we hold, sometimes unconsciously. The world is real to us only on the scale of our inner model of space, purpose, and values. To see more than this we have to exchange elementary for advanced assumptions—as we all do, inescapably, in the course of growing up.

Artists, too, see what they see by means of assumptions. Their vision, if it is sensitive and true, becomes ours also: they teach us how to see and how to enjoy. We rely upon them to help us make our perceptual grasp of the world functional, meaningful, satisfying, and communicable—even though there is often a considerable time lag between the artist's grasp and ours, for the artist's high degree of sensitivity tends to make him something of a prophet. We sometimes gain insight into our own attitudes more quickly by questioning art than by questioning ourselves. The attitudes are common—and, in the images of art, highly concentrated. Further insight is furnished by testing the postulates of artists against the conclusions of science, first with respect to the energies and processes of the physical world, second with respect to the energies and processes of the individual and society.

An essential theme of this issue is the contemporary relation between the visual arts on the one hand and science on the other. Because our modern specialization so often separates artist and scientist, neither has been always fully aware of the profundity of the other's work. Scientists and artists both reach beneath surface phenomena to discover basic natural pattern and basic natural process. Yet there is a tendency for the scientist to expect the artist to interpret literally, like some unthinking sensitive device, and for the artist to expect the scientist to think coldly and mechanically, like some unfeeling technical appliance. To a reader with an essentially scientific bent it should be insisted that the creation of a visual image in the arts is not the instinctive act of certain individuals but rather a fusion of their deepest inner workings with the messages of society, including information from the realm of knowledge and rational thought. Like the scientist, the artist uses the learning of his times in a basic way. And, again like the scientist, the artist profoundly affects our world outlook.

A fundamental transformation of our world outlook is indubitably taking place on every possible level of thinking and feeling. Less indubitably, perhaps, but demonstrably, the insight brought us by art is a partner to scientific understanding in this process of transformation. The bold generalizations of scientists, bringing formerly unconnected phenomena into larger, more general schemes impressive in their cohesion, are redefining the expanding world and keeping it accessible to our intellects. Among the echoes and parallels in other human endeavors are the brave efforts of many artists of this century to find an emotional footing upon this bewildering new world.

Science, in a sense, has been the angel with a sword, evicting us from the smaller, friendlier world in which we once moved with a confidence born of familiarity, and plunging us into a bigger, alien world where our unaccustomed sensibilities are forced to cope with a formidable new scale of events.

The responsibility is being laid on us of coming to emotional terms with the new horizons, under pain of the blackest self-punishment. Our age, no less than any other, needs to find a consistent orientation, to harmonize its inner and outer vistas. But we are trapped by a crisis of scale.

Most of our ideas and images grow out of and belong to a small scale of existence; we try to apply them to a scale that is far too big for them. We seem unable even to keep pace with events. It is as though our human capacities grew by linear increments, and the problems resulting from our activities grew by exponential increments. The limited range of signals to which our naked animal bodies are sensitive has hardly changed in the last twenty-five or thirty thousand years, but our new image of nature now harbors strange forms, such as nuclear particles and radiation, none visible to the naked eye, none relatable to our own bodies. This new nature is alien to our senses—and it is not only nature that is alien. The man-made world, after five centuries of accelerating scientific discovery and technical development, has expanded so explosively in so many directions that we seem unable to grasp its dimensions or assert authority over its dynamics. The wild growth of our cities—in physical mass, in population, in complexity of human relationships—makes them seem endowed with an independent life beyond human control. We have disrupted the atom and speared the moon, but, as we all know, there is as much apprehension over the unknown, unpredictable consequences that are released as there is joy in new vistas of what life can be.

We try to cope with the exploded scale of things without the standards that would help us to evaluate them. For this we need more than a rational grasp of nature. The extended world revealed by science and the technical world of man's own making both require mapping by our senses, the disposition of our activities and movements in conformity with their rhythms, the discovery of their potentialities for a richer, more orderly, more human life. The sensed, the emotional, are of

7

vital importance in transforming our world of chaos into order. The new setting, both natural and man-made, has its own dimensions of light, color, space, form, texture, rhythm—a wealth of qualities to be apprehended and experienced. A grasp of the new conditions, on the sensed and the emotional levels, may yield forms and images that provide a vision of contemporary reality.

In the crisis of scale presented by the complex condition in which we now live, we face two different but related obstacles to meeting its challenges. One is the corruption of our visual surroundings by cultural forces divorced from art; the dirt and clutter of the uncontrolled and ugly man-made environment infect us and numb our capacity to see. The other is the discouragement of our creative artists in the face of a surrounding chaos and a new scientific prospect, both seemingly too vast for them to comprehend.

Industrial civilization has propagated conditions that poison not only the body but also the spirit of man. We are justifiably alarmed about the dangers of radiation fallout. But the smoke, the dirt, the meagerness of the space in which men are forced to live, the lack of color and light, the corrosion of the best qualities of man's creative work—these are a fallout at least as dangerous. We speak today of safety levels, and watch out for the number of milliroentgens in our surroundings, but neither now nor in the past have we accorded recognition to the importance of the safety levels of our daily lives. We worry very little about mitigating the boredom of repetitive work—a killer of the spirit. We make no move toward arresting the waste of creative energies devoted to inane gestures or toward restoring the fading courage of man amid his progressive isolation. For the tragedy of democracy is the chaos of communication: the three-hundred-ring commercial circus of advertising, public relations, slick magazines, and fatuous entertainment. To most people ideas and values are imparted by middlemen whose objectives are crassly narrow and nonsocial.

Our sensibilities have been so starved as to have become in general untrustworthy. Some of the discourse in these pages would have been obviated if the contemporary scene were not so vast, noisy, confused, and contradictory, and also if its values were accessible, if we could all cope with its tangle of communications, uncompromised by exposure to the sights and sounds of a crudely commercial civilization. But we are compelled to use the aids of sociological and psychological interpretation as correctives to our vision in order to grasp the real value of man-created visual images. We need, therefore, more than the artist's capacity to respond strongly to aesthetic facts: we also need clear, comprehensive thinking.

As many have remarked, men who have acute sensibility and can also exert disciplined rational thinking are rare. Artists are deeply committed to their eyes, they can bring their passionate vision to the most intense focus; but as a rule they lack impeccable logic and manipulative skill in verbal communication. In addition, they are understandably reluctant to translate from their own concrete, sense-bound language into an alien and unaccommodating language of pale, abstract, verbal signs—this is not the area of their competence. The other side of the situation is the cheerful willingness of persons to compensate for their undeveloped sensibilities by making public statements about art, building elaborate speculative structures from limited or secondhand data. Such speculations, unless combined with a direct experience of the unique meanings of visual forms, are unlikely to contribute to genuine understanding. The eye has no surrogate, and the sensibility of artists' eyes is an absolute requirement for reading the potentialities for human life inherent in the new scale of events.

The task of adjustment is only part of our traffic with the expanded environment—we also need to reach out for its gifts of new insights and values. Artists have responded variously to our crisis of scale. Some have moved toward accepting its challenges, and have turned their eyes and minds outward upon the expanded world and its new promise. Others have been overwhelmed, and have turned inward upon themselves, contracting their world and widening the gap between outer and inner perspective.

Some major artists of the preceding generation—Juan Gris, Piet Mondrian, Fernand Léger, and the architects who shared their new kind of vision—opened their eyes to the wealth of the industrial civilization and tried to bridge the gap between a rational and an emotional understanding of it. They accepted science and technology as a value, and welcomed the visual forms generated by the new conditions of modern life. Artistic goals were also tools for a proposed social transformation; in a period of social upheavals and revolutions, of disillusionment and pessimism, they had an absolute faith in the future, they created an aesthetic of dynamic space and precise, clear, machine-inspired forms, and in their working theories they employed such key words as "honest," "functional," "economical," and "architectonic." They developed a deep sense of interdependence, between man and environment and between man and man, as embodied in the painting of pictures or the shaping of buildings.

We see now that these men were overoptimistic and overconfident: the problem was bigger than they knew. Creative artistic use and interpretation of the values latent in our technical

9

civilization required a profound confluence of art and science —sensibility and knowledge—a stage difficult to envisage, let alone assume. A completely successful solution of artistic problems could not develop while human minds were splintered, while men lived in a world divided—socially, politically, personally. Although the architectonic vision was one of the stirring achievements of our century, it lacked the breadth to comprehend both our outer and inner worlds.

The modern failure to achieve common boundaries is symbolized in some of the authentic documents of the recoiling mid-century mind, especially in the manner these are presented to our view. A beautiful crystalline structure in America's greatest city (itself a symbol of the finest thinking in contemporary architecture and at the same time, like the *torre* of medieval Tuscany, a boastful symbol of wealth and power) displays, in surroundings that state an absolute control of contemporary materials and techniques and a perfect mastery of the new beauty of architectural space, images of the torn and broken man. In its offices and corridors are paintings and sculptures shaped with idioms in tune with the twilight spirit that created them: surfaces that are moldy, broken, corroded, ragged, dripping; brush strokes executed with the sloppy brutality of cornered men.

To the men of today's generation, the key words of yesterday have too bold and confident a ring. Some of these men retire to the caves and jungles of the unconscious and explore contracting spirals diminishing toward oblivion. Others go slumming in inner areas of corrosion, burning, and tearing—displaced persons who tour the inner ruins much as, in the last century, the Romantics toured the ruins of the outside world. Still others mark time, finding a way of staying in the same place but keeping their sojourn interesting: these immerse themselves in gadgetry, playing inside elaborate boxes of colors, lines, and spatial layers, obsessed with the precision of relationships and the refinement of space effects, narrowing more and more the visions they had two decades ago. Rather than accept the creative challenges within the range of the visual arts, rather than learn to see a broader world, most of us, our artists included, divorce ourselves from common obligations, turn our backs on the rational, and separate man from himself, from his fellow men, and from his environment.

The artistic expression preferred at this point in time is fluid, amorphous, and undefined. Although the best among contemporary artists have created images of a shining inner structure in spite of all programs, there is spreading in this sophisticated world a new type of artistic image that has made a central principle of the unformed, the irrational, and the uncontrolled.

10

The created image is constricted in space and meaning, and is reduced to the elementary experience of the kinesthetic pleasure of the act of painting. Some painters limit their horizon to the space within physical reach: others require a direct sense of physical contact with their space-creating image. Jackson Pollock, whose work has had a major impact on the present generation, once commented, "My painting does not come from the easel. I hardly ever stretch my canvas before painting. I prefer to tack the unstretched canvas to the hard wall or the floor. I feel nearer, more a part of the painting, since this way I can walk around it, work from four sides, and literally be in the painting." The bright-colored *hortus occlusus* of the medieval painter finds its faded twentieth-century projection in this picturing of a nest, with the creative act weaving a blanket against the chilling wind of memories.

Another painter, Willem De Kooning, has written:

> The space of science—the space of the physicist—I am truly bored with by now. Their lenses are so thick that, seeing through them, the space gets more and more melancholy. All that it contains is billions and billions of hunks of matter, hot or cold, floating around in darkness echoing the great scheme of aimlessness.
> The stars I think about, if I could fly I could reach in a few old-fashioned days. But physicists' stars are used as buttons, buttoning up curtains of emptiness. If I stretch my arms next to the rest of myself and wonder where my fingers are—that is all the space I need as a painter.

Here the total world, the common world that unites the thinking mind, the motivating heart, and the acting body, is denied a unity, for such a unity seems beyond hope. It takes a special courage today to face the heavy odds of a blighted landscape; the vulgar faces of cities; the hard, mechanical rhythm of the industrial scene, so out of time with our heartbeats, our desires, our hopes; and the fantastic expanse of cosmological pattern, from ultramicroscopic to superastronomical, unrolling from the looms of science. It takes still more courage to take this whole as a whole.

Before now in history, men have risen to the creative challenge of altering human consciousness in order to orient themselves on a higher level. Through such modifications of consciousness we have become manifestly distinguishable from the biologically identical men of the Ice Age. Artistic sensibility has had its role in this process, in teaching all of us to see and in developing models and symbols from which concepts have been built.

There can be little doubt that this is an age of extraordinary vitality and promise. It calls upon artists for more than strong protest: its enormous potential for undreamed-of harmonies and

11

rhythms demands new levels of sensibility, a new capacity for unification, a new creativity. Our buildings of glass and steel rival nature's structures in their size and strength; the lights of our cities recall the glories of medieval stained-glass cathedral windows in their richness and purity; small electronic tubes rival the flowers in their delicacy and order. There are new values: the speed and precision of machines; the energy of a dynamic society; the new ranges of space opened by science and technique. There are a host of exciting new images arising in a hundred different fields of science. The new scale is not a disaster.

Machine rhythms can be tamed, they can become the rhythms of human needs. Blight in the man-made environment can be repaired, and with it the corrupting damage inflicted upon twentieth-century men. Artists can explore the new science-born horizons, make them accessible to our common perception, and develop consistent, orderly images and symbols. The public can be brought to an appreciative understanding of the minds and feelings of creative people.

Our scientific perspective, our cultural legacy, and our art too, can help bring our sensations, feelings, attitudes, and thoughts into harmonious correspondence with the broad movements of nature and society. But our transformation of ourselves and our surroundings must proceed from a knowledge that we can meet new circumstances and grow with them.

We can move once more with confidence through the world, provided we unify our experience of eye and mind. Symmetry, balance, rhythmic sequence express essential characteristics of natural phenomena: the connectedness of nature—the order, the logic, the living process. Here science and art can meet on common ground. The challenge of scale can be met only if we broaden the base from which we view and live the world. We must use our faculties to the full—with the scientist's brain, the poet's heart, the painter's eye. Through our scientific knowledge we are aware of the biological and psychological requirements of men, and so can begin the restructuring of the man-made world and restore the balance between men and their surroundings. The symbols of order needed for this major task may be drawn from the poetry of image awaiting the explorer of new horizons.

MARGARET MEAD

Work, Leisure, and Creativity

ONE OF THE CONTEXTS within which the word creativity is invoked is in answer to the question: "What are people going to do with their leisure? Can we make them more creative?" I should like first to question the usefulness of the simple dichotomy of work and leisure, with work being those things which man has to do to earn his daily bread, and leisure everything he does with the time that is left over. For if we follow this way of looking at life, peculiar to our own narrow tradition, we are then faced with placing such activities as the worship of the gods, or the performance of a tragedy, in either one category or the other. Some peoples have solved this by vocabulary. For the Balinese life consists of work—for which a harsh short word is used when it is done by low-caste people in everyday life, and an elegant word when the activity is performed by high-caste people or for the gods. The word for feast then becomes a noun from this verb which describes activity by or for those to whom one looks up. An echo of this kind of classification can be found in the English word amateur, with its implication that activities which can be performed freely by those whose livelihood comes from some other source, are lowered and tainted if done for gain.

So, we may start with the freedom to pray or carve, act or paint or sing, and end with its degradation or, as the Balinese do, emphasize not whether an activity is for pay or not, but rather who engages in it and under what circumstances. Appropriately enough there are no amateurs in Bali; there are young girls who do not dance very well, but those who dance badly are as seriously committed to the requirements of style as those who dance well; they are simply less gifted, less practiced, or less well taught. When a temple club or a raja pays for the dancing of those who dance well—while the dancing of the less gifted is simply a part of temple ritual—the payment goes not to the individual but to the group, for new musical instruments, or new costumes. The club group with a good set of dancers practices harder, gets better teachers, is in demand for more performances, and always runs the danger of suffering from popularity which will make the dancers, so continuously in demand, become conceited, stop practicing, and sink back again into anonymity. Teachers must be paid, club members who give many days to traveling performances will receive expenses, performances will be offered to the gods in the temple to which they belong. But the expert individual members do not draw their livelihood from these activities. The lines are drawn in many places, always with precision down to the last little bronze penny.

People labor, as they must, for their livelihood, for special purposes beyond a livelihood, in response to the demands of the community—as corporation and as temple—and as members of groups devoted to the arts or sometimes as individuals, grown so skilled that a dancing teacher, a musician, a carver of masks, will be frequently called away from his rice fields. But the system provides for just such freedom of movement. There are rice-harvesting clubs that may be called in to help with the harvest; there are rice-harvesting clubs that one may join if one is short of cash; exemption from work for the village or the temple may always be bought for a small "fine"; when a hundred men have been called together to chop up one pig, ten will not be missed, and the fines they pay will be useful. Sometimes when a man has a special skill, like the ability to scrape the great bronze gongs to tune them, the village may exempt him from ordinary work on the roads, and citizens of a high caste may be asked only to perform activities which are skilled, or be permitted to make contributions in kind.

Visitors to Bali, anxious to explain the interpenetration of art and life, have ventured many explanations, only to find that one simple contrast between Bali and the West is not enough, and leads instead to spurious statements about the evils of the modern world, with our slavery to clocks.

For on another South Sea island, Manus, I found in 1928 a people without clocks, without a calendar, with only the simple rhythm of a three-day market and the monthly rush of the fish over the reef, who nevertheless drove themselves from one unrecognized and unremarked year to the next, seeing feasts as harder work than days which had no feasting. To them the white man's periodicity of hours to start work and hours to stop came as a blessed relief and the Christian Sabbath as a day of undreamed-of rest. They spoke with enthusiasm of the bells which punctuated the hard labor on European-owned plantations: "When the bell sounds at noon you can stop, and you don't have to work again until the bell sounds to return to work."

The Manus live in a tropical environment, where no seasonal snows fall, but the version they have constructed of man's

14

place in nature is both puritanical and driven—and strangely like our own.

In almost comic caricature, the Manus bought and sold the artistic productions of neighboring tribes, but they made nothing beautiful themselves. Where in Bali a prince may be the best actor or finest carver of them all, and his wife excel in weaving, in Manus the richest and the poorest members of this near egalitarian society might buy and sell, but did not practice the arts for themselves.

Each well-described culture provides evidence of the many ways in which activity can be categorized: as virtuous work and sinful play, as dull work when done alone and happy gaiety when the same activity (fishing or hunting or housebuilding) is done in a group, as work when for oneself, and delight when for the gods, or as, at most, pleasant and self-propelled when done for oneself but horrid when done at the behest of the state. There are as many kinds of classification as there have been civilizations, each having its significance for the place of the arts in the life of any particular human group.

Any attempt to order these classifications must always be limited also by the perspective of the moment, by the categories within which one must address oneself to the relevant audience. One significant variable is a sense of freedom: what one does of his own free will must be separated from anything done under coercion, by the need to eat, or survive, or by the will of others. So hunting for food would be work, and hunting for the joy of the hunt would be leisure. Planting a garden for food would be work, but done for the pleasure of boasting about the size of one's cabbages, it becomes leisure activity.

The attempt to classify activities in terms of their intrinsic "creativity," so often resorted to by those who, in search of a world more hospitable to the arts, castigate the lack of creativity in modern work, brings us out little better. If we take the set of criteria so often used, work to be creative must make something new and something made must not be made too often, or the words "repetitious" and "uncreative" will be introduced. Cooking the daily midday meal is repetitious, but preparing special foods for a feast is creative. This distinction is pleasantly blurred in the house of the rich gourmet; the food that is feast food for the common man becomes daily food for him. His cook then becomes a chef and an artist. The distance from cottage to castle has turned labor into an art.

Still the idea of something made new, and rarely, recurs throughout all the confusing dichotomies and continua of many civilizations. Among one people the slight decoration of every doorway may be a craft, widely practiced, possibly lucra-

15

tive, slightly honored. But in the next tribe there may be only one man who has the skill and the will to paint a single bark panel with his version of the house decorations of his neighbors. He is not a craftsman; he practices no art grown simple and habitual by long usage; he is instead an artist, occasionally and painfully producing something new—new to him, and new to his fellow tribesmen who cluster around him. Or it is possible to introduce the same slight sense of distance and newness by a device such as that used by the Mundugumor of New Guinea, who had decreed that only a male child born with the umbilical cord around his neck might be an artist. As the tribe was small, and there was no provision that each male child so born be trained as an artist, in the end there would be only one or two men in a generation with the cultural right to paint a design on bark, which might have been a common craft, practiced often and unrewarded, among a neighboring tribe.

The gardener in England lives upon newness and difference. One flower or a border blooms earlier or later, and another is not there at all. The light catches on a new clump of larkspur, and the garden is new made. And in New Guinea the dusty old woven basketry masks are hauled out of the attic of the men's house, and made new again with fresh feathers and bright flowers arranged in new combinations, with small, graceful, painted birds made of a cork-like wood and poised lightly on swaying reed stems. Even among the puritanical Manus, where feast clothes were mourning clothes, all validated by hard earned money, and ornaments were made from the hair and bones of the dead, there was a sense of freshness in the air when they were worn. Skins usually dull from work and only dutiful ablutions shone a little to match the woven armlets that held pieces of the rib bones of the dead.

I should like to propose that we look at this element of freshness, of newness, of strangeness, as a thread along which to place the activities of the consciously creative artist, the conscious patron and critic of the creative artist, and the common man—common in the sense that he has no specified part in creation or criticism. If we make one criterion for defining the artist (as distinct from the craftsman and the trained but routine performer of dance, drama, or music) the impulse to make something new, or to do something in a new way—a kind of divine discontent with all that has gone before, however good—then we can find such artists at every level of human culture, even when performing acts of great simplicity. The conclusion has sometimes been drawn that in some societies, for example the Bush Negroes of Dutch Guiana, "every man is an artist," or, as in Bali, that "every man is a musician." Where any art has reached the state in which it is required behavior for some category of human beings (if all women must make offerings, all young men carve if they are to be eligible for marriage, or all men play some instrument in a temple or village orchestra) then the making of offerings, the carving of wooden wands, or the playing of musical instruments ceases to be a field for the artist in the simple way it was before. Those who deserve the name of artist will move on to the invention of new offerings (while their sisters make old ones) or the development of new designs or new ways for a whole orchestra (in which each musician is a faithful practitioner but not a composer) to play the old pieces.

The difference in quality between the single bark painting made by an artist in a tribe in which no one else paints on bark, painted with tenseness and desperate eagerness, and the beautifully executed traditional design of the craftsmanship of many men in the next tribe, will not give us the clue as to which tribe depends on craftsmen and which on the occasional artist to produce a painting on bark. If we have only one of each, the chastening hand of tradition may well resemble the individually disciplined vision of the single artist; the traditional will often appear to our eye—to which each is fresh—as more of an individual vision, as we are unable to distinguish between freshness to us and freshness to the man who made it. We have here two situations, one that of the difference between the painter who makes something new and the painter who executes the old with faithful skill, the other that of the spectator who, without a large set of paintings to guide him, cannot tell the single object made with great creative energy from the repetition of some object in a style grown beautiful by the contribution of many painters and many critics. We can add a third. Granted that an object has been the outcome of a single artist's or a group of artists' desire to make something new and fresh, it will then matter enormously what happens to the object.

It may be quickly destroyed, having been a stage set for a single production of a play, or a design for a triumphal or centenary ceremony to be held only once. In this case, part of the freshness will come from everyone's knowledge of the brief life that the arch of flowers, the floats of paper, the giants of confectionery, the cunningly contrived stage sets, are to have. Tomorrow or the next day, all this will be dismantled, faded, or even eaten up. Only those who are there that day will ever see it; it will linger on only in the delighted memories of those who made it—to underlie later new creations or new applications by those who saw and enjoyed it once before.

Or it may be set permanently in a special place, behind a high altar, in a palace hall, in a public building, or in one of the

17

many rooms of a private house of the very rich. Here the sense of freshness of the masterpiece is maintained by the difference between those who live near it and those who have seen it only once at some great ceremony or when they journeyed from a great distance on a pilgrimage, for a coronation, or to see a capital city, or attend the university graduation of a son. For most people, such a painting or statue will be seen only once or twice in a lifetime; those who live close to it—the rich private owner, those who attend Mass each Sunday beneath the startlingly lovely altar piece, those who work in the old Guild Hall with its murals—live and feed on the freshness which is contributed by the new visitors. The rich man takes his guests through the gallery, the resident takes a visitor to the picture gallery, or to see the village church where the vicar recounts for the thousandth time the story of an especially beautiful window. So for those who live close to a masterpiece there may be either a protective caution which blocks off a too continuous dwelling on its beauty or the reinforcement of its newness to others, so that they live a happily parasitical life on the delight of those who see it for the first time.

For several decades at the end of the last century and the beginning of this, we added a new and temporary dimension of freshness, that of partial and bad reproduction, by photography. This replaced the earlier ambiguities of copies which ranged all the way from the same picture painted by the same great master, in which all that was different was the church in which it hung or the name of the patron who ordered it, to the humble little lady traveler who painted all day in the Louvre to capture one painting, in part, and take it home as partly her own, now, for her brush had worked at it. The black-and-white reproductions of the late nineteenth century played a similar role; here the traveler sought to capture and keep for himself and those who had stayed behind a reminder of original freshness and delight. The reproduction was often no more than a hook on which to hang exclamations and judgments exchanged between men who had seen Athens and those who had not; but on the walls of those who had never been there it became a kind of promissory note of the future: "Someday, when I am grown, I will see the Colosseum, climb the hill to the Parthenon, really see the Night Watch, learn how Raphael painted." These early reproductions were not good enough to detract from the memory of the original or the promise that it might one day be seen. Faulty and incomplete and unpretentious, except when used only to prove one had traveled or had taste, they were pleasant to have on the walls, and could well compete for delight with the kind of "original" one could afford—in most cases the holiday effort of a relative who was a poor amateur painter.

18

The relationship of the arts to leisure in American nineteenth-century society was therefore quite simple; those who had leisure traveled to the places where art was to be found, those who had money sometimes bought it and brought it back, and they, or some of those who visited the museums to which it eventually found its way, learned to enjoy it. Those who had not traveled, and probably would not travel, were taken to museums as children, or shown slides, and were exposed to very tentative promissory notes in the form of black-and-white reproductions on the walls of schools. Coming from homes in which there was no temporary artistic effort to be constructed and destroyed, and no craftsmanship out of which necessary skill could be distilled, the relationship between the common man and the visual arts was almost completely destroyed. Children might be taken in groups to the Altman collection in the Metropolitan Museum, and of these some would see other work by the same painters some day, others would treat this as an experience without any meaning for themselves, and once in a while some child might make the extraordinary leap of believing that he or she might someday *paint*. To paint meant, very simply, to go away from everyone to some faraway place where paintings were made, where there were people who painted. Out of generations of this well-documented nostalgia of the man who would paint, in a civilization that made nothing of the visual arts, or failed, as England did, to recognize that gardening, which trained the eye to loveliness and the mind to criticism of form and color, was an art, have come the extremes of the present day, accentuated by our contemporary processes of exact reproduction both of lovely craftsmanship and of the isolated vision of the artist in many other lands and periods.

For almost overnight (for Americans) it has become possible to acquire reproductions, not only of the pottery and fabrics of other peoples, in which the cunning of the machine can repeat over and over what the hand once had to learn, but also of individual works, which once drew their beauty from their singleness. Van Gogh's Sunflowers blaze on a thousand walls, day after day, collecting not even a faint film of dust beneath their protective glass. From the spectator of such reproductions nothing is required. He neither fetches the paint nor carries the stones nor holds the scaffold on which the painter stands. He need make no pilgrimage, even on the subway, to see a painting. Nor is it any longer a matter of individual choice of the too brilliant reproduction which one purchases for one's own wall and becomes strangely tired of and yet lets it hang. For there are all the other walls, in the dentist's office and in the homes of all one's friends, and the bank poster on the bus.

19

What was once sought diligently and seen seldom is now staled by continuous unsought experience.

It is said that the public has never been so "interested in art." This is only too true, and yet is this interest, expressed in the reproduction of objects never meant for reproduction and totally unrelated to their owners, a way of closing the gap between artist and critic and the common man, or of widening it? The most casual visit to our campuses where "modern art" is produced by the yard would suggest that the gap is really widening while it might seem superficially to be closing.

Is it possible that what has gone wrong is just here, in the control of freshness? It is undoubtedly a good thing that many people, as children, as young adults, and as elderly people with new leisure, should be given a chance to "create," to stand before an easel and wrestle with an attempt to make the world anew. But what is happening today is that in these thousands of studio situations the painter does no such wrestling; it is not individual vision but the ability to replicate a strange commodity—individuality—which is being practiced. Like the Christmas cards of the intelligentsia, each painting must be different—a photograph of our dog instead of your dog, our children instead of your children. A slight difference, within an agreed-upon range, has been substituted for newness.

Second, the very quantity defeats us. If thousands of people are to produce in a form once sufficiently rare so that some church walls remained bare for lack of a painter and only the state rooms of the palace had murals, the sense of coming glut oppresses our spirits as we listen to the enthusiasm with which still another friend takes up painting or sculpture. There is no place to put the million individual works of those who are trying to participate in an activity where once only the rarely gifted worked.

When every man practices an art, it becomes a craft, and for crafts there is a place, either in space or in time: in space, a bed for the embroidered bedspread, coffee to be drunk from the painted cups, and soup to be sipped from the hammered spoons; in time, a delight to match the temporary structure of snow or flowers, the delicately executed Christmas card that is cheap enough to throw away at Twelfth Night. In such exercises, the common man, who may of course be a physicist or the governor of a state in his own professional personality, may experience for an hour or a day an appropriate nuance of the creativity of the artist, making something new—at the moment of making— either for later quiet, undemanding use, or for quick destruction.

But because of the plethora of reproduction, the distinction between the rare vision which must remain rare—to someone— and delight in producing form and color has been obscured.

20

It is revealing to look at the present recourse of those whose delight contains an extra component of the esoteric. On their walls are large black and white reproductions of blown-up cameos, once so small it took a microscope to appreciate them, or telephoto photographs of some detail high up on an Indian temple wall, unseen since some loving hand carved it ten centuries ago. Deprived of the individual experience of seeing a great painting for the first time, they will at least see something that no one, even the man who made it, ever saw in this way before. With the marvels of modern photography—the photographer perched at some unlikely angle where no man ever stood before to catch the sunlight on the Parthenon—the spectator participant tries to reestablish the freshness of the experience, in ways even stranger than those once used by the kind of miser prince who kept a masterpiece behind a curtain for his own eyes alone.

But this is a mere temporary expedient, for the hundred people who come to the cocktail party to appreciate the freshness of this photographic abolition of distance and scale may all go home, buy a copy of the same miracle, and put it on their walls.

Is not perhaps a different answer to be found than this abuse of freshness which is seen on every side? Is not part of the solution to be found in shifting the freshness from the singleness of the work of art, now effectively nullified by cheap and perfect reproduction, to the considered choice of the spectator? For those who wish to use part of their leisure, part of the time when they are freed from making a living, to become actively a part of the world of the visual arts, there should be a far wider temporary field—walls to be painted anew every week, stage sets for every occasion—as the Balinese work for days on beautiful panels of contrasting greens which will lose the design when the cut leaves fade to the same dullness. It will not matter then if one mural is very like another, as it does when the attempt is made to wring individuality out of an obedient reproduction of some recognized style. There will be only one mural on the wall at a time, and its freshness will be adequate for a week, to carry it along, or add pleasure to its destruction so that it can be replaced. The Balinese, who give their acclaim to the occasionally highly gifted, carry their critical appreciation in hands and feet that do not attempt the impossible but often gaily, "from delight," make beautiful things that are not meant to last.

But we will need a second development to complement this: the painter whose creativity is great enough to justify his giving his whole lifetime to it must come to include, in the vision of

21

what he does, the process of reproduction. As poets write to be printed, so painters must come out of the manuscript stage and paint for reproduction. A painting meant for reproduction is no more demeaned by reproduction than is a poem by reprinting. But a poem written only to be read by the author, designed for the single uniqueness of such perfectly realized cadence, is too precious for other lips. Poets long ago, when writing was invented, were humble enough to surrender their lovely lines to the stumbling reproductions of others, whose lips moved slowly and ineptly, as images other than the poet meant crawled or danced through their minds. Perhaps, indeed, poets were more willing to do this than we know, after centuries in which a minstrel had to repeat the same poem over and over before a different set of carousing, feasting lords. But when the poets bowed to print, their poems were quietly put away in books. Now with a recording, we can listen when we wish to a poem read beautifully, sometimes even by the poet who wrote it. But who could bear to encounter perhaps twice a day the *Ode to a Nightingale,* or one of Eliot's *Quartets,* sounding uninvited from some corner of a room, however faithfully the reader attempted to render the lines? Any lover of poetry would rebel at once against such unsought experience, and yet we acquiesce in putting vivid reproductions on our walls for the helpless visitor or captive child to stare into meaninglessness, perhaps forever.

There is a related responsibility which Americans have never taken, responsibility for the landscape which others see when they look out of their windows or walk down a street. We have so sedulously sought each his own view, swept clear of the hand of man, that we have failed to recognize to what extent our house or garden has become the "view" of others in this crowded world. We none of us take joint responsibility for the city streets, the combination of water tanks and occasional pleasant pinnacles which we call a skyline, on which our children's eyes must be fed, and so we learn to turn a blind eye to ugliness. Our unplanned towns and sprawling developments, our unwillingness to adapt a new building to the line of the buildings already there, have bred a people who expect beauty to be a piece of private property for which they take no responsibility.

These are possible steps which those who give direction to the last half of this century might well take: stress the value of participant production of ephemeral things, a mural for a night, an individual greeting card that will go quickly to an honorable grave, a sketch on the edge of a letter to a distant friend; emphasize the importance of painting *for* reproduction, rather than making exact reproductions in which the single masterpiece is still intended; protect the single masterpiece from the vulgarization of unintended, unresponsive contemplation by keeping reproductions in books that can be opened at will, or for occasional enjoyment in a temporary frame; and develop a structured responsibility for our towns and cities, in which we build the shared man-made landscape in which eyes become accustomed to beauty, rather than immune to intrusive ugliness.

SIGFRIED GIEDION

The Roots of Symbolic Expression

THERE ARE SIGNS today that we are again approaching an age of symbolism, and that a prolonged phase of naturalism is giving way to new conceptions of reality, one of multiple dimensions and renewed significances. The present revival of interest in the symbol and its meaning leads us back to its origins in prehistory. It is there that the whole process of symbolization can best be studied. Indeed, symbolization is the key to all paleolithic art, from the grandiose engravings and paintings in the caverns of southern France and Spain to small artifacts made from reindeer antlers. In every case actuality has been translated into symbolism, however realistic it may appear. This transmutation persisted throughout paleolithic art until the neolithic period, when abstraction reigned supreme.

It is only in recent years that scholarship has recognized the importance of a systematic study of the symbolic content of prehistoric art. The further we proceed in such investigations, the more we are astonished at the amazing richness of imagination displayed. Here, it seems, may be the sources of much of the imagery which has been attributed to Greek art. However, the previous work of all serious prehistorians and anthropologists has concentrated on the classification of material objects such as hand axes and other such tools. Consequently there still exist great gaps in our understanding of what symbol meant to prehistoric man.

Today the common denominator in creed and ritual that once linked man to man has lost its force. Whereas in primitive eras magic, myth, and religion provided man with a spiritual armor against a hostile environment, today he stands stripped and naked. In the effort to compensate he has had to create symbols and inner images out of himself. Half-ironically, the surrealist painter Max Ernst wrote, "In 1930, after having composed with violence and method the *Femme 100 têtes*, I was visited nearly every day by my private phantom attached to my person—the superior of birds named Loplop."[1]

Today the average man appears to have lost the key to his own being, even though he still believes that he knows what he likes and that he can express what he feels. The ruling taste of the times demonstrates the result of this loss, for it affects the entire sphere of emotional activity. The average man, whether governed or governing, has grown indifferent to the flood of surrogates, to *ersatz* in art and architecture, to falsity in expression; and this process has been called "the devaluation of symbols."[2] For a century and a half it has been apparent, and it is still going on. The decline in our community life, our helplessness in finding forms for celebration or leisure, our lack of imaginative power to develop forms to counteract the maladies of our culture—all indicate the extent of man's present disorientation.

It is not difficult to understand how this has come about. The man of today has to bear an enormous and increasing load of intellectual knowledge, while at the same time his emotional world has been steadily atrophying. His emotional apparatus has shrunk to a mere appendage, quite unable to absorb and humanize the knowledge accumulated by his brain. He stands alone. It may be that from new developments in the communal sphere some new suprapersonal spirit will emerge. But at the moment, man must rely on himself. This situation may give us a clue to the nature of those symbols which are today emerging in the work of contemporary painters and poets.

The Reawakening of Symbols

Jean-Paul Sartre (however his existentialism is regarded) is a poet with visions of what kinds of symbols are possible today. In *L'Imaginaire* he asserts that, in contrast to the situation in former periods, symbolic function is no longer derived and explained from the outside world. "We would not accept a conception according to which the symbolic function has to be added to the image from outside. The image is in essence symbolic by its very structure."[3] Without any kind of intermediary, the symbol through its very form finds a direct access to the emotions.

Forms that have no apparent significance and yet seize directly upon the senses are the dominant constituent elements of "contemporary art." These symbols differ not only from the magical potent symbols of prehistory but also from the conceptualized symbols of the Greeks. Today's symbols are anonymous; they seem to exist for themselves alone, without any direct significance. Yet they are imbued with an inexplicable attraction: the magic of their forms. In a sense, they represent a regenerative or healing process, a flight from technological frenzy. Beside these anonymous symbols or forms without direct significance, age-old symbols from the remote past have

25

been revived and integrated into new contexts, as is discerned in the work of Joan Miró and Paul Klee, among others. It would be a rewarding though difficult task to carry out some form of research which could give us an insight into the process of this development and its manifold ramifications.

It cannot be said today that the forces of symbolization no longer exist. A great picture that seizes all our senses simultaneously (as does Picasso's "Guernica") can become a great composite symbol. As we become aware of the multilayered fabric of the soul, we try to ascertain not only the limits within which logical argument operates as a reliable tool, but also the areas in which that tool cannot be used, areas of different psychic dimensions. The laws of logic have colored philosophic thought ever since the Renaissance, especially since the seventeenth century. This influence is closely paralleled in the optical sphere by the influence of perspective on our view of the world. It is just these narrow criteria of logical cause and effect and of optical perspective that the present period resents and rebels against.

One no longer has to ask why. Our eyes are not blinded to the marvelous artistic achievements of recent centuries; but we have become ever more conscious of the situation to which rationalism led us throughout the nineteenth century: that of living only for the moment, lacking all certainty regarding decisions that take on psychic dimensions. The one-way street of logic has landed us in the slum of materialism.

The Symbol in Primeval Art

Before art, man created the symbol. The name arose late— the symbol, early. It appears at the very dawn of man's urge for expression. Its first rudimentary form emerged in the Mousterian era as the traces of Neanderthal man's first attempts at a spiritual organization transcending simple materials and a utilitarian existence. Bones engraved with parallel and diagonal lines or with red circles have been found, but these are so fragmentary that no safe conclusions can be drawn from them. It is quite otherwise, however, with the small hemispherical hollows carved out of stone, called *cupules*. Prehistorians report that the earliest surviving man-made signs were found on a triangular grave slab discovered in the rock shelter of La Ferrassie in the Dordogne. These were small hollows in the slab, which was placed face down over a child's body. These hollows, which had no practical function, are a widespread phenomenon of paleolithic art whose symbolic significance is undefined.

The magic symbols that appear most frequently and over the longest periods of prehistory are simple. They consist of fragments, the part standing for the whole: a hand, for example, represents the entire human being, and the genitalia represent fertility. But it is more difficult to give meaning to the circle. It appears in a great number of forms, large and small— as cup-shaped depressions in stone *(cupules)*, colored dots and disks *(ponctuations)*, holes *(perforations)*, often varying in shape.

In primitive times symbols sometimes stood alone, though usually several were associated and interrelated, e.g., dots were related to hands, animals, or tectiforms, and *cupules* were arranged in rows or placed singly in association with an animal or upon the animal. Greater precision could thus be given to certain of the manifold meanings inherent in any one symbol, and also a single overriding meaning could be accentuated, such as the desire for increased fertility. Such designs, in which different symbols with many meanings were combined in order to stress one specific meaning—as genitalia and *cupules*—may be called "composite symbols."

In addition to simple straightforward symbols, a host of complex and entirely abstract forms were developed in primitive times. Man's power in this direction seems to have been inexhaustible, but the meanings are all the more obscure. The names given these more complex symbolic forms are mere labels —tectiforms, claviforms, naviforms. In contrast to the simpler symbols, individual imagination here seems to have been given free play, and in many cases only a single example of certain types is as yet known. These symbols are usually in the most inaccessible parts of the caverns, as at Altamira, El Castillo, and La Pasiega. The fact of their inaccessibility may be interpreted as referring to the special potency of the magic emanating from them. Even today many of these configurations exert a strangely powerful impression on the beholder, as in Altamira, where blood-red zigzag symbols as large as the drawings of the bulls traverse the whole ceiling.

Symbolization arises from the need to give perceptible form to the imperceptible. Symbolization emerged as soon as man felt the need of expressing the disquieting and intangible relation between life and death, first expressed in very primitive ways. When Johann Jakob Bachofen said that it was in the tomb that the symbol was formed, he was thinking of the Etruscan necropolis that was the starting point for his pioneer researches on symbolism.[4] His supporting material was provided by tomb reliefs, long ignored by the archaeologists, and by his profound knowledge of classical authors. Since then, both material evidence and our understanding of symbolism have increased enormously, and our newly acquired knowledge of primitive art has largely sustained Bachofen's theories.

27

Symbol and Existence

Let us repeat: the symbols of primitive art are rooted in the primary demands of human existence, in the idea of the continuity of life and death. The main purpose of primitive existence was to obtain food. Food implied the animal. Where direct attack on the animal was not successful, rituals, magic signs, and magic symbols were invented, by which man hoped to be invested with power to bewitch the animal. But the killing of beasts was not enough to ensure a continuous food supply. That depended also on the fecundity of the stock; to ensure this, primitive man was even more powerless. Only magic held out hope.

We can therefore understand that most early symbols, though they appear in highly varied, even opposing, combinations, were concerned with the perpetuation of the animal species, and in one way or another were designed to promote fertility through magic. We see this more clearly in the primitive Aurignacian than in the later and more highly developed Magdalenian era. In the former, one symbol of fertility is the vulva; it appears constantly, generally alone, but sometimes in combination with the animal whose increase is desired. Such representations of female organs have certainly nothing to do with human sexual instincts, nor do the much rarer representations of male organs, or the small female figurines with enormous breasts and abdomens, or the ithyphallic male figures. This can be substantiated, of course, only by many comparative illustrations.

Signs of a belief in the continuance of life after death appeared in the early Mousterian age. Things come to no abrupt end, and death does not completely extinguish life. Some possibility of re-entering the earthly cycle emerges, both for men and for animals—though how this is to be achieved is very unclear. In that age man lived close to his dead, who were buried within his dwelling place. Tens of thousands of years later the same custom was practiced in the Nile Delta (Merimde), just before the dawn of history. The dead influenced the fate of their descendants, they shared in the family meals. Today in parts of Polynesia it is customary to bury the dead within the dwelling or outside beneath the eaves. This area is otherwise sacrosanct. "People do not turn their backs on it, and when they lie down to sleep they orient their heads in that direction."[5]

The animal, too, possessed magic power after death. Both in the interests of the food supply and also to placate the spirit of the dead animal, it was reasonable to take steps to facilitate its return to life. "In short, everything was done as though the animal had magic powers at its command which must be propitiated or dominated by other magic forces."[6]

Symbol and Myth

Premythological man was completely embedded in the world which surrounded him. He formed one with it, he did not stand above it, he did not feel himself to be the center, but a humble element in it. His fate was ruled by powers he could not comprehend. To him the animal was a superior being, a creature greater than he, and at the same time a personification of invisible powers. All primitive symbols are rooted in this zoomorphic age. However simple or complex these symbols, they all represent invisible forces in a universe not yet reduced to a battleground between man and man.

Myths, on the other hand, are based on the relationships and destinies of men, or of men and gods. In myths, time (the succession of events) plays a determining part. In primeval times, today, yesterday, tomorrow all were one. Myths grew out of the huge transformation from the zoomorphic to the anthropomorphic age in which we still live, and thus they arose relatively late. It would be hazardous to assign any precise dates; yet from their content, the conflicts they embody, and the context in which they are described, we may assume that they roughly coincided with the first formal communities, such as the small temple settlements that flourished both in the north and south of Mesopotamia in the fourth millennium B.C.

In the Sumerian epic of Gilgamesh, the cities had already become the acknowledged centers of religion and authority, and Gilgamesh the epic hero ruled the city of Erech. According to the evidence, Gilgamesh did not live before 2700 or 2600 B.C. Therefore, the epic recording his heroic deeds can date from no earlier than about 2600 B.C. In this period a new world of gods, whose hierarchical structure precisely reflected the contemporary social order, came into being.

If we consider the situation immediately before this, as reflected in Persian and Mesopotamian pottery of the fifth millennium B.C., we find no trace of myth and the world of the gods, such as appears on the cylinder seals of the late fourth millennium. The abstract designs on the earlier pottery, with their artistic intensity and great charm, are rich in prehistoric concepts, and they have far more in common with the symbolic world of the Magdalenian era (eight to ten millennia earlier) than with the anthropomorphic myths of a thousand years later.

Yet it must not be forgotten that vestiges of prehistory still cling to the anthropomorphic myths. Like the signs and symbols in the primitive world, they indicate the eternal polarity of life

29

and death, and are embedded in the cosmos. Now all has been given anthropomorphic form, and the stars themselves have become deistic personifications. This mingling of men and gods with the cosmos is the prime characteristic of myths.

The Symbol as a Concept

It was the Greek way of thought that gave rise to the conceptual form of the symbol. The word "symbol" (itself of Greek origin) was absorbed into the most diverse languages, including Latin, although the Romans had no love for the concept it represented. The variety of meanings the concept of the symbol had for the Greeks of the classical period arises from the fact that they formed three different nouns from the original verb. Its complicated linguistic relations were set down as early as 1810 to 1812 by Friedrich Creuzer. The original Greek word *symbalon* signified the adjustment of various parts to form a whole, and its three variant meanings were "to unite; to connect; to bring separate parts together." The simplest meaning of *symbalon*, therefore, is that used by Plato, "one composed of two." The best-known example of the Greek use of the symbol is a host's gift of part of a broken coin or ring to a departing guest, while he himself retained the corresponding part, so that when these halves were later matched, the owners or their descendants could recognize one another.

The symbol became a token of relationship which had been given a special significance. Viewed objectively, no connection existed between the fragment of the broken coin and the meaning it had been given, nor was any clue perceptible to the senses—it eluded them. The symbol reassumed its suprapersonal significance and recovered its original role as the image of something that could not be directly expressed.

Schlesinger quotes this passage from Bachofen's *Gräber-Symbolik:* "Words confine infinity. Symbols guide the spirit, beyond the powers of the finite state of becoming, into the realm of the infinite world of existence."[7] Thus the symbol recovers its primitive significance: it is nameless, yet it is a powerful reality, and it is this consistent meaning that is again operative today.

Today we are no longer satisfied with mere facts and philological exactitudes. We demand more, but we are confronted by lacunae or by the work of dilettantes whose knowledge of the source materials cannot be trusted. By its very conception, the scholarship of the last hundred years was impelled to condemn all attempts in this direction and reject its advocates. This is thoroughly understandable, as archeological methods have been modeled on the methods of the dominating natural sciences. Unfortunately, despite all desire for precision, the use of purely rational methods is not possible in the historical sphere, especially in prehistory and protohistory.

Today, when the question of the inner meaning of phenomena has slowly come to the fore and history is much more identified with human destiny than treated as a sequence of events, we lack the necessary source material: a background of scholarly investigation of the meaning of symbols. Only two outstanding figures since Giambattista Vico (1668-1744) have devoted their lives to the investigation of symbols, one at the beginning and one at the middle of the nineteenth century.

Friedrich Creuzer's great work, *Symbolik und Mythologie der alten Völker, besonders der Griechen* (Symbols and Myths of the Ancients, especially the Greeks: 1810) originated in Heidelberg out of the atmosphere created by early Romantic poets such as Novalis, Arnim, and Tieck, by philosophers such as Schelling, and by scholars of various fields. Like Vico, Creuzer (1771-1858) considered language the most faithful recorder of the early periods. He developed the Greek ideas of the symbol and recognized that the symbol "encompasses the whole in an instant." From this he derived a new conception of symbol, "which we express in words as 'immediate perception': *momentane Anschaulichkeit.*"

Creuzer comes very near to Johann Jakob Bachofen when he remarks, "The symbol wants to say much, and it should express the divine. . . . In a flash the idea springs from the symbol and seizes all the senses. It is a ray direct from the depths of being and thinking, it transfixes our eyes and permeates our entire nature with an immediate perception."

Bachofen (1815-1887) surpasses all others who attempted a serious investigation of symbols during the last century by reason of his profundity and his loneliness. In his era there was no recognition of him as the discoverer of primeval religion and of matrilinear descent *(Das Mutterrecht,* 1861), and as the revealer of the forgotten influence on the human psyche of myths, language, and symbols. Neither archeologists nor ethnologists nor social anthropologists were concerned with such researches. Since Freud, however, the psychoanalysts have taken up the problem, and have influenced other disciplines, though often without the necessary knowledge. Very recently certain French prehistorians have endeavored to unravel the significance of prehistoric symbols through statistical comparsions. Even so, we are only at the very beginning of such understanding.

The Potent Symbol

The golden age of the symbol was in prehistoric times. "Since then it has been overwhelmed by the hostile pressure of rational

31

thought, which, reinforced by experience and reason itself, has steadily gained ground. . . . The *raison d'être* of the symbol lies in the human urge to express that which is inherently inexpressible."[8]

The essential nature of the symbol has always consisted in this urge to express the inherently inexpressible, but in primitive times the crystallization of a concept in the form of a symbol signified even more: the symbol was identified with the wish, the prayer, or the spell to be fulfilled. The symbol itself was reality, for it was believed to possess the power of working magic, and thus of directly affecting the course of events. The symbol portrayed reality before that reality came to pass.

Herein lies the contrast between the function of the symbol in prehistory and in later periods. In Greece the symbol was not only a means of recognition, it also developed a spiritual content and became an abstract concept. It was not an independent agent.

Bachofen calls the kinds of symbols found on Roman mortuary reliefs "reposing in themselves"—that is, complete in themselves. The symbols employed in the Christian catacombs up to the middle of the fifth century A.D. embodied the hope of future bliss: wine signified the feasts of Paradise; a dove sipping water, the soul refreshing itself in the waters of life; flowered meadows represented Heaven itself. These all point to the life beyond the tomb and are transcendental, whereas primitive symbols were neither complete in themselves nor transcendental.

It is difficult to determine the limits of symbolism in prehistory. It was believed to be a potent agent, and by force of sympathetic magic was called upon to help achieve a certain purpose, with positive results. Yet the border line between the symbol and other representations is indeterminate, as in the spellbinding forms of animals on cavern walls, with their inextricable mingling of magical intent and straightforward realism.

We are again approaching an age of symbolism. No one will deny the laws of logic; they are as valid today as yesterday. Yet we are compelled to ask: does everything come under the sway of logical reasoning? Are there not many aspects of human experience to which the cause-and-effect reasonings of logic are not applicable? In considering history—even the life history of the simplest creature—we cannot help but observe how most actions evade a clear explanation in terms of cause and effect. We can always discover certain causes after the event, but we are unable to predict a future effect of a cause, or the development of which we ourselves are a part and with which our personal destiny is unremittingly involved.

Once again we begin to recognize the wisdom of bygone

periods, when so much less was known but when the world was conceived as free and untrammeled, not caged within the bounds of logical cause and effect.

REFERENCES

1 Max Ernst, *Beyond Painting* (New York, Wittenborn, Schultz, 1948), p. 9.

2 S. Giedion, *Mechanization Takes Command.* New York, Oxford University Press, 1948. Many of the remarks that follow form part of a book, *Constancy and Change in Early Art and Architecture* (based on the Mellon Lectures of 1957 at the National Gallery in Washington), to be issued in the Bollingen Series. Its main purpose is to bring out the relation of prehistory to the first high civilizations of Sumer and Egypt, and also the relations between primeval art and the reawakening of symbols today.

3 Jean-Paul Sartre, *L'Imaginaire: Psychologie phénomenologique de l'imagination* (Paris, Gallimard, 1940), p. 128. This remark is based on the work of a Wurzburg psychologist who had experimented with forms and shapes that had no significance in themselves.

4 Johann Jakob Bachofen, "Versuch über die Gräber Symbolik der Alten," (1859), *Bachofen's Gesammelte Werke,* Vol. IV, Basel, 1954.

5 Raymond Firth, *We the Tikopia* (New York, American Book Company, 1936; 2nd edn., London, George Allen & Unwin, 1957), p. 77.

6 Lucien Lévy-Bruhl, *Le Mythologie primitive* (Paris, F. Alcan, 1935), p. 52.

7 Max Schlesinger, *Geschichte des Symbols* (Berlin, L. Simion, 1912), p. 135.

8 Théodule Ribot, "La Pensée Symbolique," *Revue Philosophique,* 1915, *49*: 386-387.

FELIX DEUTSCH

Body, Mind, and Art

FREUD WAS ONCE of the opinion that evaluations of art fall within the area of psychoanalytic research only as they reveal the psychic needs out of which art arises, the psychic material art uses and the psychic purposes it serves. However, it seemed to him that "before the problem of the creative artist, analysis must, alas, lay down its arms."[1] Nevertheless, he stated that "the forces motivating the artist are the same conflicts which drive other individuals into neurosis."[2] He suggested that the artist is probably more sensitive to psychic stimuli than most people are, and that he uses the artistic gift both to avoid neurosis and to augment it. Both uses may occur simultaneously, as the preventive function is usually the dominant one. He succeeds in achieving the highest results in the transformation of his instinctual impulses through artistic activity. As the instinctual pressure rises and a neurotic "solution" appears imminent, the unconscious defense against it leads to the creation of an art product. The psychic effect is the discharge of the pent-up emotion until a tolerable level is reached.

The true artist, as Freud concludes, is able to elaborate his daydreams and to mold them until they faithfully express his ideas of his fantasy. When he succeeds, his repressions are for the time being out-balanced and dispelled.

1

In the past two decades the interest of analysts in the psychologic aspects of artistic creation has greatly increased. Their leading exponent has been Ernst Kris.[3] At various times I have been concerned with a number of problems associated with artistic creativity. At one time I chose poetic art[4] as an example to show how the artistic expression of a poet may be determined by his neurotic traits, and how the choice of specific themes and topics by poets is intimately related to unsolved emotional problems which they unconsciously discharge in their writings. Later[5] I compared the art of interviewing emotionally disturbed patients and the method of searching into their past, where the child's undeveloped ego reigns over body and mind, with artistic activity; I pointed out the resemblance of primitive (e.g., the primary thought processes of childhood) to abstract pictorial art. More recently[6] I tried to trace the creative passion of the artist down to the synergistic sensory functions and the intersensory perceptivities of his personality. This was in accordance with Kepes'[7] concept of the language of vision: that there exists an intercorrelation, a common structural basis of all kinds of sensory languages. In other words, in artistic activity we deal with "intermodal" relations between the different senses, and the stimulation of one of these—real or imaginary—encompasses the whole organism in all its parts as a biological process.[8, 9]

In the very young child all sensory perceptions are objectless: a sound is only a noise from nowhere; a sensation of light is only a change of darkness; a smell is originally only a sensory sensation different from odorlessness; a touch, only a signal for reflectory motility adaptation. Much later these perceptions become signals to turn to or to withdraw from objects, or else they are used to regain such objects when lost, or to fuse them with imagined or symbolized objects. They become the means for an awareness of the inner and outer world and of so-called reality. Fragmentary sense perceptions are sometimes used to absorb, by means of specific faculties (smelling, hearing, or seeing), the objects of the outside world, to incorporate them, figuratively speaking, and to keep the outside world in continual contact with the body. The opposite task assigned to sense perceptions by the growing ego is to repel and exclude the objects from the bodily union by disgust or antipathy, moving away or shutting off perceptive faculties in relation to objects. The abstract image of the world becomes separated from the object-related one, and either may outgrow the other.

Visual objectless concepts rooted in the visual abstractions of early childhood can have a bearing on the development of personality. For instance, the visual perception in adults of objectless color leads to sensations in which concrete and abstract qualities are combined in a revival of early emotional experiences. The colored impression of the environment lifts the person out of his present reality. He feels depersonalized, as if he were transferred to a pictorial world resembling the environment of the past he has left behind but which he has always carried within himself. As long as the color impression is effective, the person finds himself transferred to a world more pleasing than reality is. I once made a therapeutic use of this concept. I advised patients with anxiety conditions expressed in bodily symptoms to wear red or green spectacles, respectively, depending on their patterns of reaction. This helped

35

them to escape into worlds of unreality, away from the conflicts of the real world,[10] and their current problems were modified by moods originating in the past.

The modern artist forms, reforms, and transforms the world of reality into more elementary, abstract forms. Children who are born blind illustrate the possibility of this type of transformation. A group of such children were induced to play with blocks in the shape of cylinders, cubes, spheres, pyramids, cups, and triangular and oblong shapes to test their sense of reality.[11] For each infant in this group who played with them, the simple shapes sufficed as a basis for his concept of both the real and the imagined world. The wooden objects turned through fantasies into a living world in which wooden blocks became anthropomorphized. The cylinder became personified as a man or a father; the pyramid, as a girl who wanted to have what a boy has; the cup, as a shelter where the child felt safe when putting the sphere into it; the cube, as a house (mother) with the roof —the triangular block— on top of it; the oblong block became the bed where the family sleeps. These children were fusing the reality perceived by their intact senses with the psychic reality seen with their inner eye, and they colored or distorted their sense perception of the world as suited their needs, for they live in such a confused world, with its abstract representations.[12] In this respect these children resembled the abstract artist who closes his eyes to conventional reality and blots out its accepted representations in the art product. It is the trend of modern times to see the world as a structure of energies, and matter only as a convenient but arbitrary image of our senses.

2

The sense of reality originates in the young child when he begins to project certain sensory perceptions arising in his own body upon objects he finds in the outside world. Since external objects are perceived as if severed from the body and lost, I believe that this separation leads to the continual wish in the child to restore the loss of the body's intactness and wholeness through symbolization. The pyhsiologic functions of those body parts which have become the representatives of these external objects may be modified on account of this process.

Before the development of a reality sense, the new-born child goes through a phase in which he does not distinguish himself from his environment. Individual objects or elements in the environment are not differentiated, nor are the modalities of feeling, sensation, or emotion differentiated from one another. The infant's own body is his only reality, and the sole object of

36

his interest and awareness. What occurs in such an infant is that his body is stimulated by external and internal stimuli. Sensations and feelings are aroused due to innervations in the body, acompanied by concomitant physiologic reactions and by emotions which depend on whether these sensations bring pleasure or pain. The stimuli—such as temperature changes, variations in light, and the presence of sound—need not originate in an outside object, in the strictest sense. The gratification of needs, the diminution of tension, or the abolition of pain or displeasure are connected with the increase or decrease in certain bodily sensations. The new-born child does not distinguish between external and internal stimuli, for they all seem to arise from within his own body. What is perceived via the sensory stimulus is a sensation specific for the special sense organ. This sensation, as far as the visceral organs are concerned, becomes more complicated, but is qualitatively not different. All visceral sensations are referred sensations, as if originating from other sense organs, which serve as signals either to prevent pain or announce pleasure.

Changes in bodily sensations, with their accompanying emotions of pleasure or pain depending on the gratification or frustration of inner needs, make the infant aware of his own body, or they remind him of the body of his mother, with whom he had a symbiotic relationship, and of other similar objects in his environment. These sensations in his own body bring back his feelings toward those objects he once perceived through taste, smell, hearing, vision, and touch, before his full recognition of a world separate from his own body. In this sense, the whole outer world, once imagined as belonging to the child's body, becomes to him the nucleus of his emotions and fantasies through his sensory and visceral sensations.

Eventually the infant becomes aware that the breast or bottle that supplies the milk to satisfy his thirst and hunger comes and goes. The person who has supplied this food or who holds him, keeps him warm, or rocks him is not always present and available for the instantaneous gratification of his wishes. In other words, the child has learned that what he once thought of as part of himself does not belong to him. His former bodily sensory perceptions are now recognized as percepts, and are distinguished from the self. The conception of objects stems from the ego's ability to manipulate sense perceptions in the earliest cognition of objects, such as the parental figures.

The not-self or "object" the infant recognizes is made up of what he previously perceived as going on in his own body. That was his reality. Thus one element in this developmental step is the projection onto the object of what went on in the self. In this light, an object such as "mother" would then be a projection

37

of a synthesis of bodily sensations of warmth, rocking, thirst-quenching milk, etc.

3

Psychoanalytic studies of adults and children have shown that real and imagined losses are significant emotional events of early childhood. They often lead to an attempt to regain the lost object either in fact or in fantasy. This seems to occur even in the case of the loss involved in the separation of the self image from the image of the outside world. The primitive experience that the world was once a part of the self and that gradually it was taken away or became externalized is never completely accepted. The unconscious wish to regain it, along with the sense of timelessness and omnipotence that goes with it, leads to highly charged emotional attitudes. If the child cannot be literally reunited with the lost object, the reactive fantasies or illusions may become focused on a part of the body that then becomes a representative substitute or symbol for the imagined lost object, and such a substitution functions as an attempt to regain that object.[12] Each part of the body possesses the potentiality for the symbolic expression of this type of recovery. The choice of the particular body part will depend on the size, form, and function of the organ, as well as the sensory perceptions that may serve as associative links with the lost object. The identification, of course, is unconscious in that the individual is not aware of it. The nature of the symbolization will determine the threshold of the perception of that organ. This threshold can be lowered in some individuals to zero, a condition that may be called "sensory amnesia." The unconscious may be considered as the sum total of lost sensory perceptions lowered beyond the threshold for certain sensory elements.

The symbolization substitutes for the amount of loss which the lost object represented to the individual. The degree of internalization depends on the intensity of the relationship to the lost object as well as the number of other objects symbolized in an organ system. Furthermore, the loss of an object may mobilize the need for its restoration in artistic creation.[12] The symbolization of external objects becomes the medium through which the lost objects may be re-embodied.

A specific sensory perception develops into a memory symbol, later projected onto the external object. A specific sensory stimulus may serve as a step in regaining the lost object by symbolic representation, enabling the ego to discharge the tensions created by the emotional conflict of the original loss. The symbolization of objects consists of synaesthetic constellations of sensory and visceral perceptions, inner instinctual needs connected with them, and the concomitant affects.

38

4

According to this concept, visual art originates not only from specific sensory stimuli and specific motives of the artist in the present, but also from the specific way in which the artist's personality has developed. This development includes a particular and unique history of sensory experiences and of associations between sensory and other experiences. From this point of view, the power to react to the sensory stimuli unconditionally essential for artistic creativity depends on:

1. the early fusion of specific sensory stimuli with complementary psychologic stimuli into a unit;

2. the repetition compulsion for the discharge of the tension in the specific kind of creation;

3. an ego equally receptive on several strata to these instinctual demands;

4. the irresistible need of the ego and its insistence on retrieving the loss by creating a substitute;

5. the ego's unchangeable dependence on a specific sensory stimulus for the gratification of an instinctual need which channels other sensory functions into coalition with the prevalent one.

Visual art is an attempt to redeem a lost reality. It tries to revive the pleasure or undo the pain of a past experience, real or illusory. Artistic creation is set in motion when the ego has established a particular and repeated pattern for reacting to an important unconscious conflict in that specific sensory thresholds signal the need for the recovery of what is lost. The ego mobilizes simultaneously other sensory functions as adjuvants in the recovery process.

The irritability of the total physiologic and psychologic sensory unit will determine whether the sensory signals are reliable agents for calling on all resources to unite in the drive toward artistic creation that promises the recovery of a reality lost in the past in a symbolized form.

The components of artistic expression always remain the same. Which of them will become more prominent at a given time will depend on extrinsic and intrinsic factors, the former depending on the influence of environmental, social, and cultural factors, and the latter on the development of a psychophysiologic process. Both together will vary the individual form of artistic expression. In our atomic age, in which living objects will be taken beyond the stratosphere, where they may remain for some time or even for good, and from where return is uncertain, it has to be expected that the urge for recovery of the lost reality, for its restitution—for one's own rebirth, as it were—will be forever an incentive to visual artistic creation.

5

The art productions of both children and adults illustrate the importance of the processes described above. The visual artistic expression of the child often begins with the drawing of a sphere or a circle that has the appearance of a closed hole. It represents in essence the container to which he wants to return. The drawings of childhood do not reveal the richness of adult art products. The circle represents the universal hole, the womb. It soon becomes identified with the body holes or hollow parts of the body, and hence it may gradually come to represent the mouth, eyes, ears, etc. Simultaneously the child begins to draw lines representing the protruding parts of the body. The closed circle then is filled in with these lines, and the round frame later turns into a square. Since the earliest primitive drawings are attempts to retrieve the imagined losses of objects, the early drawings of parts of the body show them sketched inside the hole, as if to keep them sheltered. Only later are the protruding parts, like the legs, arms, ears, etc., drawn outside the frame and connected with it.

It is interesting that as the ego matures and begins to act in a more self-assured fashion, the drawings may reflect this by an emphasis on straight-line configurations, although simultaneously weaker parts of the ego may offset these kinds of artistic expressions by including in the picture hollow, weblike drawings from which straight lines protrude. They finally become separated from the round web.

Thus these drawings are mirrors of the psychic development of the child. Hence, combinations of lines drawn outside the circle or square, like legs, arms, or ears, are signs of the child's increasing feeling of independence, on the one hand, and of a feeling of security, i.e., of being loved, on the other. But whatever form the drawings may take, whether they depict persons or are abstracts, the child's artistic activity derives from the instinctual need of illustrating loss and reunification.

This has been illustrated in the biographies of some great artists who showed artistic potentialities in their early childhood. However, they fell sick when they were infants. Some of them became injured in an accident which affected their vision or sense of hearing. This loss of the bodily integrity occurring just at a stage of development when the need to have the sensory faculties intact for the full grasp of the reality and of the objects therein was vital, sparked the need for the restoration of the self by imagination and symbolization.[6] In this emergency, when the ego strives relentlessly for the restitution of the loss, other sensory faculties become enhanced at their threshold, and help the defective one in the process of regaining the loss, as it were. This means a harmonization of sensory functions for the sake of the same goal.

To reformulate it: the ego tries with all its means to reach this goal and turns to other sensory faculties as allies which should join in the service of the deficient one, not only to regain the loss but also to prevent further losses. During this process the sensory organ system with the appropriate sensory modalities for artistic activity becomes and remains the focal point in the following phases of development up to maturation. The specific choice of artistic activity reflects this psychophysiologic process.

6

An ever new impetus to artistic creation appears whenever a stimulus provokes the need for a recreation of a unified reality. In visual arts such as painting, sculpturing, architecture, the eidetic faculties are in default as far as the insatiable demands on them by the ego are concerned, and they join forces with the tactile ones, turning the imagination into a visual product of art. The more sensory modalities become synthesized with the sensory faculty most fit to take the lead, the greater is the prospect of reaching the highest kind of artistic achievement.

However, there are other powerful forces which stimulate the drive for the recreation of a unified reality. Freud has pointed out that the artist is originally a man who is in danger of turning from reality because (and when) he cannot come to terms with the demand for his renunciation of infantile fantasies. But in his creation he finds a way of returning from the world of fantasy to reality. Some of these fantasies to which Freud refers are related to the child's desire to reconcile the anatomical differences of male and female, as if being born and belonging only to one sex constituted a loss. He puts emphasis on the inborn bisexuality which plays a decisive role during the passive experience of the creation. This unconscious wish for finding in the self the unification of these polarities never ends, and excludes a permanent peace of mind, since the fusion can never be accomplished. But it presses far more for its gratification and contributes to the ecstasy of creative passion of the artist in whom all sensory faculties are stirred up to create a new reality in the art product. The ground for creativity is laid in the fantasy world of the child who, if he possesses the harmony of the senses, may become an artist or even a genius, i.e., having at his disposal the inexhaustible faculties to recapture again and again the lost reality of the past.

All children show at different times, particularly during the latency period or prepuberty, tendencies to artistic activity

41

which get stranded or are given up in favor of other more timely ones due to changes in the harmony of the sensory modalities. They give the vanishing reality of the past an expression more befitting the acute needs for pleasure-pain gratification. A diffusion of the cathexis on different sensory organs (until maturity is reached) corresponds to normalcy. The artist, however, differs from other people in that his efforts to create substitutes as a way of handling his unconscious conflicts over past losses are not abortive but lead repetitively to a successful handling of the neurotic conflict.

These mechanisms are part and parcel of the process of restitution by expiation through artistic work, of procreation and destruction, of resurrection and redestruction fantasies, worked into the creative process. In creating the wholeness, these psychologic mechanisms are a *sine qua non* for the mastery of the feminine and masculine drives here involved. They become realized symbolically in the process of creating an art product, where the visual incorporation and the tactile destruction and procreation lead simultaneously to the same goal: to produce a new reality.

The true artist relives in the creative process the cravings of his infantile ego, but the quality of the final product will depend on whether his adult ego takes the lead. During creation the infantile part-egos are unleashed, and the feeling of creative passion, of fulfilling a mission can be aroused. It is as if the recreation of the wholeness had been achieved. Believing in it, the artist's narcissism has to be saturated and the feeling of loss has to vanish.

Any loss of an object calls upon the ego to retrieve it with new means, or find a substitute object. The loss revives the ambivalent conflict and reawakens the early infantile hostility to objects, the loss of which had either been threatened, desired, feared or experienced—a hostility which has to be repressed or gratified.

Feelings of revenge and grief caused by the loss can hardly be harmonized to give a satisfactory result. Loss means "having been abandoned." Revenge means to leave this object and turn to others, more dependable. The first step may lead to isolation, to preoccupation with the self as an object one can love or hate, exalt or devaluate, which can be revived and enjoyed as an alter ego, and for which one can mourn. These feelings can give new impulses to artistic creation, in order to undo in this form the previous losses.

This enticement is one of the mainsprings of the artist's preconscious need to bring the beauty of his art to perfection. It reconciles his unconscious bisexual drives. This wish cannot be fulfilled, but since he cannot cease seeking it, he carries on

42

his work. The failure of vision turns into the visual art product, "the final beauty of a wall."[13]

The drive to creation is always nurtured by a feeling of a loss, of an incompleteness. The specific choice of creating visual art for restoring what is lost comes from a certain sensory perceptive constellation centering around the instinctual need of looking, touching, grasping. These sensory modalities mold the lost reality into a new one in the art product standing for the lost objects. The artist's unconscious urge to try again and again to regain what is lost is the source of his indefatigability, which thereby appeases his guilt and reconciles the superego. This serves as self-punishment and restores the destroyed objects. Reviving them allays the mourning for their loss. In essence, it is an autogamous process to unify the feminine and masculine wishes.

The enforced labor of producing without end can be endured because it becomes a self-satisfying act that makes success possible and provides the ecstatic feeling of being a creator. The highest level of the ego-ideal is then achieved. The artist reaches the summit where he can feel free of guilt. Through his creation he has made good the loss, as if he had been responsible for it. He sees himself in his work as well as its creator. Again we arrive at the interpretation that this is a victory of narcissism because to the artist his work is equated with immortality.[6]

7

The underlying synaesthetic processes of artistic activity are in essence the recurrence of a strong, instinctual, primitive drive pressing for discharge at a given time through a specific sensory organic function within an ego able to comply at the same time with instinctual demands. The oftener in early life these instinctual urges find gratification through the same sensory channels, the more the development of an artistic personality can be anticipated. Studies of child development have taught us that artistic creation is based on a specific sensory functional ability acting in coalition with other sensory organs.

The ego may use these dependable means of expression to guarantee the symbolic restitution of earlier infantile imagined lost objects. Artistic creation then becomes the ego's unconditional choice for achieving psychic equilibrium.

The impulse to artistic creation, then, is a derivative of the instinct of self-preservation. It rebuilds the past, when the ego became traumatized by real or imagined losses. The recreative activity of the artist materializes an illusion, a kind of *déjà-vu*, which nevertheless to him remains unknown. The drive to turn the unknown into reality derives from his depressive reaction to

43

traumatic loss. Since the feeling of loss was rooted in the illusion of incompleteness in his own body, artistic creation cannot give permanent gratification because the insatiable drive to create springs from the fountains of the infantile dream life which are never emptied.

In sum: in visual art, as in any other art, the artist tries to redeem a lost reality. The result is a visual art product. The intra-psychic instinctual processes and their irresistible need for discharge set the artistic activity in motion as a kind of acting out. The degree of tension calling for release is determined by varying circumstances. The trigger is actuated by the perception of subliminal sensory sensations. The kind of production is overdetermined and depends on the fusion of these perceptions with instinctual drives, as well as on social and cultural factors. The primary sense functions involved in artistic activity then have specific thresholds, and the infantile past becomes reincarnated through the art product into conscious reality.

The atomic age in which we live is beginning to change our ideas of reality. Light falls into the darkness of the unknown world. Visions that once would have been incompatible with the conception of reality are no longer merely imaginary. Hence, new forms of visual art will emerge.

Science creates new ways of knowing. But re-search is only the resumption of the child's curious search for the unknown. In this sense, science and art are twins. Art serves as the mediator between the imagination of the child and the sense of reality of the adult. The fate of visual art in the atomic age will depend on how these trends of the mind become unified. It may well be that form will take the lead in visual art, and that sculptural and architectural creation will make inroads into two-dimensional art.

REFERENCES

1 Sigmund Freud, "Dostoevsky and Parricide," *Collected Works* (London, Hogarth Press), Vol. 5 (1950), pp. 222-242.

2 —— "Das Interesse in der Psychoanalyse," *Gesammelte Werke,* Vol. 8, p. 416.

3 Ernst Kris, *Psychoanalytic Exploration in Art.* New York, International Universities Press, 1952.

4 Felix Deutsch, "Artistic Expression and Neurotic Illness," *American Imago,* 1947, 4: No. 3.

5 —— "The Art of Interviewing and Abstract Art," *American Imago,* 1952, 9: No. 1.

6 —— "Creative Passion of the Artist and Its Synesthetic Aspects," *International Journal of Psycho-analysis,* 1959, 40: Part 1.

7 Gyorgy Kepes, *Language of Vision.* Chicago, Paul Theobald, 1951 (1st ed. 1944).

8 Walter Boernstein, "On the Functional Relations of the Sense Organs to One Another and to the Organism as a Whole," *Journal of General Psychology,* 1936, *15:* 117-131.

9 Heinz Werner and Seymour Wapner, "Toward a General Theory of Perception," *Psychological Review,* 1952, *59:* 324-338.

10 Felix Deutsch, "Psycho-physical Reactions of the Vascular System to Influence of Light and Impressions Gained through Light," *Folia Clinica Orientalia,* 1937, *1:* No. 3.

11 —————— "The Sense of Reality in Persons Born Blind," *Journal of Psychology,* 1940, *10:* 121-140.

12 —————— *On the Mysterious Leap from the Mind to the Body,* New York, International Universities Press, 1959.

13 Joyce Cary, *The Horse's Mouth.* New York, Harper & Brothers, 1959. In this novel the artist sees on every wall the mirage of a picture which he imagines and which he paints, but then leaves behind him, to go on to the next wall.

LE CORBUSIER

Architecture and the Arts

THE PAINTING that has been transmitted to us by history is partly figurative, documentary painting. It was legitimate that this painting should be documentary for the reason that no special organism, no mechanism made it possible to do any better than the clever manipulation of the brush permitted.

Painting assumed a very special role during thousands of years: for one thing, that of constituting documentary archives or perpetuating a sermon or a speech; fixing, in more or less hermetic forms, a thought, a doctrine; making a permanent fact out of a fugitive event. But in doing this, and independently of these utilitarian tasks, painting—and this is its very foundation, its destiny—fixed figurations charged with lyricism. When painting was good, this lyricism was specifically that of forms, variable and infinitely diverse, plastic harmony. To move the sensitive heart—the wholesome hearts—to evoke poetry was then the definite aim of painting and the arts.

Today we are saturated with images. That impassive machine, the camera lens, has gone beyond the human retina. This mechanism fears neither heat nor cold; it is never tired. In consequence it has the advantage of exceptional sight to such an extent that its products are a revelation to us. They permit us to enter into the mysteries of the cosmos through investigations that our human possibilities could not hope to attain.

In consequence we are swamped with images, through the cinema as well as through the magazine or the daily newspaper. Is not, then, a great part of the work formerly reserved for painting accomplished? When an epoch is about to close, when it is animated by no collective motive, it drifts into delights of intimacy and tenderness. It is natural that at that moment painting should abound, that we should see countless painters working and living well. But let us turn the page. It had to be done one day, and today is the day. We are entering on a collective period: painting is losing part of its purpose; painters are losing their clientele. And that is the dramatic situation today, an anguish of being useless.

Let us try to see if the experience undergone by painting constitutes regression or progress. When an epoch becomes collective, or is possessed by indisputable communal needs, it then witnesses the appearance of a need to edify appropriate new systems of all kinds, and above all, there is the need to construct a new type of equipment.

It is useless to recall the significance of the mechanical revolution which took place in the last century: it has ridden over the societies of the world; it has overthrown everything, disturbed everything, molded everything. It has injured everything; but at the same time, to those who know how to read the times, it has brought a certainty of approaching release from distress and crisis.

With this marvelous instrument, which will henceforth take the place of our hands and our sweat—the machine—we will equip ourselves usefully, not only for comfort—an enormous, healthy form of comfort—but also this new period of mechanical civilization will awaken in us the joys of a maximum of individual liberty together with collective inspiration.

I will mention here some of the imminent work to be done: the equipment of our country, of all countries of the world: cities, roads, villages, farms, ports, all the places men inhabit or traverse. A gigantic activity seizing upon the entire world and placing us face to face with hitherto unsuspected tasks. This equipment opens the field of a new era to architecture. Elie Faure, placing himself on the historical plane, was able to state that in times of communal preoccupations, architecture has the floor.

And so the spirit of construction becomes our great preoccupation. It will no longer give charms of an intimate order, such as easel painting could give; it will bring the means for a new life for which the great factors at stake will be sun, nature, the culture of the body and the spirit—a sort of new selection introduced into human species. A new life, and, let us imagine it, a life of physical and spiritual beauty.

But what will become of painting, of sculpture? These two major arts, it seems, should accompany architecture. Their place is there. The architecture of modern times is not only that which the reviews publishing our works show; here are only the realizations of programs made when our hand has been forced, programs of doubtful interest which, nevertheless, have made it possible to approach the study of man, of his spiritual and physical needs. It will be a new start from zero, a good cleaning up of an enormous pile of mistakes, deformations, academic laziness. What modern architecture has accomplished up till now is but trifle and trash. It is, nevertheless, an accomplished revolution.

47

If we force ourselves to think about the great new works of modern times, we note that certain aesthetic pursuits are out of date. Other tasks present themselves on a new plane; we are entering into an epic cycle, one that appeals to the spirit of art, of course, and in consequence to the artists of spirit.

We are happy to have taken part in the startling efflorescence of the most liberating painting movement that has existed for a long time, an art movement that has brought us again in contact with great epochs of art and thought throughout many lands and ages, which brings with it unequalled possibilities for the future at the very moment when painting and statuary have lost the sense of style and degenerated into a bourgeois quietude —into a decadent art, nationalized through the good offices of the ministries of the beaux-arts, themselves inspired by the academies. I am referring here to the cubist movement which, with its humorous title, burst upon us like a liberation. This liberation was so powerful that I am quite willing to see in it the spontaneous and prodigious explosion that takes place somewhere in the world when, suddenly, at some spot, in some place or other, the exhaust opens and the event springs into life.

This revolutionary event took place with clarity and divination. It was the artists who flung it at the world like a bomb from the mouth of its projector. We must recognize what the arrival of cubism meant twenty years ago. It was a consequence, of course, of the labor of predecessors, a new link added to the chain of tradition; perhaps an immediate consequence of the work of a few great experimenters of the nineteenth century.

This art has been called abstract through a disquieting misunderstanding of vocabulary. (Whenever there is a question of an artistic baptism, idiotic terms are dug up, for it is always the enemies who do the baptizing.) This art is concrete, not abstract. In France this concrete quality could not escape the fate of the spiritual life of the country; that is to say, it could not escape a fundamental activity. At the core of international production, French art, called abstract, is essentially concrete. Its realism is inside. It proceeds by layers that are deep in organic equilibrium. We find again the origin, the route, the key, to each one of its elements.

And so we find ourselves in a position to use this art. In what synthesis will this be possible? As an architect and painter, I am every day freshly absorbed in the problem: Will the plastic arts be able to incorporate themselves harmoniously in the architecture of the present time with a sufficient sense of the new reality? It is no longer a question of incorporating painting and statuary in architecture, as was sometimes agreeably done at certain epochs, principally during the times of the greatest ceremony and frivolity from the Renaissance to the present.

I believe that we are entering upon an epoch that is infinitely more serious, in which we no longer have the right to "stick something on something," but in which the pure spirit of renovation will be expressed by organisms possessing an interior mathematics, together with fixed and inalienable places where the work of art will radiate in all its power in exact concordance with the potential forces in the architectural work.

As an architect I may say that architecture is an event in itself. It can live entirely on itself. It has no need either of statuary or painting. Architecture creates shelters. These shelters answer human needs, beginning with the simple dwelling place on up through the civic, intellectual, and mystic organizations.

It has been customary, during the last twenty years, to insist that our homes have need of art and artists. There are those who feel that a dining room should be described by a basket of fruit painted or sculptured on the wall. It is my opinion that a good roast on the table takes care of that better. The home demands a great many other things that are more urgent. The tradition transmitted to us by the prints or other testimonials from the past, shows us the home life in the time of the kings, which was universally reputed luxurious. Decorations did not exist in those dwellings; the people lived in robust simplicity, which was a proof of their moral health. As for luxury, it was often of doubtful mixture. After the revolution of 1789 people wanted a bourgeois king, then a workman king.

I believe that painting and statuary will be incorporated in architecture for the reason that architecture is beginning over again at zero to reorganize everything from the skeleton through to the skin. Animating this skeleton, architecture has edified an authentic symphony through light and the manner in which this light clarifies walls; its lyricism is made of intensely real psycho-physiological events, its controls are proportion. When all is ready for collaboration with the painter and sculptor it will not be with the intention of asking frivolous things of them. When we invite to our home a guest of distinction, of dignity, of real ability, and one whom we respect, we do not surround him with noise, we listen to him and he speaks amid the silence because he has something to say. In this collaboration of the major arts and architecture, dignity is not a vain pretension.

The conclusion becomes evident: such art requires distinguished personalities and distinguished temperaments. Who is prepared for this approaching task? I am afraid of the immense art production that has remained perfectly indifferent to the contemporary architectural event. I love walls, beautiful in their proportion, and I am apprehensive at turning them over to unprepared minds. For if a wall is spoiled, if it is soiled, if we kill the wholesome clear speech of architecture by the intro-

49

duction of an inappropriate style of painting or statuary, if we are not in the spirit, but against the spirit—it will mean just so many disappointing crimes.

There are two ways for us to call on painting. One way is entirely utilitarian. I have noticed, little by little, that the revolution in the modern techniques of the building profession was bringing us to an astonishingly complex biology of the house. This complexity of the modern plan puts us in opposition to the classical square room we have known so far. Sometimes, as a result of the biological necessity of the plan, curved or oblique partitions are necessary. It is through polychromy that the sensational play, the colored epic, soft, violent, can be introduced into a house. Using just those organic necessities of the modern plan, I have seen that tumults can be disciplined by color, lyrical space can be created, classification realized, dimensions enlarged and the feeling for architecture made to burst forth in joy.

This is not yet painting; it is architectural polychromy. I can, when walls overwhelm me by their presence, dynamite them with an appropriate color. But I can also, if the place is suitable, have recourse to a painter, ask him to inscribe his plastic thought in the spot, and with one stroke open all the doors to the depths of a dream, just there where actual depths did not exist.

The second way to interest painting carries with it a more concerted intention. The architect can make his composition with an a priori desire to bring out, at a given moment, the great song of plastic lyricism. That, then, is a complex of exalted harmony. But the danger he would run would be the dualism of two plastic events badly tuned: architecture and heterogeneous painting.

In the collaboration of mural painting and statuary with architecture envisaged, a discipline is needed, specific qualities of monumentalism and considerable preparation.

If we are at present wrongly judged in our manifestations of renovation, if the contemporary arts, painting, statuary, and even architecture, are only tolerated within certain bounds, it is because the opportunity has never been given us—and I am speaking of the small home as well as the city block—to create works whose contiguous surroundings would not be offensive. We have always been put aside in the question of site, infested with vestiges of the past—whether good or bad. We began our symphony with a proportion of 1 per cent modern spirit as opposed to 99 per cent old surroundings. There was nothing to exalt us, everything was against unity, and our continual role was to appear as heavyweights, the tough guys with the dirty, muddy boots stamping into an elegant tranquil society in order to set up our ways of thinking. And so it happened that our attitude was insolent, despite ourselves. On the day when harmony will reign in sufficient dimensions, the emotion of the people, of the masses, will be awakened; they will say, "It is beautiful."

We do not ask the man of the people to be familiar with the detours in the action that has brought about the result; but he will feel the harmony, the power, the clarity which we will have put there. When favorable circumstances will finally make it possible to rid ourselves of the depressing throwbacks which are the style today; when people will have ceased to look backward, to base their convictions on the Renaissance or the splendors of other days—many of which in fact might be disputed—we will then be sure, by keeping ahead and constructing things that go together, of provoking an enthusiastic unanimity.

JOHN E. BURCHARD

Alienated Affections in the Arts

THE GREAT architectural monuments of the past seem to have involved a complex alliance of architecture, sculpture, and painting, and even the lesser visual arts as well. Save perhaps for the present, there has not been an architectural peak for three or four centuries. But on all the earlier summits (Western or Eastern), up to and including the Renaissance, we always find a rich use of the allied arts. Such a use was often but not exclusively for religious purpose, usually but not invariably pictorial, generally but not inevitably didactic, seldom but yet occasionally a mere effort at embellishment. Whatever it was and wherever it was, it seems clearly to say to us that the painters and the sculptors were in harmony with the architects and that all were in harmony with their times; that there was agreement as to what the building and its art were for and as to the hierarchy of values within this purpose.

One does not need to know for certain that the architects were in charge to feel sure that the other artists were not "free." No sculptor would choose, in perfect freedom, to try to cram human figures at one scale into the narrow triangle of the Greek pediment or onto the semicircular tympanum of a Romanesque portal, to say nothing of the boundaries of the Gothic voussoirs; nor would painters press to embrace the limitations of the geometry of a dome or vaulted ceiling. Yet the artists managed all this with little more effort than seems to have limited the men of Lascaux as they carried their animals upside down, sideways, and right side up over the rocky protuberances of the caves, or the late-fifteenth-century French artist who painted the Last Judgment on the inside of the blind façade of the Cathedral of Sainte Cecile at Albi. No artist today would consent to be bound as all the Gothic artists were by the long-standing conventions laid down by the second Council of Nicaea. Yet with all these limitations—limitations of dictated space, of dictated subjects and symbols, of an ardent conformity

—these usually anonymous artists added to the architectural miracles of their ages.

After the Renaissance all this began to peter out, although the gestures continued into the twentieth century. The Georgian, amiable as it was, was pallid in contrast to the Renaissance, and so was its art. After the Georgian, the eclectics cast building in every imaginable form; in so doing they called upon sculptors and painters to fill their pediments and tympani and altars and ceilings and walls with appropriately placed and equally eclectic work, and the painters and sculptors responded, being cast in the same mold. But there was no fire in all this, and the iconography of the portal of Princeton's chapel was quite as unconvincing as the pale murals of Puvis de Chavannes in Boston's Public Library.

In the end this languor was mercifully put to death by the modern revolutionaries. But since the burial there has been an emptiness.

The assassination was no doubt overdue. To it we owe the novel potential for another great period of architecture which has been revealed if not fully realized in the work of a number of our contemporaries. The assassins were thorough. They expelled architectural history from the curricula, where it had come to be a quarry for details and reminiscences, not a breeder of philosophy. They eliminated charcoal drawing of nudes, which had become an end in itself and not a disciplined way of understanding other and nonhuman, even abstract, problems of form. They stripped buildings of ornament, and with the ornament went the other arts. Their polemics praised physical as opposed to aesthetic functionalism, which was in fact denied. They worshiped the possibilities of using industrially standardized and machine-made materials as opposed to those that were the product of handicraft and individuality; they praised the virtues of collaboration and anonymity, the primary eminence of structure, the aesthetic virtue of economy. Seeking to set himself in the vanguard of his contemporaries and to be clearly a man of his time, noting the rapid obsolescence of ideas in science and engineering, the rebellious architect could seek a corresponding virtue in ephemeral architecture, crave new materials wherever they could be found. More importantly, the creed was based on a new vision of interpenetrated space, which it then thought, less happily, to ally with relativity; the space was elegant but the analogy fuzzy, unconvincing, and indeed unnecessary.

Looking back over the thirty to forty years of a movement all but one of whose greatest leaders are yet alive, it seems probable that the extreme positions were necessary to clear a fetid air, to empty an overcrowded stage. The leaders may even have

53

entertained their personal reservations as the iconoclasm was in progress. In any event, the positions have been shifting of late. History has come back into the curricula though in different form; the tenets of visual design are now being challenged, just as lettering and charcoal drawing were a quarter-century ago; the visual functionalism of Louis Sullivan or Mies van der Rohe or Le Corbusier is accepted as being of at least as much importance as, and as no less "true" than, literal engineering functionalism. Many of the best of the architects now recognize, as their great predecessors have done, that the most efficient plan does not necessarily guarantee the happiest architecture and that the utility of a work of architecture may be quite as closely related to the empathy of the environment it induces as to mere matters of cost or of convenience in the daily routine. This is leading to a wide range of experiments away from literal technical functionalism, involving often a straining for structural effect, a straining for decorative embellishment, a straining for a new symbolism or a new monumentality. All this is hard to assess if only because it is so self-conscious and so new. In the same current are the debates about the relations of modern architecture to the other modern arts. These have been going on for a long time, but they are as yet unresolved. Perhaps nothing new remains to be said. Perhaps, nonetheless, the main lines are still worth recapitulation.

Not very many can be found to believe that the architecture of our times has found a way to use the other arts as effectively as in the other and "great" days.

This is despite the fact that the revolutionary architects of the 1920's felt a close bond with the painters, sculptors, and even critics and historians whom they estimated to be fellow-revolutionaries. Indeed, at the Deutsche Bauhaus workers in all the visual arts toiled together in a loose confederation. A few works of Brancusi or Gabo found their way to axes of modern buildings, just as Arp and Miró and Léger found occasional walls to paint. In the most recent days a more conscious effort to embrace the other arts has been made by architects such as Saarinen, Bunshaft, Gropius, and Breuer. They have sometimes tried conspicuously to involve contemporary artists in their buildings. But it is hard to claim that these efforts have been very successful, even when they were most purposeful. It is perhaps this evidence of failure that is most disturbing, or at least thought-provoking. It is easy also to adduce any one of a number of pat reasons why things are thus, but their patness becomes less convincing as one examines them in greater detail.

We have to concede, I assume, that we have not succeeded in our time in achieving a combination of architecture, sculpture, and painting comparable to that of the earlier great periods. We may not wish to dismiss this lightly. We can dismiss it by choosing to state the obvious truth that the present is not to be measured by the past and that the lack of success is therefore irrelevant; indeed, such a success is not even desirable. If we say this, or if we insist that there actually is success, then the discussion is over. Thus, let us assume that the success is at least incomplete and that the failure is significant. We may then wish to find reasons.

It is no doubt true that the great architectural arts of the past dealt with rather unified concepts and made use of symbols that had common current meaning. Today there are clearly more concepts, of which fewer, if any, are held with any real unanimity; and there is more confusion in the symbols, too. This must be combined with the other important fact that we seem to be confused about our dominant social goals; there is nothing so universal as the service of the *polis* or the idea of life as a preparation for Hell, Purgatory, or Heaven. This in turn leads to a vagueness in the hierarchy of building types. Office buildings and factories are larger, costlier, and often finer than churches or halls of state or education. But we are not agreed about the common significance of this at any level. Even those who proclaim our age to be an age of science would be hard put to it to prove that science has any real universality as a thing to be admired, or that laboratories, for example, are in any serious way symbolic of a general will. These two difficulties combine to trouble us.

When we examine the great architectures which have used art freely and well, we notice quickly that they were in the service of a great and generally accepted human purpose, most often religious; that their arts were more than mere embellishments of surface; that they added to the symbolism the building itself had, even carried specific messages which the building could not speak. If now we have a society in which there are no such generally accepted motives, no required symbolism, no universality of understanding of the symbols which exist—indeed in the arts a jungle of private symbols—the present consequence may be inevitable.

This offers difficult questions. Shall we admit that we have no common purpose and give up? Shall we say there is a common purpose if only it could be stated? If there is a common purpose, is it then a silly notion that at least a few artists might find beliefs of the society to which they could subscribe and which they might then portray in intelligible symbols? If this should come about, will it not be important that the men whose ideas are clearly expressed in paint or in sculpture shall not be downgraded while we forgive those whose ineptitudes or per-

55

versities succeed in concealing in a merciful haze the fact that they have no ideas at all?

But first one has to define the unity and catch the symbols, and our whole trouble may be that there is and can be no unity of our times and that therefore any symbols which emerge are at best representatives of fractional truths or beliefs.

Is it possible that we have our unities and down deep somewhere our symbols which need not necessarily be new ones, and that it is only perverse sculptors and painters who are to blame for the void? One can build a fair case for this.

Others may wish to argue instead that it is the public which is perverse, not the artists. But whether one blames the public or the artist, the end is the same: the contemporary artist has almost nothing to say to most of the people of his world.

The conflict that exists in our architecture and our art may be between the individual or creative action, and the group or implementive action; between the individual client, who may even be the artist himself, and the collective client, who, even for the most self-centered architect, can scarcely be the architect alone. This is not a conflict which could have been very well comprehended in past societies of the West or East.

The idea that the individual is of such majestic consequence is really a Renaissance idea. It has not yet been thoroughly tested by time or adversity. The determination to find a man behind every badge, an inventor behind every invention, a hero to cast every shadow, is neither Egyptian nor Greek nor Roman —nor Christian. The sculpture of Chartres is not talking about a personal Christ or a personal saint or a personal emperor. When Louis IX is awarded extensive hero worship by De Joinville, it is not as a man but as a type of saintly king. The idea that a personal artist or a personal art is of any real importance is thus a new idea and a fragile one; and the Renaissance notion of *virtù* is easily corrupted, but modern artists cherish it as a first principle, as do more and more modern architects.

On the other hand, the world is becoming more and more collective. This is not anything so simple as a mere matter of socialistic distribution of economic goods, however much promoted by tax structures. Everywhere group efforts and group decisions are extended. Few signs of the last quarter-century have pointed to any other road, whether or not it looks attractive. Architectural projects have become more and more complicated, demand more knowledges and skills, and have reached the point where pure intuition can be applied only by the rare genius and on a very small work. So the architects are pressed either to work collectively or to retreat into personal expression along with the other artists. Where they follow the first course, their collective committee work is often unsympathetic to the personal artists; where they try to be individualists, their personality is in conflict with the personality of another individualist, and this conflict is serious and bitter when it involves people none of whom has any higher social ideal than the expression of his own personality.

Against the trend to collectivism the painters and sculptors seem to have been the most obdurate defenders of individuality. The more society has seemed other-directed, the more determined they have seemed to be inner-directed. In older societies artists appear not to have tried to convince every one of their uniqueness. Indeed, in primitive societies such an essay might have led to expulsion from the tribe or worse. The Greek artist or the medieval artist did not set out to state generally held beliefs in personal and incomprehensible terms, much less to deny the generally held beliefs altogether. Yet in our society, which has been moving back to collective actions that would not have seemed strange to our pre-Renaissance ancestors, the painter and the sculptor have fought hardest and most successfully to remain personal.

In their determination to be themselves they have fallen to muttering, sometimes to each other but more often to themselves. They mutter that nothing matters except what they think of the world; that if the atom bores them it must be generally boring; that it is quite immaterial anyway whether anyone else understands what they say. But at the same time they do not wish to talk *sotto voce*, so they seek the market place. In this they may have been abetted by critics and buyers. Sometimes it has seemed that the parade of not always interesting or profound individualities is most brilliant when the artists are most certain that they are not being understood. Thus it is perhaps not so much that the society rejects them as that they eject themselves from the society. Such men could not be expected to contribute to the collective task of building, nor could their messages be expected to convey any common interest and hence to be appropriate for a building which was to serve the common purpose.

But it is quite as easy to lay the blame at the door of the architects. More and more of them seem to be following the painters into individual productions which can brook no helping hand. When they acted more collectively, as was the case at the beginning of the modern movement, they nonetheless produced spaces which were seldom friendly, and often hostile, to the introduction of painting or sculpture. Perhaps the architects, then, are too arrogant with their architecture, and despite their condescensions at the end of the project perhaps they have in fact excluded the artists by the nature of their own designs. Again, a considerable case can be made for the fact

57

that contemporary architecture may not want or permit a rich collaboration.

Herbert Read has been insisting that it does not. There was, he argues, a functional necessity for sculpture in some earlier times, notably in the time of the Romanesque, when the union of sculpture and architecture was happiest. But, he continues, the modern architect likes the angularity of his buildings, does not want them "softened" by sculpture, and it does not help that the sculpture is abstract, for the principle of "no softening" is yet supreme. Thus the innate monumentality of modern geometry cannot be contravened by the other arts. Mies van der Rohe points the same way when he says that the problems of architectural design are too complicated today to permit the architect to try to take care of the other arts as well.

Is this acceptable as dogma? Is it not clear that the tyranny of Read's four-square building is already threatened by the forms of Wright, Saarinen, Goff, Le Corbusier, even Stubbins, Stone, Breuer, and Yamasaki? But even if the four-square building is accepted as dominant, might not its transparency have opened up new possibilities for art, not at all like those of the wall, the tympanum, the vault, or the voussoir? Read's conclusion is that modern times will not permit such detours, that modern building methods are themselves the denial of sculpture save as the architect himself becomes sculptor by making the whole building into one sculpture. Out of it he has concluded that painting and sculpture must go their separate ways, that this independence is a source of strength for the culture as well as a possible weakness.

Among the accusations, it is not surprising that the artists find the architects arrogant, ignoring the other arts or trying merely to add them when the project is really finished, while the architects find the artists uncooperative. Architects and artists alike who are not given to reproaching others are likely to regard their independence as inevitable and hopefully profitable as well.

The argument goes: "Painting and sculpture are freed from the shackles of architecture," and "The building can at last have its complete and solely architectural unity."

Both architects and artists might if they wished push the blame on the rest of us. A great deal could be said to show that our democratic public is apathetic toward the arts, has impeccably bad taste when it discards apathy, and perhaps most of all values the arts so little that it is unwilling to sacrifice anything for art as sacrifices were obviously made in other days. There is little doubt from the evidence of project after project that budget-conscious men, working for corporations or for congresses, have deleted the fine arts and even the trees and grass that were regarded by the designer as integral parts of architectural proposals. Is balancing the budget a nobler aspiration than cultivating the arts? Many seem to think so.

There have been times in American history when men like Charles Follen McKim set out to demonstrate that it was cheaper in the long run to have good art than to go without it altogether. But these arguments have been specious. It does cost more to bring art into a building, and this cost is often used as an excuse to reject an art which is really not wanted for other reasons. Still, there is an economic question and it is not trivial. It is strange that it should be so weighty in a nation as prosperous as America. But this is still a nation that preaches a virtue in frugality. It is not frugal to add artists to the budget, so art in some way becomes unvirtuous. This attitude has never quite left us from the days in the early eighteenth century when an observer insisted that the grain-raising Plowman was more "serviceable to Mankind, than the Painter who draws only to please the Eye." That observer and most of his colleagues preferred the carpenter to the "curious carver" and insisted that it was always better to serve the necessities of people than to try to please their fancies.

Such arguments have long prevented Americans from projecting their architectural engineering to the heights that have been reached on some parts of the European continent, or from developing their landscaping to the pitch to be found in Japan. But since the collaboration between the other arts and architecture seems to have been no more powerful in other parts of the Western world than in America, it is hard to believe that an effort to achieve better results will break in the end on the rock of cost.

It is harder to assess the matter of public apathy. Some observers think it can be corrected only by better general education in the arts. This will no doubt be helpful, but the suspicion remains that if the artists and architects do well enough they will not fail of public appreciation and that the public is right to be apathetic about a good deal of what is done. It is much harder to see how much of the trouble, if any, rests with the positive bad taste which manifests itself in so many of the objects the public seems avid to buy.

It is probably safe to say also that the new technologies, and especially the speed of travel, which make the nature of vision different than it has ever been before, may have something to do with the dilemma; but surely not much, for it poses no fundamental opposition to the conjunction of the arts and building but merely calls for different expressions and different scales and perhaps different sequences, and the arts have successfully coped with comparable changes before.

59

Finally, how are we to proceed if artists and architects and money and desire can be assembled for a common purpose; and if no reason of economics, of aesthetic theory, of individualism, of consumer taste, of atomized society, predicts in advance that we cannot again achieve an operatic architecture?

Certainly it is not to be achieved by fiat or by essays. Certainly the architect poses difficulties if he insists upon thinking of the surfaces or the spaces of his building as something to be withheld from the other artists or to be given over for filling up long after all the important aesthetic decisions have been made. It seems probable that a deeper collaboration is needed. The classic and medieval artists may have been willing to work effectively in predetermined niches, but this seems impossible for the contemporary artist. There are possibilities that the whole building is sculpture and painting but beyond the capacity of even a great architect to mold by himself; there are surely times in the study of the shape of a building when the sculptor's or the painter's notion of the best shape might assist the architect in arriving at a form that not only would later impose the least limitations on sculptor or painter, but that might in fact be the best total shape. To this only the work of Le Corbusier seems an exception, but he is the only architect who is also a painter and sculptor of quality. Full collaboration has certainly not often been sought by architects, who might not even find it acceptable. It might not be acceptable to the other artists either, for it would entail responsibilities that extend far beyond the responsibility the artist now bears when he makes art for a building, or the one he disclaims when he goes disdainfully by, headed for the gallery.

It must be conceded that these views are personal and no doubt often subjective as well. But many people think that the problems posed are real. It may be interesting therefore to mount a colloquium at long range. To do this, I have written to a number of well-known architects and artists to interrogate them about quite specific questions. They have not had a chance to talk back at one another, only to talk back to me; but the next section presents their views fairly, I believe. The questions did not seek, encourage, or expect consensus, and not much has emerged. They did not reach enough people to achieve any statistical validity. What we have is a set of preliminary unproved statements, read to an obbligato of comment on a theme which each correspondent has had to imagine for himself. The correspondents were Walter Gropius, Pietro Belluschi, and Walter Netsch, architects; Eduardo Chillida, Harry Bertoia, and Richard Lippold, sculptors; Irene Rice Pereira and

Jimmy Ernst, painters. To their notes are added opinions by Le Corbusier, Jean Gorin, José Luis Sert, Reg. Butler, and Basil Taylor, drawn from other sources. Many other voices might have been invoked and might have spoken, but the present chorus fairly recognizes the range of opinion among those with contemporary minds, although no doubt ignoring the views of those who insist that our best escape is back into an eclecticism based on history.

Views on Art and Architecture
A Conversation

Arranged by John E. Burchard—
with the participation of Pietro Belluschi, Harry Bertoia, Reg. Butler, Eduardo Chillida, Jimmy Ernst, Walter Gropius, Le Corbusier, Richard Lippold, Walter Netsch, Irene Rice Pereira, and José Luis Sert.[1]

BURCHARD: Are the present relations between art and architecture, or art and the city, less rich than they have been in other great periods?

BERTOIA: No, they are as rich today as in any other time. They may be even richer, "in the sense that we have a greater vocabulary of forms and relations, certainly not in the sense of unity. Great periods attained higher levels of unity . . . the element of time had a tendency to condense and preserve those forms and relations which gave a greater unity. The irrelevant, if any, disappeared. Whereas today the irrelevant is still with us."

NETSCH: Whether less or more is not so important as that the present relations could be much richer.

CHILLIDA: These relationships are not so close as they have been in some privileged periods of the past.

BELLUSCHI: "Our generation has not succeeded too well in integrating the Arts of Painting and Sculpture with Architecture, because they no longer convey or explain literary ideas, but are more intent on the discovery of more fundamental but less obvious visual relationships. They wish in fact to contrive personal esthetic images of the kind of universe which science is progressively unveiling to our perceptions."

GROPIUS: "Yes, and this is precisely the reason why our period cannot be called 'great' in a cultural sense. For the average man a problem like the relation between art and the city hardly exists, not, anyway, to an extent that would engage his personal interest and willingness to let it take precedence over more immediate material and practical considerations."

PEREIRA: "I feel that today there is hardly any relationship between most contemporary art and architecture." If architecture means a "structural network of relationships which give dimensionality, form and a physical objective content to space, then, I would say that, in practically all cases, contemporary art, in particular painting, is the antithesis of structural form. Whereas, architecture is a building and formulating process, which requires intellection; present day art, and this is regrettable, has been concerned with the dissolution and fragmentation of form, structural relationships and space.

"In other words, unlike architecture, most painting today has no underlying structural framework within which to construct an object. Inasmuch as structural and form-giving properties are essential for conveying meaning and content, it would seem to me that representation in the visual arts has become a pictorial expression of a flat concrete abstractiveness.

"More precisely, contemporary art, in most cases, fragments the object and negates space. There is merely a dynamism in action and a dissolution of structural form. Architecture is a dynamic of relationships which involve space, give objective reality to structural form; and, within the form, is content and meaning."

BURCHARD: Most of us do seem to agree that these relations are not as rich as they have been in the past or as they might be now. Let us ask, then, "Does it matter?"

GROPIUS: Yes. "Historic examples of a rich relationship between architecture and the arts are extremely meaningful, since they present a challenge and an incentive for us to become more articulate in our own period."

PEREIRA: "I do feel that historical grandeur is meaningful. The qualities of elegance, beauty and order endow an age with inspiration and heightened sensibilities. Ideals and goals of perfection continuously bring consciousness to higher syntheses with the evolution of thought and knowledge. Without these universal qualities both art and architecture are impoverished; originality and the great individual are missing. It is a great loss to an historical period when these universal qualities are lacking."

NETSCH: Extrapolation of historical grandeur may be valuable to history. Let future history decide how well we have done. Our solutions should be for active participation and an interpretation of our culture.

BERTOIA: "If this has any importance, it is only as a measure of comparison and perhaps it would be of interest to point out the differences and similarities, but I don't think it would contribute to our capabilities to deal with present relations."

LIPPOLD: "The truly creative man has faith in his time."[2]

REG. BUTLER: There is no absolute reason for collaboration and it should not be treated as a moral imperative. A mural may be a very poor solution to a problem which was perhaps

63

vital in the seventeenth century and which has little meaning today. Men like Mies van der Rohe have a perfect right to their classic simplicity and economy.

The arts may be either harmonious or complementary. There are many permissible sculptural activities, such as the provision of textures, nonfunctional elements, etc., "but I do not think you can expect the contemporary sculptor to involve himself in a kind of dilution of aesthetic vitality in his work in order that it may fit happily on to the surface of a stressed skin concrete building or fit into the general disposition of mass which the average building represents today. If you want to use sculpture as such, as opposed to making use of sculptural decoration, I think you have to face the preoccupations which are in the minds of contemporary sculptors, and they are as strong as those in the minds of architects. Sculptors are concerned with the creation of a statement made in inanimate matter which can be regarded as a living thing . . . which is so sensitive and vibrant with the quality of living being that you will get that horrible effect of a crucifixion if it is attached to a building. . . .

"Any architect who wants to use sculpture should not sit down, scratch his head and conjure up some kind of stylised device which fits in in some way with the conception of contemporary architecture. Use sculpture as it comes, when you like it, and when you do not like it do not worry; carry on without any sculpture, because you get rid of the moral imperative which says you ought to have sculpture and you ought to have painting."[3]

BURCHARD: Let us assume now that the relations are not rich enough and that it does matter; then we might ask who or what is to blame. Is it perhaps because there are no common visual symbols any more?

BERTOIA: There are plenty, "but they are not substantiated by a common unity of thought."

NETSCH: We have them, but they are hard to perceive in our complicated society, and more frustrating for the creative artist to reveal. . . . Our artists are well related to the world of space and science, and our symbols will not appear common until later.

BURCHARD: In the absence of other comments and in my understanding of some common symbol which would require it to be both current and clear, it seems to me we may take it that this is one of the difficulties, unless we want to say that visual symbols are no longer necessary. Is there perhaps another difficulty, that we lack any dominant social goals?

NETSCH: Probably so. We overemphasize our dramatic larger-than-individual cultural contribution, i.e., technology. We have a more diffuse and greater opportunity for petty self-expression at the expense of critical evaluation. As a society we feel no awesome premonition of doom, everlasting punishment, nirvana. Our cities are no longer dramatic social magnets save in economic terms and in the most urbane cultures; yet our art is either historical or in museums, not in squares and churches— not in the suburbs. We have more leisure time, with even more expected, and our recreation is spectator-oriented. We lack individual patrons to support artists over a period of years, with resulting creative continuity and hopeful opportunity. Our political cultural goals are confused between the individual and the group. The economics of our time does not include art as a necessity, and economics dominates our general culture. We fear controversy and dislike to be thought radical in a conservative society. We lack critical appreciation or any desire to have our work evaluated before its public appearance. Creative artists generally occupy a secondary social position. Thus historically we may be looked on as another example of a fragmented group in a fragmented world—another example of diffusion. With isolated exceptions, this is no doubt the true picture today. But it need not be our fate. Architecture and art have gone against the current before.

BERTOIA: "A dominant social goal is strongly lacking. This may produce more varied relations but not necessarily any cohesion. At best they are discontinuities in a matrix of inertia."

LIPPOLD: "Naturally, the chief requisite for the architect and artist is an agreement on the forces which unite them in spirit in a given age, and further unite them with all men alive at the same time. This demands the same faith of both. There is no need to describe again the nature of our mid-twentieth century sources of faith, because they have been discussed thoroughly before and ought to be in the blood of anyone who is wholly alive in our age of space-yearning and dematerialization. It is anyone's privilege to rebel at the evil aspects of our time and to yearn for previous faiths or await a happier future. I believe the artist and the architect cannot afford the luxury of such escape techniques."[2]

GROPIUS: "I believe that if we as a people cannot evolve a clearer picture of our common objectives and unite our moral forces behind their realization, the desire of the architect and artist to create unity will remain thwarted, and his individual contributions towards beauty and order will remain isolated. Only when a social or spiritual goal has become clearly identified in the mind of a society does it become the inner substance of its works of art. Lacking such a common objective we have, as often as not, come to accept the substitute of a preconceived formal pattern, superimposed on the living tissue of human activity, to achieve at least an external order in place of plain chaos. But such order is of a precarious character, easily uprooted and soon ignored when it remains unabsorbed by life and inexpressive of its real motives.

"But if our democratic societies have, so far, not shown enough unity of purpose and, therefore, few convincing manifestations of general cultural significance, the authoritarian societies have, in spite of strong directional control and forcible drive, contributed nothing at all to a new visual interpretation of this century. All-embracing ideas can apparently be instilled by an act of will, but they cannot be made to flower into art by decree. Culture grows from the grass roots or not at all, and when it does it creates unity in diversity, the very climate for a close relationship between all the arts."

BURCHARD: Perhaps we have such precise techniques of communication now that we really don't need visual expositions any longer?

NETSCH: "As long as we have eyes, a heart, and the eternal questions, we have a need for visual exposition—when we no longer wish to see, to think or to ask, we have no need for the many things that make us 'the fortunately endowed animal.' "

GROPIUS: "A visual symbol is a dramatic shortcut, understood instantly and intuitively, in contrast to literary prose, which logically enlightens the intellect step by step. Neither way of expression can ever be dispensed with since each reflects different aspects of human nature."

BERTOIA: "Increased literacy does not remove the need for visual messages. To my mind, literacy should increase the need for the visual expressions, provided we do not accept substitutes, namely, one medium of expression for another.... Man's deepest thoughts perhaps remain unexpressed, but he surely can exercise his intelligence in choosing, among the various media, the one best suited in coming closest to what he wants to say."

LE CORBUSIER: "Spare us from deceptive lessons upon the walls of our public buildings. The newspapers can do this task —they come out every day: the technical papers do it too—they can be filed away! Four hundred years have passed since Gutenberg performed his labours! This would be a confusion of motives: things would become out of scale. Everything, good and bad, has a right to be communicated to the public— but in a suitable form."[4]

BURCHARD: Does any of us think that we can blame the difficulty on the determined overindividualism of the painters and sculptors?

BERTOIA: Does this mean the artist of today is of a different breed from the equivalent of the "great" days? No. By all counts he is still a human being. If he behaves differently it

66

serves only to indicate the age of specialization, if not the "lack of a dominant social goal."

PEREIRA: "In the 'great' days, for instance the Renaissance, artists and architects were preoccupied with a new world-view; man and nature; a new humanism. 'Conformity' in this sense was a general or universal concept within which the artist's intellectual curiosity and senses were stimulated. Today artists are expected to mature within a preconceived theory or style. This preconceived theory is not created by the artist (who has become quite inarticulate) but by external demands, pressures and authorities who try to figure out what the artist is doing and then impose the style or form within which they expect the artist to mature.

"However, it is my feeling that contemporary architecture makes a positive contribution to the understanding of this age— love of techniques, collective living, organization, light and air, etc. Whereas, the visual arts show a dissolution of thought and the disintegration of the object and consciousness."

NETSCH: The search for technique and a calligraphy for our culture has clearly been individually approached, and probably the fractured aspect of our visual society has made this inevitable. The lack of historic participation has certainly made us rusty. But there is disappointment in talking to a well-known painter, to discover that he has no interest in participating in architecture because he feels his work is too personal. He thinks Brancusi or Giacometti might have participated because they were less personal. This unwillingness to participate is certainly a serious barrier to the richest collaboration. But I would still want to foster such individuality while limiting participation to those who I believed wished to speak.

LIPPOLD: I believe that there must be three-way collaboration between architect and artist and public. Any one can fail. "I have also, alas, frequently heard from sculptors the complaint that a true collaboration makes the sculpture nearly invisible, or forfeits it to the scale and mathematics of the building. To this I can only answer: 'Hurrah!' As in a love affair, when sacrifice of one's self to love itself opens new worlds of understanding of the human condition, so, I believe, the ascetic artist, by bending his forms to the master proportion and social creed expressed in a good building, can fulfill his social destiny."[2]

BELLUSCHI: "Non-objective Art, in my mind, is trying to define new kinds of order in the apparent chaos of human life. Modern Architecture in a way has traveled a parallel road."

GROPIUS: "One of the bequests of the nineteenth century which handicaps us today is the obsession with the idea that individual genius can only work in exalted isolation, a view which was quite foreign to other periods. It prevents the public

67

from understanding the new efforts at collaboration among architects, and between architects and artists, and constantly throws us back into unwarranted jealousies and confusions. Slow and painful are the attempts at seeking points of contact again after the long alienation between the different branches of the arts, and artists and architects cannot be blamed if they do not want to rush into this development unguardedly."

BURCHARD: I would have intensified the last question had I thought it would serve a useful purpose. I might have suggested that the dominant themes of today circle around truth-searches of science and the hope for benign applications of technology as much as they did around a Last Judgment in the thirteenth century. I might have suggested that the artists who worked with questions of the Last Judgment had more than a purely intuitive understanding of the theology involved and what the society needed to be told. I would then have added that I cannot think of an artist or architect of my acquaintance (and there are some good ones) who is not really an ignoramus about science and confused about technology, and rather proud of it. Then I would have asked why we should trust a purely intuitive understanding of science. But this would have opened up an entirely different range of issues, which might well be debated another day. Let us turn away from the poor artists and sculptors and ask the other question. Are our architects unduly arrogant, egocentric, or even autocratic, and is it this that leads them to disdain the use of the other arts and ignore the aspirations of the other artists?

BERTOIA: "If it is the autocracy of Le Corbusier, we have the best fusion of the architect, the sculptor, the painter, etc. If it is the autocracy of Mies, we have the greatest possible unity of form. If it is the autocracy of Wright, we have the best relationship of man-made to nature-made brought into harmony. If we have the autocracy of all three and many more, then we have much variety, but may find ourselves searching for unity. These examples of autocracy in architecture do not exclude the other arts. Here is ground for thought."

NETSCH: "Many artists and architects claim that our culture has no place for art in architecture. I think this means a lack of critical courage, an unwillingness to be counted; or a lethargy and conservatism which prevents the architect from including art in his concept. Good contemporary architecture denies nothing positive and in creating space accepts art."

GROPIUS: "If architects should have deluded themselves and others into believing that they hold positions of autocratic leadership, they cannot be living in the world *I* know. Anybody who has undertaken to steer a client toward architectural solutions which would transcend the merely practical and economical approach knows that he will have his hands full without trying to add proposals for collaboration with painters and sculptors. If he has such intentions, he is usually forced to hide them carefully in the beginning for fear of alienating his client right from the start. When he has finally succeeded in breaking ground, it may be too late to incorporate the artist's work organically into the whole concept. It does not normally occur to a client to look upon the architect as the natural ally of the artist and to accept his leadership as the coordinator for all the arts. His education has never offered him such insights, and it is hard to re-educate him to see things in their proper perspective after he has spent a lifetime disregarding artistic values and responsibilities."

BELLUSCHI: Modern Architecture (traveling the parallel road with modern painting and sculpture) "has found that the way to give transcendent quality to a building is to emphasize its structure and to manipulate its space sequences rather than to introduce sensuous externals as it was done in the past. The result is that the architect tends to regard with impatience and as an intruding element any work which tries to speak for itself in a place where every part is meant to be a clear, self-sufficient declaration. This is particularly true when we observe that any statement the modern artist makes is meant to be a unique expression of his personal world which must be heard on its own terms as his own 'message of discontent.'

"This fear of a confusion of voices trying to be heard has made integration between the so-called Visual Arts and Architecture a most difficult task. Only the artist-architect, as one man, could succeed in this work of integration—or perhaps a rare combination of two men whose enthusiasm is born at the same time and as a shared experience. But this kind of collaboration is rare. We must admit that pure, uncompromising Architecture is not at ease with Art, even if thirsting for it, because Art will seldom add; much more often it will detract from the purity of the architectural idea."

LIPPOLD: "To my astonishment, however, some of the seemingly most important architects to-day do not exhibit this faith [in their times] when they ask artists to collaborate with them whose work forms a most striking contrast of form and material, and denies the technological and spacial concepts of the buildings in question. I can only consider such lack of faith as pathetic as I would the use of Greek or Egyptian carvings on the portals of Chartres in order to assure its architect that it would not take off for Heaven!"[2]

ERNST: "Architectural expressions have always given the appearance of merely following the influences of other art forms. And there is no reason to believe that this impression

69

will change. No serious artist will use such an argument to downgrade architecture, because he knows that the area of public responsibility is heavier on the architect than on the artist, that the experiment in architecture is by far the more courageous because it becomes immediately public. Unlike the artist, the architect cannot discard privately any of his finished work. The architect, on the other hand, should not assume that this larger burden of immediate public responsibility entitles him to cast painting or sculpture in the same mold. It is this latter 'autocracy' which is rightfully resented even by those artists who do not object to architecture calling itself one of the arts.

"Almost all of the artists of my acquaintance are uninhibited in the opinion that most architects are deliberate in their apparent contempt for painting and sculpture; that architects seem to consider it a sign of professional weakness if their work is in need of artistic addenda; that some of them consider the artist a mere mechanic who is to carry out a visual idea for which the architect could not spare the time of execution.

"I cannot deny that more often than not I am given to similar opinions, but I must admit that I am at a loss to present any constructive plan or alternative to bring about a better working relationship. It would be folly for any artist to insist on individuality on the one hand, and to pretend on the other that a realignment of the professions is possible on the basis of a general all-inclusive plan. It will not do to deny that the more the architect takes on the character of the independent artist, the more difficult the relationship between the two must become. The situation could be resolved if the architect were content to be a benign coordinator who impersonally oversees the technical assembly of materials to fill an existing physical need for shelter. But surely no artist could expect this of another creative individual. And he would certainly consider it to be a worthless endeavor to be a part of an effort that can only result in mediocrity."

LE CORBUSIER: "The real builder, the architect, can construct the most useful building for you, because he knows most about volumes. He can in fact create a magic box enclosing all that your heart desires. Scenes and actors materialise the moment the magic box appears; the magic box is a cube; with it comes everything that is needful to perform miracles, levitation, manipulation, distraction, etc. The interior of the cube is empty, but your inventive spirit will fill it with everything you dream of—in the manner of performances of the old Commedia dell' Arte."[5]

BURCHARD: It is possible also to blame the clients, the customers, the public taste, the public frugality in the arts, the destructive influences of technology, but it is refreshing to note that none of you really wishes to stress these handicaps. Most of you admit they are there, but you seem to think them less important than the more fundamental questions already discussed, although Walter Gropius consistently asks for education, education, and education. In spite of your restraint in the argument, I hope any citizen who happens in on this discussion will think about what he himself is doing or has done to encourage a better architectural-artistic world. I would expect him to be ashamed if he can bring himself to be candid. The modern Pericles seems hard to find. But whether or not this is so, shall we end on a pessimistic note? In other words, can any one suggest that there is anything to be done?

ERNST: "All talk of finding a level on which to 'integrate' the various arts to make them more 'meaningful' is Utopian. Utopia presupposes mediocrity, conformity, and the prohibition of dreams.

"The obvious solution to any contemplation over the relationship between art and architecture appears to be no planned solution at all. The best course is to allow for continuing wider divergence, if that is what the various individual creative ways indicate. Magnetism, if any, can exist only between individual practitioners and not between the professions generally. In each case, the degree of domination, or lack thereof, can only be determined by component parties to an idea."

LIPPOLD: "A finished building with its sculpture, painting, and other 'adornments,' stands most successfully when it is 'incomplete,' waiting, like a poem, to be read. If the picture presented to the user is so complete as to exclude him, to be looked at from a distance, every detail of space, scale, and equipment so complete in itself that it substitutes for the man who would enter, then I believe that a true collaboration of 'three' has failed. . . .

"It simply means that the artist cannot embrace only the building or only the spectator. . . . Technically, he must place the scale of his work just above the scale of the man who sees it, and indicate thereby the scale of the architecture with which it works. He must also attach his work so tightly to the building, in similarity of proportion, material, and technique, that try as he might, the user cannot pry it loose (visually) and thus is forced to move through the sculpture or painting to the building, and of course, back down through it again to himself, experiencing in such unified, proportional relationships the place of all forms in our cosmic entity. . . .

"The architect's responsibility in this is simply to allow the artist to achieve this double rapport, neither asking him to

71

isolate his work from both building and user, nor asking him to substitute it for the user, or for weak areas in the design of the building."[2]

SERT: "The works of the great creators of modern art are not shown in the places of public gathering, and are only known to a select few. Our best artists are divorced from the people. Their works go from their studios to the homes of wealthy private collectors, or to the deep-freeze compartments of the museums. There they are catalogued and belong to history. They join the past before they meet the present."[6]

TAYLOR: "The notion of building as a kind of exhibition place for painting and sculpture is an undesirable one."[7]

GROPIUS: "I had a correspondence with Jean Gorin. He feels the same as I, that it is not enough to call in a number of famous artists and hand them out this or that spot in the building to be filled with a work of art. True collaboration must start from scratch, the members of the group stimulating each other, conceiving the idea in mutual exchange as the builders of the old cathedrals who were living at the site devoting their life to the task. Time was not of the essence. They changed and rebuilt until they were convinced that it was good enough. Consider, for example, the open letter Gorin wrote on 6th March 1956." A translation and paraphrase might read as follows:[8]

Del Marle said in 1952 that the question was no longer one of ornamental polychromy, something decorative, something fundamentally sensory, which would harmonize with the styles of the centuries, but rather one of an architectural polychromy, sprung from the newest evolutions of painting and architecture, a modern polychromy, characterized by rationalism, the flagrant sign of our period.

Architectural polychromy was not to be considered as an adjunct to architecture, to be more or less necessary at will; it could not let the color stand in a secondary position vis-à-vis the plan. Indeed, it did not relate to the plan but rather to space. It was not enough to put plaques of color on asbestos cement.

The synthesis of the arts cannot consist in putting sculpture and painting in appropriate architectural locations or even natural ones, even when they are very appropriate, because that is, when all is said and done, nothing but the program of a museum. We believe that the true synthesis of the arts is to be found in the architectural work itself and commences from the first stages of the conception. This was not what was done at UNESCO. Many works of art were commissioned but they were not integrated into the architectural work. Even though the execution of the work was arrested for a long time no sculptors were invited to collaborate with a view to realizing a true and constructive unity, a synthesis of the arts, as it has just been defined.

72

BURCHARD: It is no doubt the view of most artists and of a few architects such as Gropius that the synthesis will never be achieved until it is attempted from the beginning. This too is my view. But the difficulties are many and severe, as we are reminded by almost every collaborator. Indeed, most architects and most artists seem to think they are too many and too severe. It can all be summed up perhaps by a statement from—

CHILLIDA: "This problem of integration of the arts is generally badly focused. It is not a matter of adding anything to the architecture. It is rather a matter of making architecture more open to the other arts from the start or early conception of the project. Architecture, painting, sculpture, etc., are the result of different creative forces, and perhaps a careful analysis of these creative forces will be the way to obtain a closer integration in the work that is only a plastic expression of those forces.

"In a rose, for example, the function of form and color, etc., is something that originates in the seed.

"The real collaboration aiming at the total integration of the arts should result from an equilibrium of forces. I believe that this equilibrium may not be a plastic equilibrium.

"Isn't it a miracle, for example, the integration, if we can call it that, of the eyes in the face of a human being? There is something that can be an equilibrium between the physical and spiritual dimension. Volumes and surfaces find themselves balanced not by what the eyes are but by the things they do. I believe that what concerns us is the task of men who give a color to the things they look at, who see in the objects they look at, according to the images they already have inside them."

REFERENCES

1 Most of the discussion is taken from private communications by the various participants. Where they have not been paraphrased, the comments are included in quotation marks. Quotations from other, printed sources are identified by independent references.

2 Richard Lippold, "Three in One," *Balance* [National Institute for Architectural Education, 1957], *4*, 6-7.

3 In a discussion, "Architecture and the Other Arts," held at the R.I.B.A., 7 January 1958, and published under that title in *The Journal of the Royal Institute of British Architects*, February 1958, 65: 118-119.

4 Le Corbusier, "The Core as a Meeting Place of the Arts," in *The Heart of the City* (CIAM 8), edited by J. Tyrwhitt, J. L. Sert, and E. N. Rogers (New York: Pellegrini and Cudahy, 1952), p. 48.

5 Le Corbusier, *op. cit.*, p. 52, caption to Figure 50.

6 José Luis Sert, "Centers of Community Life," in *The Heart of the City*, pp. 14, 16.

7 Basil Taylor (discussion), *The Journal of the Royal Institute of British Architects, op. cit.*, p. 122.

8 Jean Gorin, *La Synthèse des Arts Majeures, Est-elle Possible?* (Mimeographed copy in the possession of Walter Gropius.)

EDUARD F. SEKLER

The City and the Arts

*. . . if one could create this,
the life of a city—it would
be wonderful!*—Picasso

WHEN WE CONSIDER the city and the visual arts of today, certain
associations readily occur; probably we shall recall a few works
of art which contribute decisively to the physiognomy of a city
—fountains for example, or statues such as Zadkine's at Rotter-
dam—and a host of minor occurrences which are part of the
urban image, including the transitory art of poster and display.
We may also remember the many attempts undertaken in
recent years to achieve in the city a fuller integration of architecture with all the visual arts, and how little has come of it.
The practice of bringing in the artist long after all relevant
planning has been done yet prevails, instead of taking advantage of his sensitivity when everything is still *in statu nas-
cendi.*

If we turn to museums and exhibitions as part of a city's
cultural life, we gradually become aware of more and more
levels of contact between the city and the arts. Proceeding
from simple contiguity in time and place to deeper interdepend-
ences, we may ask ourselves what is the role the city plays
in the artist's life and activity.

As patron, the city calls on the artist to give permanence to
collective memories and aspirations. The very beginnings of
monumental art are involved in this process. The temple artists
of the sacred city-states of ancient Mesopotamia were the first
in a long line that leads to the artists of the Greek *polis* and
the Roman Forum, to the masters who fashioned the statue of
Roland watching over the medieval market place, and to the
Renaissance artists who in their frescoes commemorated the
great moments of Florence or Siena.

On a simpler level the city may become merely a model, providing the painter with views which he chooses for their special
visual appeal, as he would a motif in a landscape. Yet beyond

74

the beauty in portrayals of cities—the golden crispness of Canaletto's light, the gaiety or melancholy of Pissaro's boulevards, the tenderness of Utrillo's grays—there may be a more intense penetration. Then the city simultaneously becomes the object and the medium of expression of a vision that, in the image of the city, surveys the entire condition of man, and thus achieves what Cézanne did for the landscape: to subsume its reality in the light of his own commitment, penetrating beneath the surface into unfathomed depths.

El Greco's brooding yet triumphant Toledo, Chagall's entranced transfigurations of Paris and Vitebsk, Kokoschka's cosmic panoramas, Delaunay's ever recurrent Eiffel tower, and Grabner's many visions of the Stefanskirche—all share one characteristic: they are not merely *vedute*, but their form is illuminated from an inner image. This inner light may glow so strongly that in its radiance the city as a model fades out completely, while the artist ceases to be concerned with the city as patron or as symbol. Yet the city is present to him all the time, not dimly in the background but as a necessary condition for the fullness of his creative experience, as one pole of maximum potential.

Another pole would obviously be the countryside with its directness in all the manifestations of life, its colors and lights, its scents and sounds as they follow the cycle of the seasons, and with man in close relation to these natural events. Here, it seems, the contemporary artist cannot be anything but a guest, an outsider, who may eventually be accepted but who carries the city with him even though he may have fled its squalor and despair, its unrest and frustration. Artists in our civilization may retire into the country, but they cannot pretend to be of the country. Between artist and city there seems to be a deep inner connection whose root is still undiscovered.

In some cases the character of the city as a work of art may be involved as representing man's unequivocal assertion in visual terms of spiritual presence. But the modern city as a whole is a work of art only in those areas where aesthetic reality can dominate physical reality. There must be a more general quality in a city that is important to the artist. Perhaps we may come closer to recognizing it if we think of it in terms of the possibilities it offers for essential choice and commitment, for that breadth of experience so many artists have indicated. Marc Chagall wrote of Paris, "At every step the city itself was my teacher in everything. The tradesmen in the market, the waiters, the porters, the peasants, the workmen—all were surrounded by something of that astonishing atmosphere of light and freedom *(lumière-liberté)* I have not found anywhere else."

75

It is sometimes assumed that the fullness of ideal city life can be brought within the reach of people not living in cities by modern media of communication and transportation. This error is based on a misunderstanding of the nature of this fullness, on the inability to distinguish between vicarious and genuine experience. The vicarious may be characterized as a tendency to maximal passivity coupled with a minimum of choice, as in watching images on a screen or listening to a program determined elsewhere. The genuine means active participation and a maximum of choice, with all the risks involved. Genuine participation and a restricted amount of choice are perfectly compatible with life in the country. But life in a city of proper size and form can provide a more complete range of possibilities for choice in matters of fundamental concern; in fact, the urban way of life alone seems to guarantee that almost paradoxical pairing of contrasts where opportunities exist side by side for a diversity of direct personal contacts and for an anonymity that is humane because not imposed.

The gamut of choice between these extremes is curtailed if the city has an inappropriate form. Every lack of differentiation in its physical pattern means a negation of choice, and thus a negation of true urbanity. An inhuman anonymity then results, that of particles in an amorphous mass, whereas a genuinely urbane anonymity is comparable to the condition of a mosaic, in which each cube contributes to the full splendor of the whole without losing any of its own lustre—in fact, the individual *tessera* only asserts its real significance within the total complex.

The artist belongs to the city, as I think, because, especially during his formative years, he needs the tension generated between extremes of choice, and the ensuing challenge of commitment that gives his work vitality. Neither city nor art can flourish in an atmosphere of vicarious experience and failing commitment. Here lies the common root of a crisis that threatens both today.

When the form of cities degenerated, and they failed to fulfill their proper function of providing a variety of experience, they were abandoned. But the flight from them often ended sadly in a no man's land, neither city nor country, whose isolation offered little that had been hoped for, and still less of what had been left behind.

When the arts lost their immediate relation to experience, there began a quest which, though initially successful, ended in a perturbing impasse: as everything not a direct formal expression of personal inner experience was abandoned, all claims of wider communicability had to be forsaken. It then became increasingly difficult to judge whether a frantic search

OSKAR KOKOSCHKA, View of the Thames, 1925-1926.
Room of Contemporary Art Collection, Albright Art Gallery, Buffalo, N.Y.

for form was not still going on long after the fading flame of commitment had ceased to illuminate the inner image. There appeared a real danger that isolation in a spiritual suburbia ridden with little formalisms and mannerisms would follow.

Fortunately, the condition is not insurmountable, since real artists quickly recognize both the impossibility of creating valid form without commitment and the need of separating true from false claims to such commitment. There is no question here of taking up nonartistic causes such as "social realism" or of mistaking conformity for commitment. A scrutiny of the work of great artists reveals the meaning of commitment in our context as an involvement which, in the act of facing reality, derives a statement of more than personal validity from inner standards of a purely personal kind. It seems to me that the demand for an involvement beyond purely personal validity— beyond the walls of any ivory tower—is an ethical postulate similar to the demand for a civic commitment.

When the artist fails, technical and formal remedies alone can help as little as in the case of the ailing city. When the city fails, it is not for technical or formal reasons but from a lack of readiness on the part of its inhabitants to embrace an urban way of life as demanding as it is rewarding. For urbanity is not to be acquired gratuitously or by any amount of training on a formal level alone, which produces nothing but a hollow like-ness. Urbanity is a reward for commitment, a reward of the same order as an artist's satisfaction with a work well done, not only in terms of craftsmanship and formal appearance but in lasting truth and power.

Artists on Art and Reality, on Their Work, and on Values

MANY A MAN has a bonfire in his heart and nobody comes to warm himself at it. The passers-by notice only a little smoke from the chimney, and go their way. . . . I am drawn more and more to the conclusion that to love much is the best means of approaching God. Love a friend, any one, or anything you like, and I tell you, you will be on the right road to learn more. You must love with a high and intense determination, with your will and your intellect, and seek always to deepen, expand and improve your knowledge, for that way lies God. If a man loves Rembrandt profoundly, then in his heart of hearts he knows God. Another man may study the history of the French Revolution, and he will not be a sceptic, for he will feel the power that shapes our ends. If you have attended the free lectures at the College of Misery, for a short time even, and have paid attention to what you have seen with your own eyes and heard with your own ears, you will reap a firm faith and learn more than you can express in words. He that hath eyes to see, let him see. Afterwards you can be a little abstracted at times, and dream awhile. I know that some become too abstracted, too dreamy, and it may quite well happen to me one of these days. They say the dreamer sometimes stumbles in this world, but afterwards he climbs up again.

VINCENT VAN GOGH *(July 1880)*

WASSILY KANDINSKY

TODAY THERE are two dangers. One is the completely abstract use of color in geometrical form (danger of degenerating into purely external ornamentalism): pure patterning. The other is a more naturalistic use of color with concrete form (danger of shallow fantasy). Thus we reach either pure abstraction (more thoroughgoing even than geometrical form) or pure naturalism. Either of these alternatives may in their turn be exaggerated. Everything is at the artist's disposal. Today is one of freedom such as characterizes great germinative periods. At the same time this freedom is of great compulsive force, since all potentialities stem from the same root, internal necessity.

That art stands above nature is no new discovery. New principles do not fall gratuitously from the sky, but are causally connected with the past and future. What is important to us is the transitory position of the principle and the way in which it can best be used. It must not be forced. But if the artist tunes his character to this note, the sound will reverberate in his work. The "emancipation" of today must advance in terms of internal necessity, which is the origin of the objective in art. Natural forms make boundaries which often are impediments to this expression. Thus they must be set aside and the freed space be used for the objective side of the form—construction for the purpose of composition. This explains the obvious trend of today which seeks to develop the constructive forms of the epoch. Cubism, as a transitory form, demonstrates how natural forms are subordinated to constructive purposes and what unessential hindrances these realistic forms are. A transition is cubism, in which natural form, by being forcibly subjected to constructional ends, becomes an impediment.

In any case, there is gradually coming into use, as the only possible road to objective form, a more denuded type of construction. It is not obvious geometrical configurations that will be the richest in possibilities, but hidden ones, emerging unnoticed from the canvas and meant for the soul rather than the eye.

The hidden construction may be composed of seemingly fortuitous shapes, without apparent connection. But the outer absence of such a connection is proof of its inner presence. Outward loosening points toward an internal merging. This holds good for drawing and painting alike.

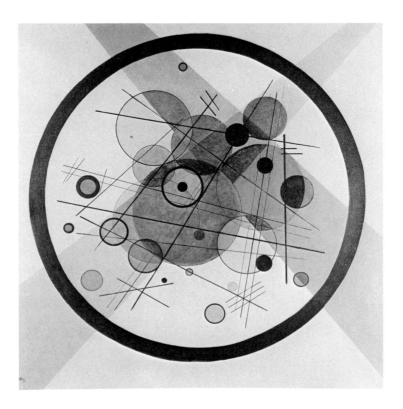

WASSILY KANDINSKY, Circles in a Circle, 1923.
Courtesy of the Philadelphia Museum of Art.

The future structure of painting lies in this direction. Those "somehow" related forms are actually very precisely bound. And perhaps this relation may even be expressed in mathematical form, only one is dealing here perhaps more with irregular than regular figures.

The final abstract expression of every art is number.

It goes without saying that this objective element is in absolute need of rational factors (objective knowledge of the craft) as a necessary cooperating force; and these objective factors will enable the work of today to say forever "I am" instead of "I was."

JUAN GRIS

THE WORLD from which I draw the elements of reality is not visual but imaginative.

Though the way of looking at the world and the concentration on certain of its aspects—that is to say, the aesthetic—has varied from period to period, the relationship of one coloured form to another—that is to say, the technique—has always, so to speak, remained fixed. I therefore believe that my technique is classical, for I have learnt it from the masters of the past.

It would almost be true to state that, with rare exceptions, the method of work has always been inductive. The elements of a concrete reality have been rendered pictorial, a given subject has been made into a picture.

My method of work is exactly the opposite. It is deductive. It is not picture "X" which manages to correspond with my subject, but subject "X" which manages to correspond with my picture.

I call this a deductive method because the pictorial relationships between the coloured forms suggest to me certain private relationships between the elements of an imaginary reality. The mathematics of picture-making lead me to the physics of representation. The quality or the dimensions of a form or a colour suggest to me the appellation or the adjective for an object. Hence, I never know in advance the appearance of the object represented. If I particularise pictorial relationships to the point of representing objects, it is in order that the spectator shall not do so for himself, and in order to prevent the combination of coloured forms suggesting to him a reality which I have not intended.

Now painting is foreseeing—foreseeing what will happen to the general effect of a picture by the introduction of some particular form or some particular colour, and foreseeing what sort of reality will be suggested to the spectator. It is, then, by being my own spectator that I extract the subject from my picture.

I do not know if one can give to this aesthetic, this technique and this method, the name of Cubism. Anyway, I make no claim to represent any particular sort of appearance, be it Cubist or naturalistic.

82

JUAN GRIS, The Lamp, 1916.
Courtesy Louise and Walter Arensberg Collection—
Philadelphia Museum of Art.

It is the appearance of the work as a whole which is its culmination, for this aspect is unknown to me. My subject, obviously, modifies the pictorial relationships without destroying or
changing them. But it does not modify them any more than a
numerical relationship is modified by the multiplication of both
quantities by the same figure.

Therefore I would say that a subject painted by myself is
simply a modification of pre-existing pictorial relationships.
Nor do I know until the work is completed just what modification it is, which gives it its character.

83

PAUL KLEE, Green-Orange Gradation with Black Half Moon, 1922.
Courtesy of the Fogg Art Museum, Harvard University.

PAUL KLEE

LET ME USE a simile; the artist, you might say, is like a tree. He has coped with this bewildering world—reasonably well, we shall assume—in his own quiet way. He knows how to find his way in it well enough to bring some order into the stream of impressions and experiences impinging on him. This orientation among the phenomena of nature and human life, this order in all its ramifications, that's like the root part of our tree.

From there the artist—who is the trunk of the tree—receives the sap that flows through him and through his eye.

Under the pressure of this mighty flow, he transmits what he has seen to his work.

His work, then, is like the crown of the tree, spreading in time and space for all to see.

Now, nobody would expect the crown of a tree to have exactly the same shape as the roots. We all know that the one cannot be a mirror-image of the other. Clearly, their very different functions, the fact that they belong to different realms —air and earth—must of necessity produce important differences in structure.

Why, then, do people deny the artist's right (which is not so much a right as a necessity) to depart from the appearance of his models? Some even go so far as to question both his competence and his sincerity.

After all, in his capacity as the trunk he only gathers and transmits what comes to him from below. He is neither master nor servant but only a mediator.

His position, then, is a modest one indeed; and the beauty of the crown, that's not the artist himself—it has only passed through him. . . . While the artist is thus concentrating on the problem of how to relate all the forms to each other as cleanly and logically as possible, so that every one of them is put in the exact spot where it is needed but without detracting from its neighbors, some layman onlooker will devastate him with the remark: "But this still doesn't look like uncle!" If he has steady nerves, the painter will say to himself, "Uncle go hang! I've got to keep on building. . . . This block I've just added, seems a bit heavy and pulls things down too much on the left; I shall have to put some sort of counterweight on the right to restore the balance."

From *XXe Siècle*, No. 9, Juin 1957. Reprinted by permission.

FERNAND LÉGER

EACH EPOCH has its own realism, invented more or less in relation to the preceding epochs. Sometimes it reacts against them. Often it continues in the same line.

The realism of the primitives is not that of the Renaissance, and the realism of Delacroix is diametrically opposed to that of Ingres.

To try to explain the why and how is impossible. It is a thing we feel, and reasons only risk confusing rather than clarifying the issue. What is certain is that there is no period of typical beauty, of superior beauty which might serve as a criterion, a base, a point of comparison. There is nothing which would permit the creative artist to turn to a past standard, in those moments when doubt possesses his heart. He can only continue in his own line of fate. His is complete solitude.

This dramatic experience is known to all those men who are condemned to invent, to create, to construct.

The mistake of the different schools is that they have wanted to establish a hierarchy of quality (the Italian Renaissance, for example); this position is untenable.

The realism varies in the fact that the artist lives in a different epoch, in a different milieu and under different conditions of general thought which dominate and influence his spirit.

For the last half century we have lived through an extremely rapidly moving period, rich in scientific, philosophical and social evolutions. This rapidity, I believe, has permitted the precipitation and realization of a new realism, one that is quite different from the preceding plastic conceptions.

It was the Impressionists who "broke the line." Cézanne, in particular; the moderns followed, accentuating the spirit of liberation. We liberated color and geometrical form and these have conquered the world. This new realism entirely dominates the last fifty years, on the artists' easels as well as in the decorative arts of the street and the home.

The original canvases which made this evolution possible are reproached with having been bought up by the dealers and the big collectors so that the general public has had no access to them. Whose fault is this? That of the existing social order. I don't intend here to go into the whole question of picture-dealers who, themselves, took a great commercial risk when they accepted the responsibility of a type of merchandise the success of which no one could foresee. Along with the big collectors it was they who made it possible for us to live, and our work is scattered throughout the whole world, thanks to them.

If our work has not penetrated to the large public I repeat it is the fault of the existing social order and not because our work lacks humanity. Under this pretext there are those who would like to burn all bridges, execute in cold blood all this painting with its painfully acquired liberation and go back to goodness knows when. The names of Rembrandt and of Reubens are cited.

Under the pretext of wanting to conquer immediately this admirable popular public whose instinct is so exact, but who is waiting to seize a new truth, there are those who would like to ship them backwards, from century to century, first in the railroad trains, then in a wheelbarrow, so as to be really "old," and then on foot.

This is an insult to the new man who asks nothing better than to understand and to go forward; it is equivalent to an official decision that he is incapable of raising himself to his new realism which is his epoch, in which he lives, in which he works, and which he has constructed with his own hands. He is told modern things are not for him. They are for the rich, specialized art, bourgeois art; nothing could be more untrue.

We have the possibility of creating and realizing a new collective mural art. We are only waiting for the time when the social evolution will permit this.

Our tastes, our traditions, go back to the primitive and popular artists, preceding the Renaissance.

From this Renaissance dates individualism in painting. And I do not think that there is anything to be gained in looking to it, if we desire to realize and renovate a contemporary, collective, popular mural art. Our epoch is rich enough in plastic raw material to furnish the basis for it.

But unfortunately, so long as the new social circumstances remain unrealized, the people will not benefit by these realizations.

By this I mean leisure—the organization, the creation of leisure for the workers—this is, I believe, the principal point of our discussion. *Everything depends on it.*

At no time in our world have the workers had access to plastic beauty for these very same reasons, that they have never had the necessary time or sufficient liberty of spirit.

Liberate the popular masses, give them the possibility of thinking, of seeing, of cultivating themselves, and we may rest assured that they will be able in time to fully enjoy the plastic novelty which modern art offers them.

This people which, every day, creates objects manufactured in pure colors, in definitive forms, with exact measures, has already discerned the possible real, plastic elements. You will find *airplane propellers* as wall ornaments in a popular dance-hall. Everybody admires them, and these propellers are very close to certain modern sculpture.

With little effort these people will feel and understand what is meant by the new realism, which has its origin in modern life itself, in its constant phenomena, in the influence of manufactured and geometrical objects, in a transposition where the imagination and the real meet and overlap, but from which all literary and descriptive sentimentalism has been banished, as well as all theatricalism that has its sources in other poetic or bookish directions. . . .

An entirely different life is made possible to the workers by the two greatest gifts which Le Corbusier has given us: the white wall and light. To learn to use them, to love them, and not be made to turn backward *in this respect also* by trying to force it to accept the stuffs, draperies and wall papers of 1900; the working-class has the right to all that. It has the right to have on its walls mural paintings signed by the best modern artists, and if it is given time and leisure it will know how to live among them and love them.

What is the representative art that is being forced on these men when they are appealed to every day by the cinema, the radio, enormous photographic cutouts and advertisings? How is it possible to compete with these enormous modern mechanisms which turn out a vulgarized art at a thousand degrees?

It would be unworthy of their comprehension to attempt to manufacture a popular painting of inferior quality under the pretext that they would understand nothing else. On the contrary, an effort should be made towards quality in a tranquil, interior type of art. We should seek a plane of plastic beauty that is entirely different from the one just described.

This doesn't hinder the fact that painters are ready to cooperate with the organizers of popular manifestations; for example, to direct the color and release it, if so desired. Pure color, dynamically disposed, is capable of visually destroying a wall. Color gives joy, it can also drive a person crazy. It can heal, in the polychromatic hospital. It is a formidable raw material, as indispensable to life as water or fire. It can exalt the feeling for action to an infinite degree. It can hold its own with a loud speaker: it is of equal size. It can be dosed, also, in infinite degrees, beginning with the nuance and ending with the explosion.

89

In this domain, in which there is the question of manifesting the intensity of life from every angle, there are entirely new possibilities—scenic, music, color, movement, light, song—all these have not yet been grouped and orchestrated to their maximum point. The man of the people is born with this feeling for beauty. The stone-mason who prefers a blue sash to a red one, commits an act of choice. His first judgment concerning modern manufactured articles is of an esthetic type. He will say "a pretty bicycle," "a pretty car," before finding out if it runs. This already enters into the acceptance of a fact: new realism. The show windows of the shops in which an isolated object holds and attracts the buyer: new realism.

All men, even the most crude, have in them the possibility of going towards the beautiful. But before the work of art, picture or poem, if leisure—I come back to it again—does not permit them to cultivate this possibility, they will remain all their life at the stage of judgment by comparison. They will prefer Bougereau to Ingres because Bougereau is better imitation. Judgment by comparison has no value, every artistic work should be judged by itself. It is an independent whole; if they are helped, they will attain it. The human crowds who claim their share, the men of the people, let us not forget that they are the great refuge of poetry.

It is they who invent this mobile and ever-new form—popular language. These people live in an atmosphere of constant verbal invention.

While their hands tighten the vise, their imagination runs ahead in the invention of new words, of new poetic forms.

Throughout the world the people have invented their language, which is their own realism. It is of an incredible richness. *It is slang*, it is the most beautiful and the most alive of all poetry. Their popular actors, their singers, use it in their neighborhood theatres. They are the masters and inventors of it. This verbal form is also an alloy of realism and imaginative transposition, it is a new realism, perpetually in movement.

And there are those who feel that this class of men has not the right to the joys and satisfactions given by the modern work of art. Those who would not give them their "chance" to lift themselves onto a new plastic plane, these men who every day invent a new language of their own . . . , this position is not tenable and these men have the right to want and to demand that times should change in order that, in their turn, they might enter the domain of the beautiful which has always been closed to them until now.

PIET MONDRIAN

PIET MONDRIAN, Pencil Drawing.
Courtesy of Harry Holtzman.

IN OUR PRESENT mechanized world, where the opposing factors of life are so strongly accentuated that only combat can bring a solution, it is illogical to attempt to experience reality through fantastic feelings. At the moment, there is no need for art to create a reality of imagination based on appearances, events, or traditions. Art should not follow the intuitions relating to our life in time, but only those intuitions relating to true reality.

Even in this chaotic moment, we can near equilibrium through the realization of a true vision of reality. Modern life and culture help us in this. Science and techniques still cause great dislocations. Our way leads toward a search for the equivalence of life's unequal oppositions. Because it is free of all utilitarian limitations, plastic art must move not only parallel with human progress but must advance ahead of it. It is the task of art to express a clear vision of reality.

JOAN MIRÓ, Young Girl Skipping Rope, Women, Birds, 1947.
Collection Museum of Modern Art, New York.

JOAN MIRÓ

WHY TALK of it? Isn't anything we could say superfluous, imprecise, for the very reason that the precision we aim at is an impossible one? What statement could ever explain these signs, these emblems, these enigmas, the discarding of these chrysalid forms forever undergoing a metamorphosis? Too many purposes, too many allusions, are involved in this reality, so fluid and so ambiguous that only those shifting forms Spinoza speaks of as altering into others can evoke and translate it into an exact language. You have only to look at these canvases to see how the images, the caprices, of the universal Fable are revealed in their fantastic or cruel grace. It is as if the artist were amusing himself behind the mask. In actuality, though, he is escaping, eluding the world in which he lives, and amid those myths that for him are the reflection and the reverse of that world, himself becomes Myth.

A MAN'S LIFE, as others know it, is not the real one, says Miró, but only a semblance they themselves construct. The real Miró is as truly what I am to myself as what others—and perhaps even I—conceive of me as being. Isn't the essential self to be found in that mysterious area where creation takes place and from which there flows an inexplicable radiance that finally comes to be the whole man? This is where reality is.

A profound, ironic reality, one that mocks what lies before our eyes—yet is what we behold. We need only see it against a light, even as faint a light as a star's.

Then everything becomes strange, shifting, at once distinct and blurred. Forms emerge even as they alter, they interchange, and thereby they create a universe of signs and symbols whose shapes move from realm to realm, they set foot on roots, themselves become roots, and in the end dissolve in the streaming hair of the constellations.

This is a kind of secret language composed of magic runes, that exists before words, and springs from that era when what men imagined and divined was far more real and true than what they saw—when that was the sole reality.

From *XXe Siècle*, No. 9, Juin 1957. Reprinted by permission.

93

JEAN DUBUFFET, Bertelé Chat Sauvage, 1947.
Courtesy of Stephan Hahn.

JEAN DUBUFFET

THIS MUCH is sure, a picture interests me to the degree I succeed in kindling in it a kind of flame—the flame of *life*, or *presence*, or *existence*, or *reality*, depending on what we take these words to mean. To be sure, it often happens with me that my picture lacks this quality. I will have put certain figures in it, no matter what—objects, people, places—they are recognizable but without being moving, they have no life (or, to use your word, *reality*). In any case, I go on working, I add and take away, I change, I revise (notice that I work empirically, like a blind man, experimenting with every kind of means), until a certain extraordinary release occurs in the picture, and from then on it seems to me endowed with this very *life*—excuse me, *reality*. How can this be accounted for? I have no idea. I never know how I have produced it, or how to repeat the same effect. It is a mysterious happening, and probably because of its very mysteriousness it drives me again and again to renew the experience each time I make a picture. Am I fooling myself? is the impression my picture gives me of containing *reality* within it (as if by some magic I had evoked a warmth, a throbbing, a breathing, so compelling as to strike fear, as if I had hit on a dangerous mechanism for creating life, without knowing how or when), is this impression true only for me, or is it equally so for everyone who looks at the picture?

This is a question I often ask myself. Sometimes it seems to me the same effect is produced on others, and then I am fairly amazed. When I see this light irradiate a picture, I feel so rewarded that I would go on making pictures with the same joy if no one but myself felt as I do about them. Take note that this awesome manifestation of life that (deluded or not), I love in a picture, this enhanced presence, this supercharged life you mean when you say *reality*, has nothing to do with the objects represented, rather it is distinct from them, pre-existent, surging up like an electric flow, without your ever knowing where it comes from. When this happens (I have often remarked, and always to my surprise, that the effect is a very stable one, contrary to what you might think, so that, once it appears, you can change and push around all the elements of a picture without weakening it), the effect persists, even if you make major alterations in the objects first chosen for representation—for example, the coffee pot becomes a person, the table a sandy beach or a field, or perhaps these are entirely eliminated—a matter of a moment with a scraper or a rag—even if the place they did occupy is now merely indeterminate or vacant, the original objects remain mysteriously alive and *real*. I would even say that at this moment, when the life principle functions at full force and even the slightest details the painter chooses to introduce into the picture, however sketchily, are endowed with an intense *reality*, that his work becomes thrilling. He has the strong impression—all right, all right, call it a delusion, maybe it is a delusion, but for him it is an undeniable fact—that his hand is bewitched and that a superior power has come to his aid, thanks to which a miraculous *reality* animates everything he has put into the picture, even—here's an added complication—where its outlines are especially vague and equivocal. At this moment he no longer feels he is responsible for the picture, it has acquired a life of its own, it takes over, as if he were allowed to be a mere onlooker of a marvelous spectacle. He may even reach the point of asking himself (people unacquainted with art and how it is created laugh at this) what is this or that line appearing? is it an object? what object? a living creature? or just some irregularity in the landscape? or is it a phenomenon from realms till now unknown? All the better if the literal intention of the picture is now in suspense: from this moment on an intense *reality* suffuses it, now it becomes a highly potent means of evoking and relating all sorts of ideas, a means of conveying an awareness of kinships, resemblances, identifications—a means of meditation.

From *XXe Siècle*, No. 9, Juin 1957. Reprinted by permission.

JOSÉ ORTEGA Y GASSET

THE NEW SENSIBILITY, it seems to me, is dominated by a distaste for human elements in art very similar to the feelings cultured people have always experienced at Madame Tussaud's, while the mob has always been delighted by that gruesome waxen hoax. In passing we may here ask ourselves a few impertinent questions which we have no intention to answer now. What is behind this disgust at seeing art mixed up with life? Could it be disgust for the human sphere as such, for reality, for life? Or is it rather the opposite: respect for life and unwillingness to confuse it with art, so inferior a thing as art?

96

ALBERT CAMUS

But the artist's rebellion against reality, which is automatically suspect to the totalitarian revolution, contains the same affirmation as the spontaneous rebellion of the oppressed. The revolutionary spirit, born of total negation, instinctively felt that, as well as refusal, there was also consent to be found in art; that there was a risk of contemplation counterbalancing action, beauty, and injustice, and that in certain cases beauty itself was a form of injustice from which there was no appeal. Equally well, no form of art can survive on total denial alone. Just as all thought, and primarily that of non-signification, signifies something, so there is no art that has no signification. Man can allow himself to denounce the total injustice of the world and then demand a total justice that he alone will create. But he cannot affirm the total hideousness of the world. To create beauty, he must simultaneously reject reality and exalt certain of its aspects. Art disputes reality, but does not hide from it. Nietzsche could deny any form of transcendence, whether moral or divine, by saying that transcendence drove one to slander this world and this life. But perhaps there is a living transcendence, of which beauty carries the promise, which can make this mortal and limited world preferable to and more appealing than any other. Art thus leads us back to the origins of rebellion, to the extent that it tries to give its form to an elusive value which the future perpetually promises, but of which the artist has a presentiment and wishes to snatch from the grasp of history.

97

PIERRE SOULAGES, January 10, 1951.
Collection Museum of Modern Art, New York. Acquired through the Lillie P. Bliss Bequest.

PIERRE SOULAGES

Neither the various appearances of things nor things themselves are reality.

Man's relationship with the objective world, his sensitivity, his myths, his ideas, the social structures they clash with—these are reality.

When we experience, when we live the relationships of colors, forms, space, structures, the rhythms that are the artist's domain, we encounter a new way of reacting to the world, of experiencing and understanding it, and thus new relationships between man and the world, a new reality, appear.

The painter's experience of the world pervades his work. Since painting is a poetic experience, it transfigures the world—the picture is a metaphor.

Even though this painting may seem dissociated from the world, still it is the world that bounds it and gives it its meaning.

From *XXe Siècle*, No. 9, Juin 1957. Reprinted by permission.

JEAN HÉLION

. . . mais par un curieux retour des choses, c'est aujourd'hui de cette notion de représentation qu'on a perdu le sens. C'est sur elle qu'il convient de s'expliquer.—Pierre Bru-guière ("La Nouvelle Querelle des Images," *Cahiers du Sud*, no. 305, 1er semestre, 1951.)

REPRESENTATION is a very old, and at present a rather revolutionary technique for approaching the meaning of life through its forms.

Painting thus becomes an act of adoration, an avowal of faith in the validity of existence.

The real is bottomless, and representation an endless pursuit. One trusts the eyes. They think more quickly, subtly and precisely than does the mind alone.

To paint is to achieve a harmonious continuity through the model, the palette, the mind, and the canvas.

In practice, one wades through mud with heavy fingers: I mean colors. Superb mud.

But to give life, on canvas, to what is alive in the world requires the greatest effort of imagination. Indeed, it is a desperate venture. Even the best figurative painting fails to capture the much more luminous coincidence of the spiritual and the material which the artist had foreseen in his spell of inspiration.

JEAN HÉLION,
Roofs, 1959.
Courtesy of the artist.

The roofs that I see all day from my terrace overlooking Paris.
More than a landscape, it is a mask.

This ocean of angles, holes, and bumps: a continuity made of parts. The color it seems to be; the colors it provokes in me.

The roofs do not completely hide the earth under their dead waves. Walls of stone emerge like the banks of a river. Chimney pots float on the edges like corks.

The skies shine superbly in every sheet of metal roofing.

Daylight slides on the tiles and slates, to fall bluish in the courtyards, and meet brown and green rising from underneath.

But the roofs also make up the prop of the sky. Immensity rests upon their shoulders and somehow reshapes them.

Clouds above. Clouds do not evolve at random. The landscape of the skies answers the landscape underneath. In a painting, a cloud is born out of the color the skies have become, and it is also designed by the rhythm binding all the elements in the composition.

I have never worked on a more difficult subject.

Hollow and full like a skull, and already so much of a design. Its very geometry is misleading, and must be both understood and broken down.

Painting the roofs is not describing the various building techniques but seizing the sign they make in space: a sign both obvious and mysterious, like a Chinese ideogram, and yet clearly, for anyone, the portrait of these roofs.

But are the roofs spontaneously "Cubist," or was "Cubism" influenced?

101

JEAN HÉLION, Portrait of a Singer, 1959.
Courtesy of the artist.

"The face of my old friend the singer is a landscape."
It has hills and valleys, peaks and ravines. In the trihedron of the nose, eyebrow, and cheek, space enters. The upper lip somehow closes the fourth side, thus producing a hollow prism.

One must concentrate in order to grasp this figure, but it is so powerful that it completely defines a person.

The eye inscribes itself at the top, delicately; and the power of sight seems distributed among all the planes leading to it.

A head is also a sort of ball into which space enters, here and there. The skull underneath. That object is curiously carved by hand: it bears the marks of a thumb everywhere. Flesh is draped over it, here tightly, there loosely.

A face demands a maximum of attention. It is the most intense part of creation and offers an endless interplay. Not a wrinkle that does not reveal far more than fatigue of the skin. The chin answers the back of the head and its sides; and below it, the knees.

A head is as much the top of a man as it is the limit of all the space surrounding it.

Opposite me sits my friend. Drawing his face, I recognize everything I ever had an intimation of. Perhaps this is why it has been said that man is created in God's image.

Features are not engraved on his face. They originate in every part of his person, and also beyond him. His own typical expression may reside in a few points, but it is confirmed everywhere.

It is not more important to identify the model as a person than it is to show how this person defines the world that produced him.

Art seeks the point in space where the obvious and the remote coincide.

103

JEAN HÉLION, Plowed Earth, 1959. Illustration for a poem by André du Bouchet.
Courtesy of the artist.

Plowed earth is much like the sea, and like the roofs. It is also made up of foreheads, eyebrows, and cheeks.

And what can be more spontaneously abstract?

It is without limits. The face of a man is an isloated sign, concentrated.

Plowed earth is not flat, but plays within the surface. It has no center: instead, a continuous rhythm, broken and overturned and always felt throughout.

Yet it is also the anonymous *mask* of the earth.

Tufts of grass here and there. Twigs? Lines?

No two heaps of earth are alike, though produced by the same machine in the same field.

They are as different as human heads, and one feels that it is for the same reason.

On every slanting face, a reflection of the sky recalls the blade of the plow.

These lines, taken from notebooks,
were written while painting.
Words, but meant to command the brush,
not to comment.
Or passwords, to be forgotten when the
narrow gate is opened.

104

JOSEF ALBERS, Structural Constellation K 44.
Courtesy of the artist.

JOSEF ALBERS

WHEN I PAINT and construct, I try to develop visual articulation. I do not think then about abstraction, and just as little about expression. I do not look for isms, and not at momentary fashion.

I see that art is essentially purpose and seeing *(Schauen)*, that form demands multiple presentation, manifold performance.

I do not see that forced individualism or forced exaltation is the source of convincing formulation of lasting meaning.

In my own work I am content to compete with myself, and to search with simple palette and with simple color for manifold instrumentation.

So I dare further variants.

105

THEODORE ROSZAK, Invocation II, 1950.
Courtesy of the Pierre Matisse Gallery.

THEODORE ROSZAK

THE FORMS that I find necessary to assert are meant to be blunt reminders of primordial strife and struggle, reminiscent of those brute forces that not only produced life, but in turn threatened to destroy it. I feel that if necessary one must be ready to summon one's total being with an all-consuming rage against those forces that are blind to the primacy of life-giving values. Perhaps, by this sheer dedication, one may yet merge force and grace.

It is altogether possible that society may be on the threshold of a great transformation—and while its external circumstances may remain relatively unchanged, I believe we will witness vast shifts in emotional and moral outlook. It is not without possibility, too, that in the next most important phase of our century we will again see the emergence and meaning of the baroque symbol, revealing a psychic life of organic growth, that itself has the power of regeneration and transcendence.

It seems to me that the baroque symbol may be interpreted from either of two aspects. The early phase, when the budding is most closely related to the sharp Gothic thrust, the herald of its appearance; or the latterly phase, when the ripe fruit, ready to fall, disintegrates and deposits its seed again.

My interest and feeling for the baroque is for that of its inception, when it is closest to the Gothic thrust. In contemporary visual terms, it expresses itself at once as—sharp and undulating—assertive and pulsating—defiant and hopeful. The rhythm between the discipline of the classic and the emotional stirring of the baroque may well establish a new synthesis toward the completeness of man and his hopes for the fullness of life.

Sculpture and architecture have always symbolized unified institutions and unified man. Painting with its subtle mutations of change and broad versatility flourishes best within an atmosphere of suspension and discord. This explains in part why painting is still the dominant voice in these times. But, I believe we are faced with the prospect of an impending cycle of social change that is already indicated by the growing presence of a New Architecture and New Sculpture.

Malraux describes in his *Twilight of the Absolute* the necessity for the contemporary artist to discover his moral values through his own work. Personally, I think this has always been the case in the past as it is now—with this exception—that the contemporary western artist is faced with the more exacting problem of choices, as compared with his predecessors who had their range circumscribed by the "absolute doctrine" of religious and moral values. If art is called upon to uphold the conscience of those who practice it, as Malraux suggests it may, then surely it must contain more than the "self-sufficiency" of plastic values inherent in the media, alone.

It seems to me that the sculptor as well as the painter must strive to break through the variety of change (that can take place in any period and generally does) and try to arrive at a significant value, basic and indestructible, for the widest range of human sensibility.

Malraux's statement obliquely supports the larger question of the relationship between form and subject matter, and in the light of my past experience, particularly with my former use of non-objective forms, I have frequently been asked how I feel about subject matter for the modern sculptor. I would like to talk briefly about this question, by referring to a specific work, and I feel that the *Whaler of Nantucket* may serve as a familiar jumping-off point. But first I would like to replace the term "subject matter" with the word "content," and for this reason: subject matter as we have come to know it tends to relate itself to an immediate external—one might say a superficial—aspect of an object or event. For me, it suggests a fleeting, fragmentary kind of identity. Content, on the other hand, bears upon the core structure of an experience and grows from the center out, whether it be in terms of formal space building, or whether it is central to an orientation of feeling, quality of mood, or direction of an expression.

Content seen this way suggests organic growth, and becomes an endless source of visual suggestion for the sculptor. But, does such distinction between content and subject matter affect the artist and his work today?

Well, the fact that we are living at an historic moment that in part expresses itself in valid forms of an eclectic nature, would seem to suggest many possibilities. For my part, visual ideas must contain and transcend formal limits. The consideration of content as related to subject matter not only implies planting a seed of structural and spacial extension, it also presupposes

108

operation of an emotional apparatus that reaches out toward growth, is adaptable to change, and finally evolves toward maturity. Obviously, this transformation cannot be accomplished automatically, by the plastic possibilities of the medium, alone. One has to work at it. One has to bring it up to other and wider areas of human experience. One has to think and feel through a whole body of accumulated attitudes until one conjures a vivid sense of the total quality of the form, and invokes its image in the mind. I would say at this point that one is finally guided by an intuitional sense of order that prods the imagination into action. Its first intimations are felt through one's own psychological requirements that subsequently link larger patterns of social and cultural reference. In purely visual terms, it is really a question of coming to grips with, and challenging, the stuff of the imagination. In this sense, there are many sources and centers that can be tapped.

I believe there is an amazingly strong analogy to be drawn between the content of poetry and the content that I speak of as related to sculpture. In sculpture, we are dealing with a form that presents visual meaning within a changing source of light and the movement of the spectator. It constantly produces illusions of shifting shapes and images. Hence, like poetry, sculpture is fraught with structural and visual ambiguities that are resolved by reconciling opposites in its constant pursuit of a visual metaphor.

I think, then, that a medium such as sculpture, able to integrate diverse poles of meaning, can reveal significant suggestions of imagery that cross or fuse from one generation to another the rich source material of legend and myth.

MARCEL DUCHAMP, Study for the King and Queen, 1912.
Courtesy Louise and Walter Arensberg Collection—
Philadelphia Museum of Art.

MARCEL DUCHAMP

LET US CONSIDER two important factors, the two poles of the creation of art: the artist on the one hand, and on the other the spectator who later becomes the posterity.

To all appearances, the artist acts like a mediumistic being who, from the labyrinth beyond time and space, seeks his way out to a clearing.

If we give the attributes of a medium to the artist, we must then deny him the state of consciousness on the esthetic plane about what he is doing or why he is doing it. All his decisions in the artistic execution of the work rest with pure intuition and cannot be translated into a self-analysis, spoken or written, or even thought out.

T. S. Eliot, in his essay on "Tradition and Individual Talent," writes: "The more perfect the artist, the more completely separate in him will be the man who suffers and the mind which creates; the more perfectly will the mind digest and transmute the passions which are its material."

Millions of artists create; only a few thousands are discussed or accepted by the spectator and many less again are consecrated by posterity.

In the last analysis, the artist may shout from all the rooftops that he is a genius; he will have to wait for the verdict of the spectator in order that his declarations take a social value and that, finally, posterity include him in the primers of Art History.

I know that this statement will not meet with the approval of many artists who refuse this mediumistic role and insist on the validity of their awareness in the creative act—yet, art history has consistently decided upon the virtues of a work of art through considerations completely divorced from the rationalized explanations of the artist.

If the artist, as a human being, full of the best intentions toward himself and the whole world, plays no role at all in the judgment of his own work, how can one describe the phenomenon which prompts the spectator to react critically to the work of art? In other words, how does this reaction come about?

This phenomenon is comparable to a transference from the

111

artist to the spectator in the form of an esthetic osmosis taking place through the inert matter, such as pigment, piano, or marble.

But before we go further, I want to clarify our understanding of the word "art"—to be sure, without any attempt at a definition.

What I have in mind is that art may be bad, good, or indifferent, but, whatever adjective is used, we must call it art, and bad art is still art in the same way as a bad emotion is still an emotion.

Therefore, when I refer to "art coefficient," it will be understood that I refer not only to great art, but I am trying to describe the subjective mechanism which produces art in a raw state—*à l'état brut*—bad, good, or indifferent.

In the creative act, the artist goes from intention to realization through a chain of totally subjective reactions. His struggle toward the realization is a series of efforts, pains, satisfactions, refusals, decisions, which also cannot and must not be fully self-conscious, at least on the esthetic plane.

The result of this struggle is a difference between the intention and its realization, a difference which the artist is not aware of.

Consequently, in the chain of reactions accompanying the creative act, a link is missing. This gap, representing the inability of the artist to express fully his intention, this difference between what he intended to realize and did realize, is the personal "art coefficient" contained in the work.

In other words, the personal "art coefficient" is like an arithmetical relation between the unexpressed but intended and the unintentionally expressed.

To avoid a misunderstanding, we must remember that this "art coefficient" is a personal expression of art *à l'état brut*, that is, still in a raw state, which must be "refined" as pure sugar from molasses, by the spectator; the digit of this coefficient has no bearing whatsoever on his verdict. The creative act takes another aspect when the spectator experiences the phenomenon of transmutation: through the change from inert matter into a work of art, an actual transubstantiation has taken place, and the role of the spectator is to determine the weight of the work on the esthetic scale.

All in all, the creative act is not performed by the artist alone; the spectator brings the work in contact with the external world by deciphering and interpreting its inner qualifications and thus adds his contribution to the creative act. This becomes even more obvious when posterity gives its final verdict and sometimes rehabilitates forgotten artists.

112

NAUM GABO

Since the publication of this lecture* by the Philosophical Library in New York and in other publications in France and England, a controversial discussion has arisen around the term "image" as used in my lecture.

The idea of the image has been advanced by me from the very beginning of the constructive ideology in art. "We know that everything has its own image, chair, table, lamp, telephone, book, house, man—they are all entire worlds with their rhythms and their orbits." (*Realistic Manifesto*, 1920.) It was one of the main points of my ideological disputes with the so-called "Productivist" group, led by Tatlin.

These discussions have now flared up again and I notice that opinions are divided in two directions. Some have already accepted this term in relation to the abstract or non-objective art without further question and, I am afraid, without much consideration about what the term "image" means. It is often taken as meaning the same as the term "symbol."

The others are reluctant to accept it for philosophical reasons, interpreting the term as an ultra-idealistic philosophy leading to a kind of mystic-solipsism or some such idea. Therefore I hold it necessary to dispel this confusion and to define what I mean by the term "image."

Our thinking and perception are creative acts (they are thus autonomous). The primary stage of these creative acts consists of building up in our consciousness distinct images of everything we perceive or think of; only when we suceed in getting a clearly defined image of them, do we know them. Images are thus the building blocks of our consciousness and in their entirety constitute that which we call reality.

Symbols however are auxiliary, secondary elements in the process of our thought and communication. We build them up

*The Trowbridge Lecture of 1948 at Yale University.

113

either as a short cut to that which we already know and of which we already have a clearly defined image, or we build them up in places where we have to skip those crevasses in our path of thinking where the completely unknown comes in our way and we are incapable of creating a clearly defined image of it.

Symbols thus signify that which is commonly known or that which is entirely unknown. A few instances may help to explain these definitions. For instance, we see an object growing out of the earth which has a particular shape, color, and characteristics, different from another object. We have a clearly defined image of the one and of the other. From our repeated observation of these two objects we have got the images of both of them and we now can give them names—we call one "lily" and the other "rose." We know the image of the lily and the image of the rose so well that we can use the word "lily" alone without describing all the details of that image of lily and in our communications we can be sure that we will be understood by others. The words "lily" and "rose" are then serving us as symbols for something of which we have already succeeded in creating a clear image.

To go over to the world of ideas—let us take the word Christianity. The idea of Christianity has been created by us in our history, with our mythology and in our epics so intensively and so exhaustively that we have a clearly defined image (in this case conceptual image) of Christianity, so much so now that, without fear of being misunderstood we use the sign of the cross as the symbol of Christianity. The cross has become the short cut of a communication (or conception) of an idea with a clearly defined image.

But when we take a term like infinity—we do not know what it is, we do not know its characteristics and its reality is highly problematic; yet, for some reason, in our thoughts it is persistent and also for some unknown reason we don't dare to exclude it entirely. It is with us as a crevasse and we have to jump over it, taking for granted that it exists. But the image of it is nonexistent. We use the word "infinity" or this sign ∞ as a symbol of something entirely unknown.

This is the meaning of the term image in comparison with the term symbol as I understand and use them.

Art does not deal with unknowns. Art strives to create an image of that which was unknown, making it thus known, and therefore it would be an error to explain abstract art as a new kind of symbolism. In my work, at any rate, there is nothing symbolic.

114

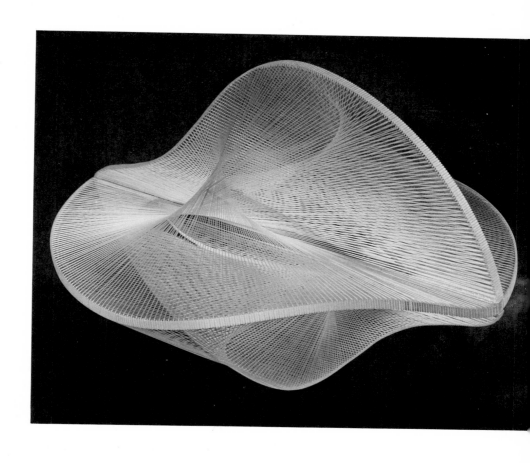

NAUM GABO, Linear Construction in Space, 3.
Courtesy of the artist.

JEAN ARP, Automatic Drawing, 1916.
Collection Museum of Modern Art, New York.

JEAN ARP

Your implied question as to why I work cannot be answered. You could ask with equal justification why I exist at all. It is my opinion that the mind serves only a very small fraction of human happiness. The most astounding fruits of the mind have brought humanity boundless misfortune. I find most of the "great" discoveries of our time gruesome and unwholesome.

I write fairy tales, and the content of my sculptures is also fairy tales and dreams. Read my poems, and in them you will find the best interpretation of the content of my sculpture.

In creative art I always look for collaboration. To this end it is not necessary to establish guild laws, as in the Middle Ages. Collaboration as I understand and have practiced it with Sophie Taeuber, Theo van Doesburg, Magnelli, Sonia Delaunay and Mortensen has created designs and other works which for the most part have been reproduced in periodicals and portfolios. I interpret collaboration in the widest sense of the word. It should be connected in particular with architecture. When I created my last large work for UNESCO, however, I discovered unfortunately that architects hardly spare the time to discuss in earnest with the painters and sculptors. On the occasion of my last stay in Cambridge (Massachusetts) I hope to have brought to a happy conclusion the design of the walls in the Harvard Graduate Center in cooperation with Walter Gropius and his collaborators.

The 'thirties, during which I created the "papiers déchirés" represented experiences most important for my work. They clarified within me the boundaries between certainty and uncertainty, day and night, between the absolute and the relative, between calligraphy and nature.

117

STUART DAVIS

THE SCOPE of Subject Matter indicated by the title of this essay could be taken as formidable and even alarming, but as a Scholar without Scholarship, I find it more convenient to take a Do-It-Yourself attitude and simply follow the Instructions on the package of my own experience.

In line with that decision, I feel able to make the categorical statement that The Place of Painting in Contemporary Culture consists entirely of what each artist emergently makes it. In my understanding the word Culture means a Subject Matter for art, as opposed to the notion of it as an Historical Imperative which makes the Rules, and then Scoops the Artist before the Algebra of his Dream has become a real Event. The Predictions of Cultural Determinism might allow the Artist to read his own Obituary in the Morning Paper, so to speak, but at the same time it would rob the Artist of his Birthright of the Enjoyment of it. But when culture is understood to be simply a splendid Environment of Events with no questions asked, the role of Painting seems much less Macabre, and can even be considered quite attractive. By the foregoing I think I have succeeded in changing the title of this occasion to one more suited to my ability in dealing with it. It now reads, "The Place of Culture in Contemporary Painting."

Contemporary Culture as a Subject includes the Past in the form of the Past and Present Individual Formulations of it. These exist on the same plane of our Awareness with what is Uniquely Immediate to the Twentieth Century. The latter includes New Lights, Speeds, Sounds, Communications, and Jazz in general, as the Ornaments of daily Experience. Their continuous presentation to the Front Page of our Common Sense constitutes a Montage Perspective—a Short Cut to the necessary Implementation for Knowing you are Alive. It holds the promise of an Automation Psychology suited to the Know-How for a Pre-Fabricated Humanism. It suggests a Button for the Correct determination of Obligatory Moral Categories.

118

STUART DAVIS, Visa, 1951.
Collection Museum of Modern Art, New York.

And then of course there is Modern Art with its Natural
Giants of Painting in the last fifty years. That too is a laminated
Fact in the Cultural Subject Matter for Today's Artist with a
normal Appetite for the Air-Conditioned Now. The Continuity
of Culture exists as a Sequence of Unconsidered and Unlicensed
Choices and Identifications by Artists. They reserve their
Faculty of Consideration and Comparison for the Mathematics
of Tangibility which gives to Choice its forms as Public Currency. The Painting itself is the Responsible Social Act of the
Artist, and is one of the surest, most direct forms of Communication known to man.

At one time or another, including the present, this question
of Communication has been Viewed-with-Alarm by Scholars,
Critics, and others occupying a position Tangent to the Main
Point. They are fond of saying that the Content of much of
Modern Art is Perversely Cryptic, disassociated from the inter-
ests and observations of the Citizens, and that its Visual Idiom

is impossible to Translate. In effect they demand of Art an Audit and Notarized Itemization of its Contents. I regard this as the Wrong Approach. It is not the Property Assets of the Painting's Subject which are the Measure of its Civic function, but rather the Unsolicited Blueprint of the picture's Shape-Identity—a Photostat of the Individual's Deed of Ownership to the Enjoyment of his own Senses.

There is nothing more Universal in Experience than Enjoyment, but Art is simply *one* of the Techniques for its Social Communication and Use. To propose that the worth of Art stands in Direct Ratio to the Universality of its Appeal is a fairly meaningless Proposition. It represents basically an un-Democratic impulse to coerce not only the Artist but the Audience as well. In effect it would deprive the Individual of his Right to Free Choice of Technique in Creative Social Communication. It is necessary that the Right to Hate Art as well as to love it be preserved and that the current Popularity of the Aptitude Test be respected. In brief, since Modern Art is very well understood by Millions who are impelled to concern themselves with it—why quibble?

My personal guess as to the Meaning and Enormous Popularity of Modern Painting goes somewhat as follows:—I see the Artist as a Cool Spectator-Reporter at an Arena of Hot Events. Its continuing appeal to me since the Armory Show of 1913 is due, I believe, to its American Dynamics, even though the best Reporters then were Europeans operating in terms of European Identifications. Fortunately, we have our own share of Aces today. In his Professional Capacity the Modern Artist regards the subject of Subjective Feelings as a Casualty and never confuses them with the Splendor of the Continuity of Process, the Event itself. I see the Paintings as being made by Competent Workmen outside the self—not as a Signed Convulsion communicating an Enormous Capacity for Frustation with the Outside. I am aware that a number of excellent Artists today might seem to fall into the latter category and would regard my remark as offensive. But Offense is no part of my intention which is entirely one of Notation. I believe that there is a vast Audience which, like myself, is more interested in the Scenery than the Familiar Furnished Room of their own Short-Circuited Emotional Wiring.

I think that if the Contemporary Artist, with a reasonable amount of Taste for the Excitement and Impact of contemporary Culture in the sense I have indicated, will make his Report to the very Hip People—then both Art and Culture will do all right.

120

OSKAR KOKOSCHKA

THE MAJOR problem confronting the artist, now and in the past, is whether or not he is gifted enough to apprehend the real, and communicate it directly, in a manner articulate enough to convey his vision to others.

The vision of reality must not be confused with realism—the by-product of materialistic philosophy, the main road of the intellectual, the moral and social school of the Enlightenment—for realism is concerned with the purely superficial aspects of life, and such philosophical directives suit only those moonstruck members of modern democracy who, having discarded traditional roots, seek escape from the disquieting nature of life. Unfortunately, the trend of modern thought is in itself absolutely incompatible with artistic activity because it favors mechanization at the expense of humanism.

For example: in spite of the fact that a large portion of the general public has accepted—without any visible resistance—the experiments of the so-called nonobjective artists, which in large measure are a fashion of the New World, and although this movement of "modern" art has seized hold on the minds of thousands of painters and sculptors all over the world, this art eliminates man, avoids facts, and has no meaning for other people, to whom it conveys only nothingness, often in a verbose and dithyrambic jacket.

In the light of western civilization—or more accurately, that of the Greco-Latin and Anglo-Saxon cultures into which I have been born—I can reaffirm that the vocation of the artist today is to give back to man his lost place in nature. Man is not an automaton functioning by mathematical laws, bred with fixed mental patterns he is driven to obey, as dialectical materialism would have us believe. In the evolutionary process the anthropoids developed not only calves on their legs but also a conscience—to whose voice they may listen if they wish.

If I may be allowed a paradox, I would say that although adjustment, behaviorism, and conformism (which seems largely a Russian-American phenomenon) may temporarily ease the individual's role in life, nevertheless these concepts must end in a blind alley. It is up to the artists to decide which way to go.

For the simple reason that we have to face facts.

Life is not a still life. Inevitably it ends in death, experienced individually.

121

If man's immanent anxiety is not allowed to express itself in creative activity, which is its only natural outlet, then at the slightest stir of instability, the suppressed unquietness of the mind must erupt in neurosis, as is happening in our machine- and gadget-minded civilization. Modern man is without mental roots, thanks perhaps in part to the doubtful blessing of the rapid multiplication of the human species in a merely technical civilization. In no civilized society of the past can we see such outbursts of mass mania, world wars, world-wide destruction, the slaughter, liquidation, or transfer of whole ethnic groups. Certainly the invention of fire-making (not to be underrated as offering a chance for man's survival) did not strike the cave dwellers with panic. Yet the invention of an atomic cook-stove may well be a logical step toward the annihilation of all life on earth.

The best means for a young man to become an artist, as I consider, is for him not to conform to any fashion whatever, but to learn to see facts as an *individual*. In the end, nonobjective art may serve no purpose.

If there are any real talents among the hundreds of thousands of those privileged ones who need not work in factories or at a desk, but who can create painting and sculpture, may they use their God-given gifts to enable others to see reality as human creation. Such an effort, of course, demands more than merely dribbling molten metal on other hardware fragments or splashing good colors on good canvases—which could be used in a more Christian way to clothe the social outcast. Remember those poor chimpanzees who are now forced to do "modern" painting in their cages in the zoos of Baltimore and London, and soon everywhere, as the fashion goes. Would they do this freely in their forests?

I would say to the aspiring artist: by all means, let us be humble in this our period of astounding progress. See, our grandmothers did not think themselves the equals of the giants of the civilized past because they illustrated their letters with charming pen, crayon, or brush records of the visual experiences of their families, their travels. This art simply belonged to their education, and was acquired by most people as naturally as the art of writing and reading. And what about the astonishing works of the needle, the loom, the potter's wheel, the pen knife, or the metal work of the peasants of the past? Even the ornaments of primitive peoples evolved out of the facts of their observation.

The young people everywhere must learn the forgotten art of seeing life with their own eyes.

122

BEN SHAHN

I HAVE NO QUARREL with scientific skepticism as an attitude. I am sure that it provides a healthy antidote to fanaticism of all kinds, probably including the totalitarian kind.

But as a philosophy or a way of life it is only negative. It is suspicious of belief. It negates positive values. Aesthetically, it refuses to commit itself.

For society cannot grow upon negatives. If man has lost his Jehovah, his Buddha, his Holy Family, he must have new, perhaps more scientifically tenable beliefs, to which he may attach his affections. Perhaps Humanism and Individualism are the logical heirs to our earlier, more mystical beliefs. Or it might be that you have something better to offer. . . . But in any case, if we are to have values, a spiritual life, a culture, these things must find their imagery and their interpretation through the arts.

123

QUESTIONS are fiction, and answers are anything from more fiction to science-fiction.

Questions are dream, answers are dream interpretation, and they both have independence, beauty, and truth—especially the questions. But question *and* answer (like dreaming about dream interpretation) is nightmare.

I call myself The Inspector, and my profession is: discovery of questions—my questions being my symptoms, so to speak, as well as the symptoms of others. In other words, my answer.

SAUL STEINBERG, Three Drawings.
Courtesy of the artist.

PAUL & ANN RAND

Advertisement: Ad Vivum or Ad Hominem?

All that has any significance is the depth and validity of an experience out of which art comes; if it comes out of mere consciously clever ratiocination, it is foredoomed.—Alfred North Whitehead[1]

NEVER IN the history of mankind has a visual artist been subjected to such a barrage of sensory experiences as is the commercial artist of today. As he walks through that urban landscape for which his art is designed, he is bombarded with a fusillade of news and noise. He is not merely in contact with people, he is nearly trampled by them. His own art forms (billboard, sign, and advertisement) do not communicate with him, they scream at him from all sides in a crazy cacophony. He is confronted with a massive multiplicity of things—of products and events. Unlike other artists, he cannot detach himself from nor ignore this environment—it is his world. He works in it, with it, and for it.

Can the advertising artist, overwhelmed as he is by so many stimuli, have those deep and valid experiences which are the necessary basis for a genuine art? Such an artist—whose activities range from industrial design to typography—may be loosely described as a sort of professional folk artist; but he differs from the latter, not only in being dependent upon the demands of a mass market and upon using mass means for producing his work, but also in being part of a vastly different cultural climate. The folk artist flourished in relatively stable societies steeped in tradition, in which, although he himself might often remain anonymous, his work was accepted as a normal ingredient of the social matrix. Today, not only do we ask whether the popular artist produces good work, but also whether he should or can be an artist at all. This question is most often discussed in terms of technological change and economic strictures. Yet primarily it is not so much that certain elements within the environment have radically altered, but that our entire way of life and our ways of thinking, feeling, and believing have become utterly different.

The total upheaval in the structure and content of life, an-

127

nounced with such portentous rumblings by the Industrial Revolution, has been with us for a long time, yet we have still not found our bearings. Perhaps "change" is the key word in this new world. Today we are committed to change at so dizzying a speed on all levels, in all directions, and within the lives of all individuals that we are reeling under its impact. We scarcely have time to apprehend changes, let alone evaluate them.

This, however, is precisely what the popular artist has to do if he wants to work effectively. Change is his milieu. As an artist for industry, he designs the myriad products of an industrially productive age. As a painter, he is rarely, and often only incidentally, accepted by men of business. What has aesthetics to do with selling? The probable answer is: very little, directly; indirectly, perhaps a great deal. The commercial artist who wants to be more than a "stylist" must either become clear as to what his cultural contribution may be, or else be overwhelmed by the demands of clients, myths about public taste, consumer research surveys, etc.

To men of former ages, the meaning of life was, so to speak, "given," in part by the relatively unambiguous definition of the individual's vocational role. Clearly, life has meaning for man not only in terms of goals but also in terms of his doing, his functioning as a productive human being. If the artist fails to find goals or cannot manage to function within the cultural

PAUL RAND, Poster.
Courtesy of the artist.

25 Queens   Boite Nature   to Dad…with pride

climate, not only is his art "foredoomed" but so is he. Precariously perched between economics and aesthetics, his performance judged by the grimly impersonal yet arbitrary "Does it sell?" the commercial artist has great difficulty in finding his artistic personality, let alone asserting it. But art has often been practiced under severe constraints, whether those of the community, the church, or the individual patron. Under almost any conditions, short of absolute tyranny, art usually manages to prevail. Even if Lorenzo de' Medici had hated art, it is hard to imagine that Michelangelo would not have found some way to make sculpture and to paint. The artist—easel painter or designer—if he is genuinely committed to his vocation, does not need to be given a reason for existence: he is himself the reason.

Unfortunately he does not always recognize this fact. There are those who believe that the role the designer must play is fixed and determined by the socio-economic climate. He must discover his functional niche and fit himself into it. I would suggest that this ready-made image ignores the part the artist (or for that matter the carpenter or housewife) plays in creating the socio-economic climate. This creative contribution is made by everybody, willy-nilly, but it can become a far more significant one if the individual is aware that he is making it.

Such awareness, furthermore, is a basic source of that human dignity and pride which are prerequisite for the artist's attainment of creative status. The individual who feels himself a hapless, helpless pawn in some obscure life game obviously has trouble believing in either himself or the worth of his endeavor. Unquestionably, as men or artists, we must be able to adapt ourselves to environmental conditions, but we can do this only within certain limits. I would say that an understanding of man's intrinsic needs, and of the necessity to search for a climate in which those needs could be realized is fundamental to the education of the designer. Whether as advertising tycoons, missile builders, public or private citizens, we are all men, and to endure we must be first of all *for* ourselves. It is only when man (and the hordes of individuals that term stands for) is *not* accepted as the center of human concern that it becomes feasible to create a system of production which values profit out of proportion to responsible public service, or to design ads in which the only aesthetic criterion is "How sexy is the girl?"

If the popular artist is confronted too fast by too much, is split, is high-pressured, and is a part of a morally confused and aesthetically apathetic society, it is simple enough to say he can do something about it—but the bigger question is how.

First of all, perhaps, he must try to see the environment and himself in relation to it as objectively as possible. This is not easy. Where the "I" is involved, either specifically or generi-

129

cally, all kinds of resistances are aroused. It is much simpler and often more agreeable to see ourselves and the world through pastel-colored glasses. But if the artist does tumble into the swirling sea of confusion that surrounds his small island of individuality, he can at best only keep his head above water—certainly he will not be able to direct his course. He will no longer have a chance to develop the independence of thought necessary for making valid judgments and decisions.

If he can think independently and logically, the popular artist may come to see continuous and accelerating change, not as confusion compounded, but as the present form of stability. He may also be able to distinguish between the appearance of change and true change.

For the commercial artist such a distinction is vital. As a product designer he is increasingly required to consider what has been called "the newness factor"; as an advertising designer he is told by the copywriter that the resultant product is *New! Amazing! Different! The First Time in History!* All too often this "newness" has nothing to do with the innovation that is genuine change—an invention or an original method of doing or a mode of seeing and thinking. "Newness" frequently consists of contrived and transitory surprise effects such as pink stoves, automobile fins, graphic tricks. The *novelty-for-novelty's-sake* boom, with its concomitants of hypocrisy, superficiality, and waste, corrupts the designer who is taken in by them.

The differentiation of fact from fiction gives the commercial artist a basis for the far-reaching decisions he must often make. It is because of his relationship to industry that these decisions have effects far beyond the immediate aesthetic ones. When the artist designs a product, not only are millions of industry's dollars risked, but so are the jobs of those people involved in making the product. Even the graphic artist by "selling" a product helps secure jobs as well as profits. Under these circumstances it becomes a matter of social responsibility for the commercial artist to have a clear and firm understanding of what he is doing and why.

The profession or job of the artist in the commercial field is clear. He must design a product that will sell, or create a visual work that will help sell, a product, a process, or a service. At the same time, if he has both talent and a commitment to aesthetic values, he will automatically try to make the product or graphic design both pleasing and visually stimulating to the user or viewer. By stimulating I mean that his work will add something to the consumer's experience.

While there is absolutely no question that talent is far and away the most important attribute of any artist, it is also true that if this talent is not backed by conviction of purpose, it may

130

never be effectively exercised. The sincere artist needs not only the moral support that his belief in his work as an aesthetic statement gives him, but also the support that an understanding of his general role in society can give him. It is this role that justifies his spending the client's money and his risking other people's jobs, and it entitles him to make mistakes. Both through his work and through the personal statement of his existence he adds something to the world: he gives it new ways of feeling and of thinking, he opens doors to new experience, he provides new alternatives as solutions to old problems.

Like any other art, popular art relates formal and material elements. The material elements may be of a special nature, but, as in all art, the material and the formal are fused by an idea. Such ideas come originally from the artist's conscious and unconscious experience of the world around him. The experience that can give rise to these ideas is of a special kind. As Joyce Cary says, "The artist, painter, writer or composer starts always with an experience that is a kind of discovery. He comes upon it with the sense of a discovery; in fact, it is truer to say that it comes upon *him* as a discovery."[2] This is reminiscent of Picasso's admonition not to *seek* but to *find*. What both men are saying is that the very act of experiencing is for the artist a creative act; he must bring enough to the experience for it to lead him to a discovery about its nature, a discovery he will try to embody and transmit in a work of art. Surfeited by sensory stimuli, the artist today will be helpless to convert experience into ideas if he cannot select, organize, and deeply feel his experiences.

Ideas do not need to be esoteric to be original or exciting. As H. L. Mencken says of Shaw's plays, "The roots of each one of them are in platitude; the roots of *every* effective stage play are in platitude." And when he asks why Shaw is able to "kick up such a pother?" he answers, "For the simplest of reasons. Because he practices with great zest and skill the fine art of exhibiting the obvious in unexpected and terrifying lights."[3] What Cézanne did with apples or Picasso with guitars makes it quite clear that revelation does not depend upon complication. In 1947 I wrote what I still hold to be true, "The problem of the artist is to make the commonplace uncommonplace."[4]

If artistic quality depended on exalted subject matter, the commercial artist, as well as the advertising agency and advertiser, would be in a bad way. For a number of years I have worked with a cigar-manufacturing company whose product, visually, is not in itself unusual. A cigar is almost as commonplace as an apple, but if I fail to make ads for cigars that are lively and original, it will not be the cigar that is at fault.

What is important about visual ideas is that they express the

131

artist's experience and opinions in such a way that he communicates them to others, and that they, in turn, feel a sense of discovery on seeing the work, a sense similar to the artist's own. Only this can enrich the spectator's personal experience. Further, in the case of the graphic artist, these ideas must be so conceived as to help sell the product.

The artist is certainly not alone in facing these problems: they confront the businessman, the scientist, and the technologist. Nor is he alone in his creative drive. The popular artist who sees the world as dominated by mechanistic thinking run amuck, and himself as the machine's victim, feels powerless and alienated. This is unrealistic. The creative, the imaginative, even the aesthetic nature of science is now widely recognized.

If there is reassurance for both artist and scientist in the recognition of this similarity, there is actual danger in the ignoring of it. The mechanistic view of the world saw society as governed by laws similar to what were then believed to be the absolute and immutable "laws" of natural science. It tended to divorce social forces from the actions and decisions of man. The continued popularity of such an attitude is to my mind far more menacing than the physical achievements of science and technology. It is my belief that if we are at the mercy of "social forces," it is because we have put ourselves there. If we have become, or are becoming, "slaves of the machine," it means that we have acceded to slavery.

Even in the astonishing world of the computer and the simulation machine, it must be remembered that, at least initially, it is we who will give them a program. The kind of service they render depends on our decisions, on what we think (given their capacities) they ought to do. The key problem is not with any machine or with technology in general, it is with the "ought.' For both scientist and artist, as well as the industry that brings them together, it is a matter of over-all aims, specific purposes, and values. It is up to us to decide what we want.

Perception—how we see something—is always conditioned by what we are looking for, and why. In this way we are always faced with questions of value. A turbine must be "scientifically" designed in order to operate, but to design it at all was at one time a matter of decision. Such decisions may or may not be based on needs, but they are surely based on wants. Products do not have to be beautifully designed. Things can be made and marketed without our considering their aesthetic aspects, ads can convince without pleasing or heightening the spectator's visual awareness. But should they? The world of business could, at least for a while, function without benefit of art—but should it? I think not, if only for the simple reason that the world would be a poorer place if it did.

The very *raison d'être* of the commercial artist, namely, to help sell products and services, is often cited by him as the reason he cannot do good work. To my mind, this attitude is just as often the culprit as is the basic nature of the work. The commercial artist may feel inferior and therefore on the defensive with respect to the fine arts. There is undoubtedly a great and real difference between so-called fine art and commercial art, namely, a difference in purpose—a fact that must be recognized and accepted. But there is nothing wrong or shameful in selling. The shame and wrong come in only if the artist designs products or ads that do not meet his standards of artistic integrity.

The lament of the popular artist that he is not permitted to do good work because good work is neither wanted nor understood by his employers is universal. It is very often true. But if the artist honestly evaluates his work and that of the other complainers, he will frequently find that the "good work" the businessman has rejected is not actually so "good." The client can be right: the artist can be self-righteous. In accusing the businessman of being "antimodern" the artist is often justified. But many times "it's too modern" simply means that the client does not know what he is really objecting to. Unbeknown to himself, the client may be reacting to excessive streamlining, an inappropriate symbol, poor typography, or a genuinely inadequate display of the product. The artist must, without bias, sincerely try to interpret these reactions.

If there is nothing wrong with selling, even with "hard" selling, there is one type that is wrong: misrepresentative selling. Morally, it is very difficult for an artist to do a direct and creative job if dishonest claims are being made for the product he is asked to advertise, or if, as an industrial designer, he is supposed to exercise mere stylistic ingenuity to give an old product a new appearance. The artist's sense of worth depends on his feeling of integrity. If this is destroyed, he will no longer be able to function creatively.

On the other hand, it is surely more consoling to the commercial artist to see himself betrayed by the shortsightedness of commerce or to believe he is forced to submit to "what the public wants" than to think he himself may be at fault. The artist does not wish to see himself as either so indifferent to quality or so cowed by economic factors that he has taken the easy way out—just do what the boss says, and maybe give it a new twist. Yet actually it may not always be the lack of taste on the part of client and public that accounts for bad work, but the artist's own lack of courage.

To do work of integrity the artist must have the courage to fight for what he believes. This bravery may never earn him a

133

medal, and it must be undertaken in the face of a danger that has no element of high adventure in it—the cold, hard possibility of losing his job. Yet the courage of his convictions is, along with his talent, his only source of strength. The businessman will never respect the professional who does not believe in what he does. The businessman under these circumstances can only "use" the artist for his own ends—and why not, if the artist himself has no ends? As long as he remains "useful," the artist will keep his job, but he will lose his self-respect and eventually give up being an artist, except, perhaps, wistfully on Sundays.

In asking the artist to have courage, we must ask the same of industry. The impetus to conform, so widespread today, will, if not checked, kill all forms of creativity. In the world of commercial art, conformism is expressed, for example, by the tenacious timidity with which advertisers cling to the bald presentation of sex, sentimentality, and snobbism, and by such phenomena as the sudden blossoming of fins on virtually all makes of American cars. The artist knows he must fight conformity, but it is a battle he cannot win alone.

Business has a strong tendency to wait for a few brave pioneers to produce or underwrite original work, then rush to climb on the bandwagon—and the artist follows. The bandwagon, of course, may not even be going in the right direction. For instance, the attention and admiration evoked by the high caliber of Container Corporation's advertising have induced many an advertiser to say, "Let's do something like Container," without considering that it might not be at all suited to his needs. Specific problems require specific visual solutions. This does not mean that an advertisement for a soap manufacturer and one for Container Corporation cannot have much in common, or that a toaster cannot be designed in terms of the same sound principles as a carpenter's hammer. Both ads and both products can be made to fulfill their functions and also to be aesthetically gratifying; both can express respect for and concern with the broadest interests of the consumer.

It is unfortunately rare that the commercial artist and his employer, be it industry or advertising agency, work together in an atmosphere of mutual understanding and cooperation. Against the outstanding achievements in design made possible by such companies as Olivetti, Container Corporation, IBM, CBS, El Producto Cigar Company, CIBA, and a comparatively few others, there stands the great dismal mountain of average work. The lack of confidence that industry in general evinces for creative talent and creative work is the most serious obstacle to raising the standards of popular art. Business pays well for the services of artists who are already recognized and are consequently "successful." Success is a perfectly legitimate

134

reward for competence and integrity, but if it is a precondition for acceptance, it leaves the beginner and the hitherto unrecognized innovator in an economic *cul-de-sac*. Moreover, when business merely asks for something just "a little bit better" or "a little bit different," it may well inhibit not only artistic creativity, but also all forms of creativity, scientific and technological included.

From a long-range standpoint, the interests of business and art are not opposed. The former could perhaps survive without the latter, for a time; but art is a vital form of that creative activity which makes any kind of growth possible. We are deluged with speeches, articles, books, and slogans warning us that our very survival as free nations depends on growth and progress—economic, scientific, technological. The kind of climate that fosters original work represents an over-all attitude, a general commitment to values that uphold and encourage the artist as well as the scientist and the businessman.

REFERENCES

1. [Alfred North Whitehead], *Dialogues of Alfred North Whitehead, as recorded by Lucien Price* (Boston: Little, Brown and Company, 1954), p. 70.

2. Joyce Cary, *Art and Reality* (New York: Harper & Brothers, 1958), p. 1.

3. H. L. Mencken, *Prejudices: A Selection* (New York: Vintage K58, Alfred A. Knopf, 1958), pp. 27 and 28.

4. Paul Rand, *Thoughts on Design* (New York: George Wittenborn, Inc., 1947), p. 53.

135

EDWARD STEICHEN

On Photography

MANKIND IS FACED with a staggering abundance of words and images adding up to a complexity of political, scientific, economic, social, and cultural problems which no single human being can possibly assimilate. From birth to death we all function on the basis of our individual and unique genetic make-up. The future artist, as an infant, comes without an IBM card that lists and qualifies his aptitudes or indicates how the enormous influences of environment will shape his native equipment. It is only in the retrospective consideration of the artist's life work that the germ of the ultimate masterwork becomes evident even in his earliest work.

In a somewhat similar manner each period in the arts is the result of its inheritance of a past subjected to the conditioning pressures of the present, and it is only in the distant future that we shall be able to measure and evaluate the importance of what the art of our recent decades has contributed or added to the history of the arts and the culture of our period. The works of individual artists in any period or in relationship to works of other periods are only momentarily avant-garde devices. These soon become academic routine, and are often used to saddle the next generation. The fundamental relationship of great art in all periods has more basic similarities than differences. The images created in the caves of Lascaux and Altamira have a deep kinship with those coming from the studio of Picasso, and if we can skip conditioning and prejudices, what looks like radical differences between Li Lung Mien and Mark Tobey can also be translated into kinships.

Today it would seem that the painting and sculpture of our time has achieved an almost complete break from the long accepted traditions of literal representation, and has assumed an individual and personal freedom that discards all past disciplines.

Long before the birth of a word language the caveman communicated by visual images. The invention of photography gave visual communication its most simple, direct, universal language. We are only beginning to recognize generally and accept the potentialities of photography as an art medium, but as a visual means of mass communication it has become a force, and stands without a peer.

The importance of the art of photography as mass communication has been amply demonstrated by the exhibition produced by the Museum of Modern Art under the title, The Family of Man. This exhibition, in nine editions, has already been seen by some seven million people in twenty-eight countries—and it is still circulating. The audiences not only understand this visual presentation, they also participate in it, and identify themselves with the images, as if in corroboration of the words of a Japanese poet, "When you look into a mirror, you do not see your reflection, your reflection sees you."

Almost from the beginning, photographers have experimented with the production of images that imitated, or were inspired by, the prevalent concepts of other art media. Today a sizable percentage of the more talented younger photographers are probing and experimenting in new areas, creating images carrying connotations and meanings beyond, and often only indirectly related to, the objects represented. The photographers working in motion pictures with animated images in the realm of abstraction and surrealism, and with the added advantages of sound, are making a signal contribution to the modern use of photography as an art medium. As photography I would include color images directly projected on a screen by colored beams of light, even when made without the intervention of the camera.

It is quite possible that some richly imaginative and energetic young abstract painter may be even now experimenting with the highly developed photographically animated cartoon techniques coupled with related sound to open new horizons and areas in the domain of aesthetic imagery. In recording this as a possibility, I must give emphasis to the fact that a few photographers who have been exposed to the same heritage as the painters, as well as to the present-day impingements of science and of aesthetics in the arts, are now taking advantage also of the available technical advances to carry them toward these beckoning new image horizons.

BORIS KAUFMAN

Film Making as an Art

WHEN THE artist attempts to put a subject matter into visual form, he has to rely on his intuition, his feeling for the subject, and his knowledge of the medium he is to employ. A painter has nothing between him and the canvas but paint and brushes to express what he has to say. If the same condition applied to the art of the cinema, better pictures would be made. However, the complexity of this medium should not preclude the cinema's being a form of art. If an art form is defined by its ability to express by its own means, then the cinema deserves to be called an art.

Its title as such has been defended or denied since its invention. The importance of this question is not a purely academic one, but is of the essence. It is true that the commercial aspect of the cinema obscures the issue, and the fact of its being a mass entertainment, one that involves compromises, tends to obscure it the more. Yet an artist involved in the making of a picture has to believe in cinema as an art precisely so as to be able to carry through his task under the pressures of convention, of schedules, or a budget, and to bring his work to the spectator in a relatively pure form. After all, the screen is only a blank canvas that once in a while reflects an authentic work of art.

If the cinema is merely entertainment, the methods of making, viewing, and judging films will be guided by certain standards. The whole question as to art is then void of meaning, since most pictures that contain elements of story as well as acting and pictorial value will qualify as good or bad entertainment. If, on the other hand, the cinema is an art form, those criteria are no longer valid. The miscellaneous elements that enter into a film cease to exist by themselves: they must fuse into a whole, each contributing to the final expression.

Does the cinema in pure form exist? In the days of avant-garde film making, an artist trying to tell a story in visual form had to rely on the specific means of the medium. The picture succeeded or failed within those limitations. Very often what was a failure in itself was nevertheless a step forward, enabling the next effort to start from there. Each attempt at exploring and enlarging the horizon of the cinema grew into an impressive body of data of experimentation in the field of expression. If at present the complexity of film making obscures its art form, it does nevertheless exist as an art. It is contaminated by borrowed forms from the theatre, from literature, music, etc., it is plagued by gimmicks, tricks, and other substitutes for the real thing. Sound is used not to enrich, but to explain, color not to give an added dimension, but to reproduce natural colors. In general, cinema art is used not to create the visual climate of a drama, but merely to register a screen play on film.

There is one refuge for the cinematographer who is unwilling to conform: the so-called art films, made with little money, often with the makers' own. In a few cases they succeed in taking a step forward. The trouble with this field is its failure to reach large audiences and thereby earn the perpetuation of the same sort of effort. It is also subject to the dangers of narcissism, sterility, and the amateurism that may go with a lack of monetary means.

There seems to be no escape from the fact that the cinema is an industry married to an art form. As an art form it either survives, or is exterminated by the requirements of industry.

Is the cooperation of both industry and art possible in the cinema without mutual detriment? To answer this question, some of the realities of film making will have to be examined. It is generally understood that making a movie is a risky enterprise. The problem of how to lure the lost audience back from TV sets into the half-empty theatres has puzzled experts in the major studios as well as the independent producers. Let us pass over the superproductions that do not suffer from budgetary headaches and concentrate on a few independent attempts to re-establish contact with the elusive spectator lost to the box office. It should be obvious that to attract him, without gadgets and substitutes but by means of content and artistry, integrity in making such a film must prevail. This may seem apparent on paper, but experience shows that under the slightest pressure the people initiating this effort will give in, even before the need exists. This readiness to abandon the very elements that make a good film is responsible for many an abortive effort that might otherwise have succeeded.

What panics producers in this situation? The budget—meaning schedule, or speed of production. But speed at what cost, and at the cost of what? There is nothing wrong in a producer's emphasizing efficiency in operation. The present trend, however, of equating a cinematographer with a technician willing to abandon all attempt at being creative from the outset (because creativeness means complication or interference with the

139

primary aim of production, o.g., to make money above all) is something else. Unfortunately this trend no longer applies to the quickies alone. Producers allegedly planning a film with meaning, with aspiration to the real thing, shy away from any mention of "artistry," for the word has become a scarecrow. This discarding of all potential quality in favor of expediency excludes the very possibility of a film's being worthwhile.

Does this mean that good features cannot be made on low budgets? Not in the least. Time and again modest-budget films have proven as good or better than high-budget superproductions.

What, then, are the prerequisites for a happy production? A realistic schedule, with sets and locations ready on time, the careful selection of key men and crew, planning and anticipation—coordination. These few requisites, taken for granted in any other industry, have still to be accepted in motion pictures. Yet these few are essential in order to free time and energy for the creative effort—the only one that pays off.

In adapting a screen play for its visual form, a cinematographer has at his disposal a large vocabulary of cinematic language. Very often, however, this language is hardly used. Instead, a verbal continuity is illustrated with images, or the visual continuity is considered so insufficient that it is explained with excessive verbosity. As a result, both visual and verbal continuity are weakened. This could not happen if the cinema were indeed considered a self-sufficient art form. The basic continuity then would be the visual one, by the use of words, music, color, so as to reinforce and not explain, to counterpoint and not repeat.

The value of silence when there is no need for words has been almost forgotten. The value of words used sparingly and only when needed is seldom understood. Any true art form is suggestive. If everything is said about a subject, it leaves the audience with nothing to do but swallow already predigested matter. If the grass is green and the sky blue, nothing is left to the imagination. If a gesture suggesting an emotion is immediately explained in so many words, it loses its intended value. If a musical phrase overpowers the total expression, it throws the whole out of balance. To deserve the leading role in film making, the visual continuity has to live up to its own validity and use its own means of triggering perception and emotion. To use such means opens the infinite world of expression.

While in painting the infinite number of potential compositions finally stabilizes in a single permanent one, in a motion picture scene this composition lasts only a fraction of a second. Composition changes throughout the scene with the change in relationship between the camera and the objects, the actors, the background. In a dynamic composition the distribution of weight within the frame changes constantly. In the lighting, the graduation of black and white (or the chromatic scale) offers a variety of combinations that are limited only by the artist's judgment of the dramatic value. As for the visual continuity, a scene may be compared to a link in a chain representing a sequence—or a "word" in a cinematic phrase—each link having a specific weight or intensity, translated visually through composition and lighting. This continuity can be fragmentary, formed by cuts of close-ups, long shots, etc.; or it can take a legato form—the so-called fluid camera technique—when the moving camera combines several camera set-ups in one continuous scene. The choice of either method is not a casual one, but is determined by the style of the picture.

The language of the cinema is implicit—not explicit. Images logically unrelated to the scene can be used to evoke identical emotion. For example, in "Apropos de Nice" we discovered that the images of the *Promenade des Anglais* conveyed the same emotional impact as did the baroque statues in the cemetery in Nice, and could be "cut together" without affecting the logic of the statement. The procession of the children in the revolt scene in "Zéro de Conduite," shot in slow motion, conveyed a sensation of the heavy reality of a dream. When at the tea party in Bunuel's "L'Age d'Or" the servant girl is set afire, the event goes unnoticed by any one. Yet the implication of the burning maid together with the total absence of any reaction to it is stronger than any explanation could be.

In using free associations of images of equal potential, the cinema is elevated to the level of poetry or music, and is liberated from dependence on means borrowed from other forms of expression. The cinema transcends without effort the frontiers of reality and fantasy. It can move in three dimensions, even in a fourth—that of time. It can build a world from zero (in a studio), or it can select, interpret, or distort the reality outdoors.

In the studio the work is done under controlled conditions. The elements that are to go into a scene are determined and fused together into a harmony designed to express and to impress. A series of scenes forming a sequence all have to be of a certain intensity and consistency of mood, visually sustained through composition and lighting. At its best, lighting is comparable to painting, and each lighting arrangement is like a stroke of the brush.

Shooting on location represents a different problem. A certain location is preferred because of its authenticity of background. A cinematographer voluntarily gives up total control, for he

141

must cope with the inconveniences and interference of the outside world. Not all the elements of the location selected fit the scene; some have to be eliminated or subdued, others emphasized. The cinematographer has to subtract rather than add. Conditions are changing throughout the day, therefore it is harder to maintain consistency. Yet the vitality of the real world as interpreted by an artist often offers more than the controlled artificiality of the studio.

A bland reproduction of reality, however, is not an art form, unless a process of attraction and rejection takes place. Only those elements that are pertinent to the subject matter should be amplified, while the rest must be reduced. Light and physical shape—unlike those in the studio—are of a given quantity and quality. In determining the angle, the cinematographer limits the quantity to the fragment he chooses. Then making the composition gives the scene weight. The existing light, being of a given quantity at a given moment, can be filtered, partly intercepted, or boosted. Thus a degree of control is possible on location.

Obviously, the choice and control of the location should be deliberate, not accidental. Yet the whole approach has to be flexible and not rigid. The unpredictable can be turned to advantage if properly made use of, or an accidental element may become the clue to the mood or the motivation. For example, the artificial smoke in the park in "On the Waterfront" was not used for visual effect alone: the leaves burning in the iron baskets gave me a pretext for carrying the whole sequence within a specific mood. I used smoke to de-emphasize the background and to draw full attention to the foreground action. Thus consistency was maintained throughout two days of shooting, in changing atmospheric conditions.

Improvisation is an important part of shooting on location. Rigidity of preconception is incompatible with the full use of location. It is a pity that in the naked reality of picture making there is so little room for improvisation. When attempted at all, the improvisation is conspiratorial and tacit among the people concerned. They have no assurance of success. But there is no creativity in the sure thing of a beaten track.

There is little original writing for the cinema. The subject matter is usually secondhand, derived from a novel, a short story, a play, or else already expressed through some other medium. Adapting a subject to a new form of expression deprives it of the freshness of its primary form. The adaptation itself is not always perfect, but needs corrections during the making of the picture. Even at its best, a screen play has to be interpreted and shaped into cinematic form.

142

At this point it is necessary to restate the real meaning of the term, cinematic form. Indeed, what is cinematography? Is it just photography more or less skillfully executed? The trend of today's production is just that. As long as the action is competently registered on film, the task is accomplished. Only rarely is a cinematographer required to do more. As a result, you get a play photographed on film. The action and the photography exist side by side without anything in common: the cinematography is reduced to the status of a kinescope in TV. Therefore, it is necessary, at the risk of being called old-fashioned, to redefine what the medium really is. It may be helpful to those who have never heard this, as well as to those who do know but need reminding.

No matter how good the story is, it will remain merely a good story—or novel, or play—unless it is shaped into a form inherent to the medium. The real cinematography is inspired by the same vision that makes the picture worthwhile. It is invisible because it is integrated into the whole, like notes of music in a chromatic accord. Whether brilliant, dull, desolate, or gay, it is always in harmony with the basic emotional context of the scene. It is not something added, but is integral, and therefore the picture reaches the spectator with a totality of expression. The best cinematography cannot help being indifferent, unrelated, or even opposed to the very purpose of a scene unless it is motivated by the same rational and emotional impulse that moves the writer, the director, the actor. Cinematography is at its best when it creates the visual climate suitable to the dramatic situation. If consistently maintained throughout a picture, the result is a style that belongs to that particular picture. Therefore, cinematography cannot be standardized, nor its style in one picture applied to another without becoming conventional. In the same way, an artist chooses a palette that best suits his picture.

If the cinema is to survive as a medium of expression, it must maintain and develop its own specific form of art. Its failure to realize this will be suicidal—and needlessly so.

143

ROBERT GARDNER

A Human Document

THERE WAS something about the "old lady," as she came by default of the imagination to be called, which defied description. This may have been one reason she seemed from the very beginning an ideal subject for film. Age had all but erased the customary signs of sex. Her only clothing was a clump of frayed rags that she clutched between her legs with ancient modesty; sometimes she could pull it apart enough to wrap a piece around her waist and maybe over her shoulders, but usually she was concerned only about her loins.

Like the rest of her people, she was small, perhaps sixty-five or seventy pounds. In filming, there is always a problem of conveying a true indication of scale; on the screen the head of a fly can look like a monster, and a toy boat on a tiny pool like a ship at sea. This may be why there are so many pictures of anthropologists with their hands on pygmies' heads. So size was the first thing to be considered, the first problem to be solved— especially by some one three times larger. Sometimes when she was picked up she would protest and ask if she was going to be thrown away.

Her skin was like the bark of one of the common but infrequent desert trees, grey and wrinkled. It hung in folds and seemed to subsist in a detached way, drawing food and moisture from somewhere else than the body it still encased. Once she lost her way crawling back to her bed in the rain and blazed her leg on an assegai that someone had not properly put away. Under the hard skin her flesh was orange and wet but did not bleed. She had long feet and hands, these being the only organs which functioned at her command. She had to see with her hands and she had to be propelled by her feet. She was blind and nearly alone. Her vast and incalculable age seemed a mockery of those who lived about her, and her being there was a constant source of irritation as well. She had lived too long and could not now find food, or even, when it was given to her, eat it very well. Often, instead of asking for food, she would sweep away the little twigs and bits of straw that lay on the sand near her and scoop a few handfuls of it into her mouth.

The grains would spill over her chin and leak out of the corners of her mouth, but she managed to get enough to be satisfied.

To sit all day watching her was like waiting for someone to "come to life." She rarely spoke except to ask, "Where is my pipe?" or "When are we going to Nyae Nyae?" Nyae Nyae was where she was born and where she had had her children. She wanted to go there now because she felt that if she did she would be happy once again. But she could not get there by herself and there was no one among her own people who wanted to take her.

She spent most of her time asleep, occasionally shifting and adjusting her handful of clothing so as to protect herself from the cold night wind and the drying sun of the day. At first she was allowed the use of one of the little straw and branch shelters these people put up in the winter. The one she lived in belonged to her nephew by marriage. It was used to store the immense assortment of broken goods and worthless junk he had collected at a farm where he had once worked for a short time. She enjoyed this privilege even though it could not have been very comfortable lying on the boxes and bottles that contained her nephew's property. Then one day her bowels opened without warning and her nephew, swearing, dragged her off his possessions, and then his possessions out of the little house. Later the same day she crawled back to it, finding her way with the help of insulting directions and, perhaps, the smell of her own indiscretion. She lived alone in the house from then on and she could keep it the way she wanted.

Near her were the same little houses of other people who were all in some way her kin. Usually these houses are not more than ten yards from one another, and altogether they might number from ten to twenty-five. Except for the animals, both large and small, that live around these tiny villages, the only sounds are those of people, the thin murmur of their whispering conversations, food being eaten or gotten ready to eat, a pipe or a mother's breast being sucked, children screaming with delight or hunger. The "old lady" lay as if she heard nothing. The complicated pattern of life that flowed and eddied around her seemed to have no relation to her own. Only when one of the younger women teased or rebuked her for her foolish and useless old age did she show any sign of even wanting to be included. She would piteously haggle for consideration, her voice cracked and monotone. She rarely succeeded in stimulating sympathy and would subside amid the burst of renewed acrimony her pleas invariably provoked.

As time passed, she grew accustomed to the alien sounds of intruders, though the noise of the camera motor troubled her for quite a while. It usually began whenever she started to

145

"come to life." Her long periods of rest were interrupted by times when the one or two inescapable physiological activities that had not ceased had to be performed. These were the events of her day, and it upset her to be joined in them by such a clamorous witness. At first she lay back, hoping the noise would stop and she could have privacy. But the camera was more constant than her taunting young relatives, and perhaps, because the camera never raised its voice, she detected in it no malice or contempt. Later she talked to the camera, asking it for water, or tobacco, or some fire. It nearly always responded with what she wanted. One day she was given a cigaret which she put into her mouth burning end first. She smiled lightly at her own folly and bore no resentment whatever.

Her diet continued to be mainly sand, which she ate with as much relish as anything else she might be given, such as some soup made from the husks of a meaty nut all the other people were eating at this time of year. But it embarrassed her to eat sand in front of the camera. Everyone laughed at her insane fondness, and she tried to hide her craving. But finally she gave up attempts at deception and surrendered openly to this final lust of hers. When she had finished eating, and had sucked violently and mostly unsuccessfully on a crude pipe she stuffed with some borrowed tobacco, her long fingers would reach out to find shade and she would crawl to it, pushing with her feet and leaving a trail like a dry and broken tree stump dragged from its roots. As the sun moved across the sky it would find her and usually wake her and prod her into a new retreat. Sometimes, though, it was too low to disturb her and she would lie in it and absorb its warmth. Often she would be visited by butterflies that always love the sun, especially if there is the simultaneous excitement of some nearby moisture. Wherever two of her limbs had been crossed or where the flap of one of her empty breasts had lain on some other part of her, little patches of moist skin would tantalize the dancing butterflies. They would seem to hover ecstatically in the invisible vapors, drinking in the feeble steam of her being. Then they would flutter off to a drier place such as her ear or knee. She moved so little and so stuporously that these creatures never panicked and would drift away when neither light nor liquid remained.

Weeks passed, during which no change could be detected in her circumstances or condition, though around her people and events moved with the ordinary intensity of everyday life. In the house next to hers a new bride had recently given birth to her first child. Then, late at night, in spite of the beads that had been put around its fat neck and in spite of the rich milk that dripped from its mother's breasts, its eyes dulled and its cries weakened and it quietly died. The father, unstrung by his fate, threw his bow, arrows and assegai, broken to pieces, into the desert. The mother took her digging stick and her spoons and bowls and "spoiled" these things too. The next morning, after they had buried the child under the same tree where it had been born, without a single necessity of life they set out for another place, to begin again. Everyone who lived around them went away the same day, because these people never stay near a place where someone has died. Now, when they had all left, the "old lady" was indeed alone.

If there had been no foreigners in their midst, she would not have been left in this way. When a group is forced to move, as frequently happens when the seasons change and the foods each brings must be found in different places, the people cannot take those who are too old to walk, but they leave them food and water and put thorn branches over the entrance to their house, not to keep the old ones in but to keep the jackals and hyenas out. It is also told that these old people are hit on the head and then their houses are burned down on top of them. But no one could remember seeing this happen.

With the "werft," as the collection of these people's houses is called, abandoned, not a sound could be heard except for the drumming of the taut folding wings of dung beetles as they flung themselves on and off the ground in reckless and incongruous flight. For several days there was nothing moving near the "old lady" except the beetles, even the camera was still. The beetles were clumsy, dogged and truculently unconcerned with anything but the ball of dung they grasped between their legs and seemed to roll forever in all directions. She wasted in the silence of abandonment, her inertia a concentrated mockery of the camera. What began with such certain promise came ineluctably to lose its certainty. She lay, and her incessant stillness made her more and more remote. Apparently, film is at its best when it confronts motion and development. It should seek frenzy, not quiescence. This accounts perhaps for the extraordinary perfection of *The Miracle of Flowers*, in which, in seconds, a plant rises out of the ground, gives bud and blooms. Suppose one tried the same technique with the "old lady." One-turn-One, one turn, one picture, every ten seconds or every ten minutes, and she would have looked the same at the end of a day's turning as at the beginning. The time and the considerable amount of film that would have been taken might be justified by a compromise between Léger's hope of making a twenty-four-hour document of a married couple and Jacquetta Hawkes' idea of making one that would cover the entire life span of a single human being. The absurd impracticality of both ideas reinforced the dubiousness of this plan. Obviously,

147

no man or woman is going to permit a camera to see them as they see themselves, and no man or woman is going to allow themselves to be forever shadowed by photographers. And if they will, who would want to see it? Any idiot can take a picture, can sit with a camera on his knee or propped on the ground and wait for his subject to move. It doesn't matter what the subject is, either, because it's much easier to watch through a lens than through one's own eyes. The lens alienates and separates. The man with a camera sees with a different perspective, and most of the light that might have affected his own perception is mercifully intercepted by a moving band of light-absorbing silver particles that can be safely stored away for future viewing.

But the "old lady" wasn't even moving any more, except to eat the bowl of mealie meal brought to her every day since she had been left alone. She didn't like it very much but she ate it anyway, and her dark fingers would lighten as she dipped them with hot porridge into her mouth. By now every visible corner, wrinkle, and crack of her being had been photographed and the camera was useless.

One day as she slept, so still was she, it seemed even her death would defy the camera. I realized it was for this I was waiting, for a sign of death, not life, a flower falling back into the earth, not opening out of it.

She lived, and in a short time her people came back to their old houses, and she went back to eating sand and smoking their tobacco. Though she still weakened in health, she gained in spirits, for the terrible loneliness said to kill these people when they are not together no longer afflicted her.

At about this time, too, the expedition decided to move. We were leaving the desert to go home. For several months the lives of these people had been witnessed by cameras. Thousands of feet of film had been exposed and were already on the way to the processor. Every meaningful motion, glance, and detail to be discerned was somewhere in approximately one hundred miles of unedited footage. There would be miles of the "old lady," more miles of not so old and young women digging in the desert for their wild vegetables, playing with their children, cooking, eating, sleeping, arguing, doing everything they knew and wanted to do. There would be miles of men and boys, hunting, clowning, going into trance and coming out of trance, being erotic, being mean, and being sad. There would be a body of film that contained the visible portion of an entire culture, its people and its things. The cameras had done everything, within the limitations of the people who used them, that they could. There were thousands upon thousands of fragments of a larger time and place being taken away, which belonged

148

to the past of these people, and there was a problem, now, how some parts might be fitted together to tell about their present and future.

Since the trucks were going north and some of the people lived in that direction, as many as possible were given a ride. Among those who came were the "old lady" and her recently returned relatives. She was now too weak even to crawl and too uncertain a bundle to be just picked up. She was put into a blanket, which I carried, holding on to its four corners like some preposterous stork. Her relatives steadied her into a crevice on top of the truck, and it started out for Tchum-Kwi, one of the central waterholes of Nyae Nyae. We were there by mid-afternoon. Some would stay and others would go farther east, probably immediately, because there was not enough food at this place for everyone.

Late that afternoon just as we were departing, the "old lady" lay on her side, still covered with the ashes that had blown over her from the fire she had slept by the night before. She was tasting a mouthful of sand that, in this place, is whiter and maybe saltier than elsewhere. There was a faint sign of satisfaction on her face, and I knew, as well as I knew that I would kill her when I cut the film, that she would die in Nyae Nyae.

GEORGE AMBERG

The Ambivalence of Realism

Fragment of an Essay

Chaque époque a son réalisme.
—Fernand Léger

DURING the cinema's formative years, many tentative notions
about the nature of the motion picture became unchallenged
stereotypes. In this accidental way, "realism" acquired a peculiar meaning in filmic parlance and practice. It originated in
the momentous discovery that the moving image is capable of
creating an illusion of reality far more suggestive than is conceivable in the traditional arts. Unfortunately, the discovery of
this unprecedented potential was made by people unable to
appreciate its artistic significance but well able to exploit its
popular appeal. Thus, from the very beginning, the new medium
was dominated by the ambition to produce on film the closest
possible equivalent of the visual world. And since the cinema
could do this miraculously well, it became the art of imitation
in the least Aristotelian and the most literal meaning of the
term: it became the realistic medium *par excellence.*

As justification for the persistence of this direction, it has
been maintained that realism is inherent in the medium, owing
to the fact that cinematography is a technical process, producing
likenesses of the material world. Without many qualifications,
the claim is neither right nor wrong; it is, however, incomplete.
Some authentic quality of the original object is apt to carry over
into the photographic image, whether by accident or by design.
To deduce therefrom that cinematic realism is validated by
physical reality as such is to carry the argument to the absurd.
Its best refutation is Erwin Panofsky's pithy statement that "the
problem is to manipulate and shoot unstylized reality in such
a way that the result has style"—which is precisely what Maya
Deren calls the "creative use of reality." Stylization is a matter
not only of aesthetic principle or creative vision, but also of
degree. Even the ostensibly literal screen image becomes sty-
lized in the process of transmutation, if only because the reduc-

This paper contains material from a book in progress, a comprehensive
study of the theory and aesthetics of the cinema, to be published by the
University of Minnesota Press under the title *The Captive Eye.*

150

tion from three-dimensional reality to the plane surface renders it physically different from the original to which it refers. But it does not mean, of course, that it has style.

The particular literal form of realism prevailing in the average production has no more genuine authenticity, either factual or artistic, than the spectator has been conditioned to concede; it is as surely a convention as Italian opera. But it is a useful, possibly an indispensable, convention because it allows the identification of stereotypes, signifying good or evil, ocean or desert, cops or robbers. It would be an exaggeration to define them as meaningful symbols; they are merely convenient abbreviations, obviating imaginative or intellectual effort. While "special effects" credits hint broadly that we may and indeed can be optically deceived, assurance is gained from the knowledge that the motion picture deals first and foremost with physical reality. The techniques of illusion are superimposed, as it were, upon a solid foundation of fact. To a large extent, this accounts for the audience's confidence in the supposed authenticity of the projected image and, by analogy, for its acceptance of the total film situation as "real."

Underlying the implicit belief in the validity of realism is the contention that "art mirrors life," and that the better it mirrors, the better it is. This position holds just enough half-truth to be hard to refute, and thus to support the aesthetic prejudices of the mass audience. Because the film presents recognizable likenesses, and because this is the one element in art which everyone feels entitled to judge, the movies have habituated the public to a realistic criterion of art. The most frequently used terms of appreciation are not evaluative but descriptive, such as "natural" or "real" or "lifelike." Whatever else those criteria may signify, in the first place they are regarded as a measure of the film's authenticity as well as an appraisal of its honesty (as a representation of life). One depends on the other, the moral affirmation compensating for a lack of aesthetic discrimination, the pseudo-aesthetic approval confirming the presence of moral integrity. What is characteristic for those qualifications is that they avoid reference to emotional involvement and ethical commitment. One cannot help suspecting that the film events occur in an emotional void, not in addition to but instead of the spectator's individual experience and expectation of life—so much so that the cinema functions frequently not only as an art-surrogate but even more as a life-substitute.

The elaborate strategy of realism, developed and perfected in the film studios over the years, is more than a bagful of technical tricks: it is a cunning device *to make facts sell fiction.* The encounter with the unfamiliar, the illicit, the daring, the impossible, or the improbable within a verifiable frame of ref-

151

erence allows the audience to enjoy the experience as though it were authentic. This compromise between the quest for truth and the quest for wonder, a compromise that is uniquely cinematic, provides a neat solution for the average spectator's ambivalent attitude toward vicarious gratification. For, on the one hand, he craves to be carried away into experiences transcending his own limitations; on the other, he is haunted by the fear of becoming the victim of a fraud. Fearful or skeptical he may be, but critical reasoning hardly ever enters into the situation.

The moving pictures, comparable to certain religious images, are essentially *likenesses taken on faith*. It is not as absurd as it may sound, that a reputable reviewer should commend an actor for his "extraordinary likeness to Christ." Under the proper physical and psychological conditions (as they prevail in the movie theatre), visual experience seems incontrovertible. The public would probably accept a square wheel, provided it were visually corroborated. While manifesting a virtually unlimited tolerance for improbable premises, the audience is rigorously exigent in its demand for the explicit form of pictorial documentation which is supposedly objective and authentic—the presupposition evidently being that only the visual (and audible) world is "real." The suggestion that cinema, as an imaginative extension of reality beyond physical reality, may have artistic authenticity would be lost on the average spectator.

Realistic motion pictures, fulfilling those particular conditions to perfection, are rarely distinguished by originality and vision. The more they resemble one another, the more successful they are. They rely on conventional behavior patterns, familiar character prototypes, and stereotyped wish-situations, all of which allow a high degree of identification with the screen events and situations. This is the essential purpose. This, in the most personal guise, is the public's definition of realism, although the implications are not consciously realized. A shell of caution surrounds the core of excitement. For good or bad reasons, depending on the motivation, films of this genre avoid penetration in depth in favor of expansion on the surface. Conveyed with the tremendous persuasive power of the moving magnified image, even these films became frightfully "real" at times. Not that they are verifiably real; they are merely plausible *idealizations of reality*, "as good as real." Indeed, it is impossible to suppress the subliminal awareness that screen reality is at most a "literal transcript of the world of reality" and not this world itself. No matter how convincingly "true to life" by the audience's definition, how evil the villain or how virtuous the heroine, how passionate the embrace or how bloody the fight, how happy the ending or how dead the corpse—the suspicion is present that what occurs on the screen is only make-believe.

Why, then, does the audience so obstinately persist in the thinly veiled delusion that it is "facing reality," literally as well as figuratively, when involved in movie action? The answer is obvious: for the general public, the alternative is not a choice between art and life, since the cinema is not appreciated as art and life is taken for granted, or between truth and falsehood, since this is not the crucial issue in a fictional film. The choice lies simply between a motion picture that appears "real" and one that does not. Film "realism," with this popular significa-tion, does not refer to reality as either actuality or verifiable fact, or even as an imaginative transformation of actuality, but as a *metaphor for wishful thinking*. In this spurious way, the cinema fulfills the vague yet urgent needs of the "lonely crowd" that used to go empty until the movies filled the void.

This is a modest result for so large and costly an apparatus. Probably one should not, in all fairness, expect the spectator to face and recognize himself every time he goes to the movies. There is, however, an ironical twist in the public's tendency to conclude from the observation of cinematic realism that the cinema succeeds where art fails. It is not within the scope of these brief remarks to refute the error. Nevertheless, it should be clearly appreciated that the critical fallacy of this vastly popular opinion is not the explicit belief in the doubtful visual evidence of reality, but the implicit rejection of art.

MAYA DEREN

Cinematography: The Creative Use of Reality

THE MOTION-PICTURE CAMERA is perhaps the most paradoxical of all machines, in that it can be at once independently active and infinitely passive. Kodak's early slogan, "You push the button, it does the rest," was not an exaggerated advertising claim; and, connected to any simple trigger device, a camera can even take pictures all by itself. At the same time, while a comparable development and refinement of other mechanisms has usually resulted in an increased specialization, the advances in the scope and sensitivity of lenses and emulsions have made the camera capable of infinite receptivity and indiscriminate fidelity. To this must be added the fact that the medium deals, or can deal, in terms of the most elemental actuality. In sum, it can produce maximum results for virtually minimal effort: it requires of its operator only a modicum of aptitude and energy; of its subject matter, only that it exist; and of its audience, only that they can see. On this elementary level it functions ideally as a mass medium for communicating equally elementary ideas.

The photographic medium is, as a matter of fact, so amorphous that it is not merely unobtrusive but virtually transparent, and so becomes, more than any other medium, susceptible of servitude to any and all the others. The enormous value of such servitude suffices to justify the medium and to be generally accepted as its function. This has been a major obstacle to the definition and development of motion pictures as a creative fine-art form—capable of creative action in its own terms—for its own character is as a latent image which can become manifest only if no other image is imposed upon it to obscure it.

Those concerned with the emergence of this latent form must therefore assume a partially protective role, one which recalls the advice of an art instructor who said, "If you have trouble drawing the vase, try drawing the space around the vase." Indeed, for the time being, the definition of the creative form of film involves as careful attention to what it is not as to what it is.

Animated Paintings

In recent years, perceptible first on the experimental fringes of the film world and now in general evidence at the commercial art theaters, there has been an accelerated development of what might be called the "graphic arts school of animated film." Such films, which combine abstract backgrounds with recognizable but not realistic figures, are designed and painted by trained and talented graphic artists who make use of a sophisticated, fluent knowledge of the rich resources of plastic media, including even collage. A major factor in the emergence of this school has been the enormous technical and laboratory advance in color film and color processing, so that it is now possible for these artists to approach the two-dimensional, rectangular screen with all the graphic freedom they bring to a canvas.

The similarity between screen and canvas had long ago been recognized by artists such as Hans Richter, Oscar Fishinger, and others, who were attracted not by its graphic possibilities (so limited at that time) but rather by the excitements of the film medium, particularly the exploitation of its time dimension—rhythm, spatial depth created by a diminishing square, the three-dimensional illusion created by the revolutions of a spiral figure, etc. They put their graphic skills at the service of the film medium, as a means of extending film expression.*

The new graphic-arts school does not so much advance those early efforts as reverse them, for here the artists make use of the film medium as an extension of the plastic media. This is particularly clear when one analyzes the principle of movement employed, for it is usually no more than a sequential articulation—a kind of spelling out in time—of the dynamic ordinarily implicit in the design of an individual composition. The most appropriate term to describe such works, which are often interesting and witty, and which certainly have their place among visual arts, is "animated paintings."

This entry of painting into the film medium presents certain parallels with the introduction of sound. The silent film had attracted to it persons who had talent for and were inspired by the exploration and development of a new and unique form of visual expression. The addition of sound opened the doors for the verbalists and dramatists. Armed with the authority, power, laws, techniques, skills, and crafts which the venerable literary arts had accumulated over centuries, the writers hardly even paused to recognize the small resistance of the "indigenous" film-maker, who had had barely a decade in which to explore and evolve the creative potential of his medium.

* It is significant that Hans Richter, a pioneer in such a use of film, soon abandoned this approach. All his later films, along with the films of Léger, Man Ray, Dali, and the painters who participated in Richter's later films (Ernst, Duchamp, etc.) indicate a profound appreciation of the distinction between the plastic and the photographic image, and make enthusiastic and creative use of photographic reality.

The rapid success of the "animated painting" is similarly due to the fact that it comes armed with all the plastic traditions and techniques which are its impressive heritage. And just as the sound film interrupted the development of film form on the commercial level by providing a more finished substitute, so the "animated painting" is already being accepted as a form of film art in the few areas (the distribution of 16 mm. film shorts to film series and societies) where experiments in film form can still find an audience.

The motion-picture medium has an extraordinary range of expression. It has in common with the plastic arts the fact that it is a visual composition projected on a two-dimensional surface; with dance, that it can deal in the arrangement of movement; with theater, that it can create a dramatic intensity of events; with music, that it can compose in the rhythms and phrases of time and can be attended by song and instrument; with poetry, that it can juxtapose images; with literature generally, that it can encompass in its sound track the abstractions available only to language.

This very profusion of potentialities seems to create confusion in the minds of most film-makers, a confusion which is diminished by eliminating a major portion of those potentialities in favor of one or two, upon which the film is subsequently structured. An artist, however, should not seek security in a tidy mastery over the simplifications of deliberate poverty; he should, instead, have the creative courage to face the danger of being overwhelmed by fecundity in the effort to resolve it into simplicity and economy.

While the "animated painting" film has limited itself to a small area of film potential, it has gained acceptance on the basis of the fact that it *does* use an art form—the graphic art form—and that it does seem to meet the general condition of film: it makes its statement as an image in movement. This opens the entire question of whether a photograph is of the same order of image as all others. If not, is there a correspondingly different approach to it in a creative context? Although the photographic process is the basic building block of the motion-picture medium, it is a tribute to its self-effacement as a servant that virtually no consideration has been given to its own character and the creative implications thereof.

The Closed Circuit of the Photographic Process

The term "image" (originally based on "imitation") means in its first sense the visual likeness of a real object or person, and in the very act of specifying resemblance it distinguishes and establishes the entire category of visual experience which is

156

not a real object or person. In this specifically negative sense—in the sense that the photograph of a horse is not the horse itself—a photograph is an image.

But the term "image" also has positive implications: it presumes a mental activity, whether in its most passive form (the "mental images" of perception and memory) or, as in the arts, the creative action of the imagination realized by the art instrument. Here reality is first filtered by the selectivity of individual interests and modified by prejudicial perception to become experience; as such it is combined with similar, contrasting or modifying experiences, both forgotten and remembered, to become assimilated into a conceptual image; this in turn is subject to the manipulations of the art instrument; and what finally emerges is a plastic image which is a reality in its own right. A painting is not, fundamentally, a likeness or image of a horse; it is a likeness of a mental concept which may resemble a horse or which may, as in abstract painting, bear no visible relation to any real object.

Photography, however, is a process by which an object creates its own image by the action of its light on light-sensitive material. It thus presents a closed circuit precisely at the point where, in the traditional art forms, the creative process takes place as reality passes through the artist. This exclusion of the artist at that point is responsible both for the absolute fidelity of the photographic process and for the widespread conviction that a photographic medium cannot be, itself, a creative form. From these observations it is but a step to the conclusion that its use as a visual printing press or as an extension of another creative form represents a full realization of the potential of the medium. It is precisely in this manner that the photographic process is used in "animated paintings."

But in so far as the camera is applied to objects which are already accomplished images, is this really a more creative use of the instrument than when, in scientific films, its fidelity is applied to reality in conjunction with the revelatory functions of telescopic or microscopic lenses and a comparable use of the motor?

Just as the magnification of a lens trained upon matter shows us a mountainous, craggy landscape in an apparently smooth surface, so slow-motion can reveal the actual structure of movements or changes which either cannot be slowed down in actuality or whose nature would be changed by a change in tempo of performance. Applied to the flight of a bird, for example, slow-motion reveals the hitherto unseen sequence of the many separate strains and small movements of which it is compounded.

By a telescopic use of the motor, I mean the telescoping of

157

time achieved by triggering a camera to take pictures of a vine at ten-minute intervals. When projected at regular speed, the film reveals the actual integrity, almost the intelligence, of the movement of the vine as it grows and turns with the sun. Such telescoped-time photography has been applied to chemical changes and to physical metamorphoses whose tempo is so slow as to be virtually imperceptible.

Although the motion-picture camera here functions as an instrument of discovery rather than of creativity, it does yield a kind of image which, unlike the images of "animated paintings" (animation itself is a use of the telescoped-time principle), is unique to the motion-picture medium. It may therefore be regarded as an even more valid basic element in a creative film form based on the singular properties of the medium.

Reality and Recognition

The application of the photographic process to reality results in an image which is unique in several respects. For one thing, since a specific reality is the prior condition of the existence of a photograph, the photograph not only testifies to the existence of that reality (just as a drawing testifies to the existence of an artist) but is, to all intents and purposes, its equivalent. This equivalence is not at all a matter of fidelity but is of a different order altogether. If realism is the term for a graphic image which precisely simulates some real object, then a photograph must be differentiated from it as *a form of reality itself*.

This distinction plays an extremely important role in the address of these respective images. The intent of the plastic arts is to make meaning manifest. In creating an image for the express purpose of communicating, the artist primarily undertakes to create the most effective aspect possible out of the total resources of his medium. Photography, however, deals in a living reality which is structured primarily to endure, and whose configurations are designed to serve that purpose, not to communicate its meaning; they may even serve to conceal that purpose as a protective measure. In a photograph, then, we begin by recognizing a reality, and our attendant knowledges and attitudes are brought into play; only then does the aspect become meaningful in reference to it. The abstract shadow shape in a night scene is not understood at all until revealed and identified as a person; the bright red shape on a pale ground which might, in an abstract, graphic context, communicate a sense of gaiety, conveys something altogether different when recognized as a wound. As we watch a film, the continuous act of recognition in which we are involved is like a strip of memory unrolling beneath the images of the film itself, to

158

form the invisible underlayer of an implicit double exposure.

The process by which we understand an abstract, graphic image is almost directly opposite, then, to that by which we understand a photograph. In the first case, the aspect leads us to meaning; in the second case the understanding which results from recognition is the key to our evaluation of the aspect.

Photographic Authority and the "Controlled Accident"

As a reality, the photographic image confronts us with the innocent arrogance of an objective fact, one which exists as an independent presence, indifferent to our response. We may in turn view it with an indifference and detachment we do not have toward the man-made images of other arts, which invite and require our perception and demand our response in order to consummate the communication they initiate and which is their *raison d'être*. At the same time, precisely because we are aware that our personal detachment does not in any way diminish the verity of the photographic image, it exercises an authority comparable in weight only to the authority of reality itself.

It is upon this authority that the entire school of the social documentary film is based. Although expert in the selection of the most effective reality and in the use of camera placement and angle to accentuate the pertinent and effective features of it, the documentarists operate on a principle of minimal intervention, in the interests of bringing the authority of reality to the support of the moral purpose of the film.

Obviously, the interest of a documentary film corresponds closely to the interest inherent in its subject matter. Such films enjoyed a period of particular pre-eminence during the war. This popularity served to make fiction-film producers more keenly aware of the effectiveness and authority of reality, an awareness which gave rise to the "neo-realist" style of film and contributed to the still growing trend toward location filming.

In the theater, the physical presence of the performers provides a sense of reality which induces us to accept the symbols of geography, the intermissions which represent the passage of time, and the other conventions which are part of the form. Films cannot include this physical presence of the performers. They can, however, replace the artifice of theater by the actuality of landscape, distances, and place; the interruptions of intermissions can be transposed into transitions which sustain and even intensify the momentum of dramatic development; while events and episodes which, within the context of theatrical artifice, might not have been convincing in their logic or aspect can be clothed in the verity which emanates from the reality

159

of the surrounding landscape, the sun, the streets and buildings.

In certain respects, the very absence in motion pictures of the physical presence of the performer, which is so important to the theater, can even contribute to our sense of reality. We can, for example, believe in the existence of a monster if we are not asked to believe that it is present in the room with us. The intimacy imposed upon us by the physical reality of other art works presents us with alternative choices: either to identify with or to deny the experience they propose, or to withdraw altogether to a detached awareness of that reality as merely a metaphor. But the film image—whose intangible reality consists of lights and shadows beamed through the air and caught on the surface of a silver screen—comes to us as the reflection of another world. At that distance we can accept the reality of the most monumental and extreme of images, and from that perspective we can perceive and comprehend them in their full dimension.

The authority of reality is available even to the most artificial constructs if photography is understood as an art of the "controlled accident." By "controlled accident" I mean the maintenance of a delicate balance between what is there spontaneously and naturally as evidence of the independent life of actuality, and the persons and activities which are deliberately introduced into the scene. A painter, relying primarily upon aspect as the means of communicating his intent, would take enormous care in the arrangement of every detail of, for example, a beach scene. The cinematographer, on the other hand, having selected a beach which, in general, has the desired aspect—whether grim or happy, deserted or crowded—must on the contrary refrain from overcontrolling the aspect if he is to retain the authority of reality. The filming of such a scene should be planned and framed so as to create a context of limits within which anything that occurs is compatible with the intent of the scene.

The invented event which is then introduced, though itself an artifice, borrows reality from the reality of the scene—from the natural blowing of the hair, the irregularity of the waves, the very texture of the stones and sand—in short, from all the uncontrolled, spontaneous elements which are the property of actuality itself. Only in photography—by the delicate manipulation which I call controlled accident—can natural phenomena be incorporated into our own creativity, to yield an image where the reality of a tree confers its truth upon the events we cause to transpire beneath it.

Abstractions and Archetypes

Inasmuch as the other art forms are not constituted of reality itself, they create metaphors for reality. But photography, being itself the reality or the equivalent thereof, can use its own reality as a metaphor for ideas and abstractions. In painting, the image is an abstraction of the aspect; in photography, the abstraction of an idea produces the archetypal image.

This concept is not new to motion pictures, but its development was interrupted by the intrusions of theatrical traditions into the film medium. The early history of film is studded with archetypal figures: Theda Bara, Mary Pickford, Marlene Dietrich, Greta Garbo, Charles Chaplin, Buster Keaton, etc. These appeared as personages, not as people or personalities, and the films which were structured around them were like monumental myths which celebrated cosmic truths.

The invasion of the motion-picture medium by modern playwrights and actors introduced the concept of realism, which is at the root of theatrical metaphor and which, in the a priori reality of photography, is an absurd redundancy which has served merely to deprive the motion-picture medium of its creative dimension. It is significant that, despite every effort of pretentious producers, directors and film critics who seek to raise their professional status by adopting the methods, attitudes, and criteria of the established and respected art of theater, the major figures—both the most popular stars and the most creative directors (such as Orson Welles)—continue to operate in the earlier archetypal tradition. It was even possible, as Marlon Brando demonstrated, to transcend realism and to become an archetypal realist, but it would appear that his early intuition has been subsequently crushed under the pressures of the repertory complex, another carry-over from theater, where it functioned as the means by which a single company could offer a remunerative variety of plays to an audience while providing consistent employment for its members. There is no justification whatsoever for insisting on a repertory variety of roles for actors involved in the totally different circumstances of motion pictures.

Photography's Unique Images

In all that I have said so far, the fidelity, reality, and authority of the photographic image serve primarily to modify and to support. Actually, however, the sequence in which we perceive photography—an initial identification followed by an interpretation of the aspect according to that identification (rather than in primarily aspectual terms)—becomes irreversible and confers meaning upon aspect in a manner unique to the photographic medium.

I have previously referred to slow-motion as a time micro-

161

scope, but it has its expressive uses as well as its revelatory ones. Depending upon the subject and the context, it can be a statement of either ideal ease or nagging frustration, a kind of intimate and loving meditation on a movement or a solemnity which adds ritual weight to an action; or it can bring into reality that dramatic image of anguished helplessness, otherwise experienced only in the nightmares of childhood, when our legs refused to move while the terror which pursues us comes ever closer.

Yet, slow-motion is not simply slowness of speed. It is, in fact, something which exists in our minds, not on the screen, and can be created only in conjunction with the identifiable reality of the photographic image. When we see a man in the attitudes of running and identify the activity as a run, one of the knowledges which is part of that identification is the pulse normal to that activity. It is because we are aware of the known pulse of the identified action while we watch it occur at a slower rate of speed that we experience the double-exposure of time which we know as slow-motion. It cannot occur in an abstract film, where a triangle, for instance, may go fast or slow, but, having no necessary pulse, cannot go in slow-motion.

Another unique image which the camera can yield is reverse motion. When used meaningfully, it does not convey so much a sense of a backward movement spatially, but rather an undoing of time. One of the most memorable uses of this occurs in Cocteau's *Blood of a Poet,* where the peasant is executed by a volley of fire which also shatters the crucifix hanging on the wall behind him. This scene is followed by a reverse motion of the action—the dead peasant rising from the ground and the crucifix reassembling on the wall; then again the volley of fire, the peasant falling, the crucifix shattering; and again the filmic resurrection. Reverse motion also, for obvious reasons, does not exist in abstract films.

The photographic negative image is still another striking case in point. This is not a direct white-on-black statement but is understood as an inversion of values. When applied to a recognizable person or scene, it conveys a sense of a critically qualitative change, as in its use for the landscape on the other side of death in Cocteau's *Orpheus.*

Both such extreme images and the more familiar kind which I referred to earlier make use of the motion-picture medium as a form in which the meaning of the image originates in our recognition of a known reality and derives its authority from the direct relationship between reality and image in the photographic process. While the process permits some intrusion by the artist as a modifier of that image, the limits of its tolerance can be defined as that point at which the original reality becomes unrecognizable or is irrelevant (as when a red reflection in a pond is used for its shape and color only and without contextual concern for the water or the pond).

In such cases the camera itself has been conceived of as the artist, with distorting lenses, multiple superpositions, etc., used to simulate the creative action of the eye, the memory, etc. Such well-intentioned efforts to use the medium creatively, by forcibly inserting the creative act in the position it traditionally occupies in the visual arts, accomplish, instead, the destruction of the photographic image as reality. This image, with its unique ability to engage us simultaneously on several levels— by the objective authority of reality, by the knowledges and values which we attach to that reality, by the direct address of its aspect, and by a manipulated relationship between these— is the building block for the creative use of the medium.

The Placement of the Creative Act and Time-Space Manipulations

Where does the film-maker then undertake his major creative action if, in the interests of preserving these qualities of the image, he restricts himself to the control of accident in the pre-photographic stage and accepts almost complete exclusion from the photographic process as well?

Once we abandon the concept of the image as the end product and consummation of the creative process (which it is in both the visual arts and the theater), we can take a larger view of the total medium and can see that the motion-picture instrument actually consists of two parts, which flank the artist on either side. The images with which the camera provides him are like fragments of a permanent, incorruptible memory; their individual reality is in no way dependent upon their sequence in actuality, and they can be assembled to compose any of several statements. In film, the image can and should be only the beginning, the basic material of the creative action.

All invention and creation consist primarily of a new relationship between known parts. The images of film deal in realities which, as I pointed out earlier, are structured to fulfill their various functions, not to communicate a specific meaning. Therefore they have several attributes simultaneously, as when a table may be, at once, old, red, and high. Seeing it as a separate entity, an antique dealer would appraise its age, an artist its color, and a child its inaccessible height. But in a film such a shot might be followed by one in which the table falls apart, and thus a particular aspect of its age would constitute its meaning and function in the sequence, with all other attributes becoming irrelevant. The editing of a film creates the

163

sequential relationship which gives particular or new meaning to the images *according to their function*; it establishes a context, a form which transfigures them without distorting their aspect, diminishing their reality and authority, or impoverishing that variety of potential functions which is the characteristic dimension of reality.

Whether the images are related in terms of common or contrasting qualities, in the causal logic of events which is narrative, or in the logic of ideas and emotions which is the poetic mode, the structure of a film is sequential. The creative action in film, then, takes place in its time dimension; and for this reason the motion picture, though composed of spatial images, is primarily *a time form*.

A major portion of the creative action consists of a manipulation of time and space. By this I do not mean only such established filmic techniques as flashback, condensation of time, parallel action, etc. These affect not the action itself but the method of revealing it. In a flashback there is no implication that the usual chronological integrity of the action itself is in any way affected by the process, however disrupted, of memory. Parallel action, as when we see alternately the hero who rushes to the rescue and the heroine whose situation becomes increasingly critical, is an omnipresence on the part of the camera as a witness of action, not as a creator of it.

The kind of manipulation of time and space to which I refer becomes itself part of the organic structure of a film. There is, for example, the extension of space by time and of time by space. The length of a stairway can be enormously extended if three different shots of the person ascending it (filmed from different angles so that it is not apparent that the identical area is being covered each time) are so edited together that the action is continuous and results in an image of enduring labor toward some elevated goal. A leap in the air can be extended by the same technique, but in this case, since the film action is sustained far beyond the normal duration of the real action itself, the effect is one of tension as we wait for the figure to return, finally, to earth.

Time may be extended by the reprinting of a single frame, which has the effect of freezing the figure in mid-action; here the frozen frame becomes a moment of suspended animation which, according to its contextual position, may convey either the sense of critical hesitation (as in the turning back of Lot's wife) or may constitute a comment on stillness and movement as the opposition of life and death. The reprinting of scenes of a casual situation involving several persons may be used either in a prophetic context, as a *déjà-vu*; or, again, precise reiteration, by inter-cutting reprints, of those spontaneous movements,

164

EDWARD STEICHEN, The Maypole, 1932.
Collection Museum of Modern Art, New York.

BORIS KAUFMAN, Scene from "L'Atalante" (at dusk).
Courtesy of the artist.

BORIS KAUFMAN, Scene from "On the Waterfront" (smoke drifting through the scene).
Courtesy of the artist.

MAYA DEREN and ALEXANDER HAMMID, Scene from "Meshes of
the Afternoon."
Courtesy of the artists.

expressions, and exchanges, can change the quality of the scene from one of informality to that of a stylization akin to dance; in so doing it confers dance upon nondancers, by shifting emphasis from the purpose of the movement to the movement itself, and an informal social encounter then assumes the solemnity and dimension of ritual.

Similarly, it is possible to confer the movement of the camera upon the figures in the scene, for the large movement of a figure in a film is conveyed by the changing relationship between that figure and the frame of the screen. If, as I have done in my recent film *The Very Eye of Night*, one eliminates the horizon line and any background which would reveal the movement of the total field, then the eye accepts the frame as stable and ascribes all movement to the figure within it. The hand-held camera, moving and revolving over the white figures on a totally black ground, produces images in which their movement is as gravity-free and as three-dimensional as that of birds in air or fish in water. In the absence of any absolute orientation, the push and pull of their interrelationships becomes the major dialogue.

By manipulation of time and space, I mean also the creation of a relationship between separate times, places, and persons. A swing-pan—whereby a shot of one person is terminated by a rapid swing away and a shot of another person or place begins with a rapid swing of the camera, the two shots being subsequently joined in the blurred area of both swings—brings into dramatic proximity people, places, and actions which in actuality might be widely separated. One can film different people at different times and even in different places performing approximately the same gesture or movement, and, by a judicious joining of the shots in such a manner as to preserve the continuity of the movement, the action itself becomes the dominant dynamic which unifies all separateness.

Separate and distant places not only can be related but can be made continuous by a continuity of identity and of movement, as when a person begins a gesture in one setting, this shot being immediately followed by the hand entering another setting altogether to complete the gesture there. I have used this technique to make a dancer step from woods to apartment in a single stride, and similarly to transport him from location to location so that the world itself became his stage. In my *At Land*, it has been the technique by which the dynamic of the *Odyssey* is reversed and the protagonist, instead of undertaking the long voyage of search for adventure, finds instead that the universe itself has usurped the dynamic action which was once the prerogative of human will, and confronts her with a volatile and relentless metamorphosis in which her personal identity is the sole constancy.

169

These are but several indications of the variety of creative time-space relationships which can be accomplished by a meaningful manipulation of the sequence of film images. It is an order of creative action available only to the motion-picture medium because it is a photographic medium. The ideas of condensation and of extension, of separateness and of continuity, in which it deals, exploit to the fullest degree the various attributes of the photographic image: its fidelity (which establishes the identity of the person who serves as a transcendant unifying force between all separate times and places), its reality (the basis of the recognition which activates our knowledges and values and without which the geography of location and dislocation could not exist), and its authority which transcends the impersonality and intangibility of the image and endows it with independent and objective consequence).

The Twentieth-Century Art Form

I initiated this discussion by referring to the effort to determine what creative film form is not, as a means by which we can arrive eventually at a determination of what it is. I recommend this as the only valid point of departure for all custodians of classifications, to the keepers of catalogues, and in particular to the harassed librarians, who, in their effort to force film into one or another of the performing or the plastic arts, are engaged in an endless Procrustean operation.

A radio is not a louder voice, an airplane is not a faster car, and the motion picture (an invention of the same period of history) should not be thought of as a faster painting or a more real play.

All of these forms are qualitatively different from those which preceded them. They must not be understood as unrelated developments, bound merely by coincidence, but as diverse aspects of a new way of thought and a new way of life—one in which an appreciation of time, movement, energy, and dynamics is more immediately meaningful than the familiar concept of matter as a static solid anchored to a stable cosmos. It is a change reflected in every field of human endeavor, for example, architecture, in which the notion of mass-upon-mass structure has given way to the lean strength of steel and the dynamics of cantilever balances.

It is almost as if the new age, fearful that whatever was there already would not be adequate, had undertaken to arrive completely equipped, even to the motion-picture medium, which, structured expressly to deal in movement and time-space relationships, would be the most propitious and appropriate art form for expressing, in terms of its own paradoxically intangible reality, the moral and metaphysical concepts of the citizen of this new age.

This is not to say that cinema should or could replace the other art forms, any more than flight is a substitute for the pleasures of walking or for the leisurely panorama of landscapes seen from a car or train window. Only when new things serve the same purpose better do they replace old things. Art, however, deals in ideas; time does not deny them, but may merely make them irrelevant. The truths of the Egyptians are no less true for failing to answer questions which they never raised. Culture is cumulative, and to it each age should make its proper contribution.

How can we justify the fact that it is the art instrument, among all that fraternity of twentieth-century inventions, which is still the least explored and exploited; and that it is the artist —of whom, traditionally, the culture expects the most prophetic and visionary statements—who is the most laggard in recognizing that the formal and philosophical concepts of his age are implicit in the actual structure of his instrument and the techniques of his medium?

If cinema is to take its place beside the others as a full-fledged art form, it must cease merely to record realities that owe nothing of their actual existence to the film instrument. Instead, it must create a total experience so much out of the very nature of the instrument as to be inseparable from its means. It must relinquish the narrative disciplines it has borrowed from literature and its timid imitation of the causal logic of narrative plots, a form which flowered as a celebration of the earth-bound, step-by-step concept of time, space and relationship which was part of the primitive materialism of the nineteenth century. Instead, it must develop the vocabulary of filmic images and evolve the syntax of filmic techniques which relate those. It must determine the disciplines inherent in the medium, discover its own structural modes, explore the new realms and dimensions accessible to it and so enrich our culture artistically as science has done in its own province.

The New Landscape

Lichtenberg Figure,
Pattern of Electric Sparks.
Courtesy of A. R. von Hippel.

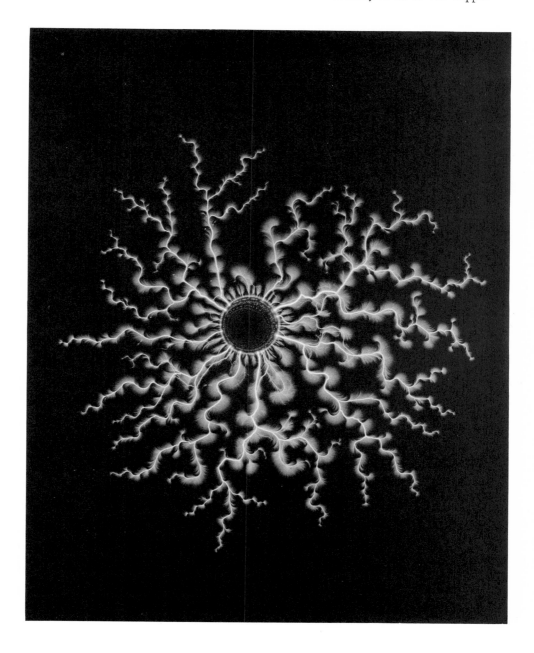

Growth Patterns of Crystals
of Silicon Carbide. The Role of
Crystal Defect Shown by
the Growth of Crystals
from a Saturated Solution.
Electron Micrograph.
Courtesy of the General Electric
Research Laboratory.

Cathode-Ray Oscilloscope Patterns.

Uranium Metal under Polarized Light.
Courtesy of H. P. Roth.

X-Ray Photograph.
Courtesy of the Eastman Kodak
Research Laboratory.

Copper and Calcium Carbonate.
Photomicrograph.
Courtesy of L. C. Massopust.

Aerial Photograph of Ocean Floors.
Courtesy of the
Aero Service Corporation.

On the next page:

Cleared Leaf.
Courtesy of I. W. Bailey.

PAUL WEISS

Organic Form: Scientific and Aesthetic Aspects

SCIENCE is usually understood to depict a universe of strict order and lawfulness, of rigorous economy—one whose currency is energy, convertible against a service charge into a growing common pool called entropy. Indeed, in its totality and in the long-range view, reality does ask a price for everything it offers. But on a smaller scale, in the short-range view, the outlook is less dismal and forbidding. Payment can be deferred, and notwithstanding the minus in the final balance sheet, there are in the account factors whose emphasis is on upsurge, growth, and gain, ignoring the downdrafts of drudgery, death, and decay. There is the lavish splendor of animate nature, proliferating luxuriantly at the expense of solar energy. And there is man, its highest creative product, exploiting and thriving bodily on those lower creatures. As his body extracts selectively from nutriment just those substances beneficial for its growth, so does man's spirit gain inspiration from the one-sided concentration on the constructive and uplifting phases of nature's course. In fact, man's spirit cunningly designs forever new devices to accentuate them.

Now if a scientist may be allowed for once, like people in other walks of life, to overstep his competence, then I dare submit that art is man's supreme device to serve this end: the tool of his creative spirit to break out from the strait jacket of a drab world of realities, in which he figures as but an item in nature's merciless accounting system, into an imaginary world of unbounded ideals and schemes, where nature's laws of cause and effect, of rise and fall, of gain and loss appear suspended. Art seems to be man's striving to temper and to come to terms with nature.

"Coming to terms" implies an adversary. Yet man, whatever else he be, is a part of nature. So his artistic world cannot be one of sharply demarcated opposition to his natural world, but rather must be viewed as a fluid and continuous extension of his domain as ordinary member of animate nature, subject to all the limitations of biological reality, into a realm of irreality of his own making, stripped of those limitations. And

181

since artistic endeavor is thus a direct organic outgrowth of nature, its elements are of necessity the same as those of primitive biological experience. The tonal elements of music are no different in kind from those of warning or mating cries; lines and colors of nonobjective paintings are borrowed from the lines and colors that in the context of biological reality delineate, mark, and identify an object as prey or mate or enemy; and gastronomic treats are but recombinations of elements of chemical perception built into our biological organization for the vital, if lowly, task of screening the useful from the harmful in food for nourishment. These are truisms, and I doubt whether anyone would question them. Nature is credited with the supply of elements, but then man's fantasy is purported to take over to recombine them freely in novel patterns of his own creation.

Here is that sharp schism that needs blurring—and blurring from both ends. On the one hand, nature provides much more for our aesthetic sense than elements; and on the other, the free inventive recombination of elements for the creation of emergent novelty is not a privilege of man, though he has carried it to culmination, but is ingrained deeply in all works of nature. Because the schism is due as much to a certain "elementarian" brand of scientific orthodoxy as to the pretentious tenets of "aestheticians," I feel impelled to try to rectify the lopsided perspective at least from nature's end in what a scientist—at least this scientist—would rate as a realistic view.

The argument will go about as follows: the universe is built and operates as a hierarchy of dynamic systems and subsystems, each with a defined degree of stability, individuality, autonomy, and durability on the level or in the order of magnitude in which it exists—from stellar bodies through populations, organisms, organs, cells, genes, molecules, atoms, down to subatomic particles. Those less conversant with the facts of science—and even some in science—have been deluded by a sort of shorthand atomistic vernacular, dating back to Democritus, into believing that nature in its scientific version is really nothing but a mechanical conglomeration of elementary colliding particles. As far as substance and energy are concerned, this formulation might be a passable one; yet it does no more than set the frame within which natural events must hold themselves—injunctions, in a sense, as to what must not happen. It can yield no specific information on just what will happen in given circumstances. The latter can be obtained only from observing and learning directly the behavior of the specific groupings in which the elements are combined into higher entities; the elements are no longer to be conceived as blind and independent agents, but recognized as forcibly restrained in

182

their potential randomness by the higher collectives to which they belong. And it is the orderliness of these restraints which imposes upon the group the over-all regularity of pattern which marks the system as more than a pile of items assembled at random.

This rule of order distinguishes organization from chaos. It must prevail wherever the activities and interactions of component parts are to be integrated and harmonized in the interest of serving the operation and preserving the integrity of the more complex unitary system. The nature, character, and state of the system as a whole remain conservatively stable beyond the flux and variations of its parts, which individually are unpredictable but whose constellation, though varying from moment to moment, is so regulated that the total pattern of activity remains essentially unaltered.

The living organism is such a system; so is each of its constituent cells. A cell remains basically the same despite the continuous reshuffling and exchange of its molecular populations; an organism remains essentially the same despite the incessant shifting, loss and renewal of its member cells—just as a community can retain its character and structure despite the turnover in population from birth, death, and migration. These being natural systems of supra-elemental order, the establishment of the various rules of order controlling elemental behavior in such systems is as imperative a scientific task as is the description of the elements themselves.

Thus scientific realism has come to correct its former faith in a naïvely mechanistic atomism by attesting the reality of regulated supra-elemental entities, which can be adequately known and treated only in their own right as integrated wholes. The existence of wholes, in which parts take appointed places in mutual harmony consonant with the total pattern and task, is an established fact of nature, not a privileged property and invention of the human mind.

This, then, concludes my argument. If nature were atomized and inherently chaotic, only creative mind could see and carve into it and from it those patterns of higher order to which we concede consistency and beauty. But nature is not atomized. Its patterning is inherent and primary, and the order underlying beauty is demonstrably there; what is more, human mind can perceive it only because it is itself part and parcel of that order.

But beauty to us connotes something more than sheer orderliness. It specifies a particular kind of orderliness. It postulates order compatible with uniqueness. This may sound like a paradox. The concept of order and regularity is something we can gain only through recurrences—the repetition of events in our

183

experience; yet uniqueness refers to the singular and nonrecurrent. The paradox resolves itself if one considers the true hierarchical structure of nature, as outlined in the foregoing; for this admits of a measure of invariability, stability, and durability in a higher-level system, notwithstanding the variability and changing constellation of its more elementary components. In short, in nature the same over-all effect can recur with lawful regularity, although the detailed events by which it is attained will vary from case to case in ever novel constellations—hence, be unique. All water runs downhill to the ocean, but the exact course of each rivulet and river is unique.

The lessons of a balanced view of nature can thus be summarized in a formula which bears a close resemblance to—and in my opinion is the root of—an aesthetic code: order in the gross, and freedom, diversity, and uniqueness in the small, are not only compatible but are conjugated. This principle is exemplified in all processes of nature whose products have aesthetic appeal. A few examples are presented haphazard in the following. They have been culled from a larger list illustrated in an earlier article.[1] The main points made there were the following.

(1) The pleasing aspects of organic forms stem from their high degree of general regularity combined with an infinite variety of detail. (2) The order expressed in the developed form, however, is but the result of the orderliness of the underlying formative processes which have led to the formed product and have left their imprint on it: what we read in the finished form is the historic record of its formation. (3) Even if two organic systems were to start out in absolute identity, the fact that in their subsequent developmental histories they would be faced with nonidentical incidents and environmental contingencies would necessarily make for divergence in the details of their final products. (4) Yet, since their over-all results still turn out to be reasonably similar, we realize that capricious and unpredictable deviations from the standard course must have been kept, if not strictly in line, certainly within a safe margin by the governing action of their respective systems, which resist disruption; a system owes its orderly self-realization and self-preservation to its very capacity to moderate or compensate the excesses of its members. (5) The over-all result thus gives us the satisfying impression of a collective task well accomplished by the harmonious cooperation under mutual control of members of a group which, but for these restraints, would yield blind chaos. (6) The viability of an organic form depends on the precarious balance between rigidity of over-all design on the one hand and flexibility of adjustment left to its execution on the other; too much aberrance one side or the other would

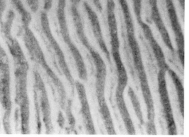

1

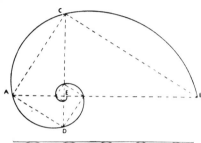

2

3

4

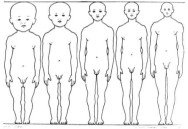

5

6

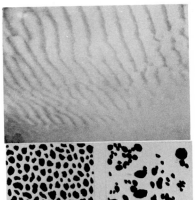

7

8

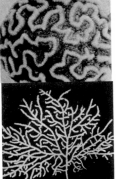

9

10

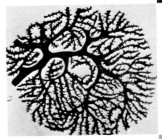

11

12

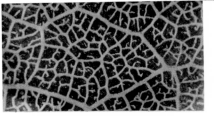

13

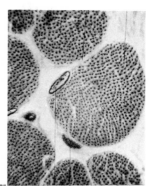

14

15

16

17

18

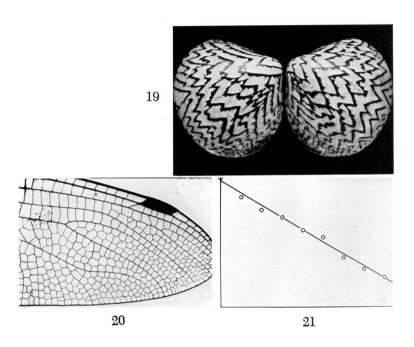

19

20

21

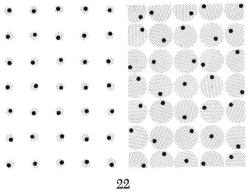

22

jeopardize survival. This is the biological foundation of what we call "sense of proportions."

Let us now turn to practical examples. They deal with forms of organisms and their parts—form in the sense of the orderly disposition of parts in space. A lengthwise section through a snail's shell (Fig. 1) shows a pattern of astounding regularity: the pattern and proportions of coiling remain the same from turn to turn, while the dimensions increase in a steady progression. The shell being the incrusted growth record of the animal, its beauty simply reflects the rule of order in the growth process. It is not surprising that for nearly 250 years, since the days of Réaumur, the subject of mollusk shells has attracted the joint attention of biologists, mathematicians, and students of design. In general, this growth pattern conforms to a curve known as a logarithmic or equiangular spiral. It has many remarkable properties, for instance the one shown in the diagram (Fig. 2), which illustrates that the ratio of any two successive segments meeting at identical angles (in this case 90°) is constant. As the curve lengthens or "grows," the geometric similitude of successive sectors is preserved. What this implies in actual fact is simply that the width of the turns increases at a fixed ratio to their length. (The actual value of the only ratio satisfying this condition is 1.618:1.)

The beauty of the shell, which lies in its law of growth, has thus been reduced to mathematical formulation. The value of 1.618 has been the subject of serious as well as playful speculation. It is related to what the Greeks termed the divine section, now better known as the golden mean. It gives the proportions of a rectangle in which the smaller side bears the same relationship to the larger one as the larger one bears to the sum of both. Art and architecture of the antique and Renaissance have made ample use of this highly satisfying proportion. But its biological sense lies in its intrinsic relationship to the logarithmic spiral.[2]

Growth that is steady and equal in all directions ("proportional"), as in this first example, leaves the impression of continuing evolution, which lets our fantasy, once it has grasped the law of growth, extrapolate the momentary product before us into imaginary forms of the same shape gigantically enlarged. Perhaps this "open-endedness" adds vividness to our impression. What we then see is no longer the static product, but the dynamic process that has produced it and carries on into a distant future—the specimen being but a sample stage from a time course of unending change, but change within a rather rigid law that stipulates proportionality.

In most forms of organisms the law of growth is much less simple. For instance, if one compares the proportions of the human body at various ages from birth to maturity in reference to the length of the trunk as unit (Fig. 3), one notes that the head grows relatively more slowly, while the extremities grow significantly faster. If carried further than it goes in man, this process of disproportionate growth may lead to rather grotesque forms, as for instance in the fiddler crab (Fig. 4), in which one claw tends to outgrow the rest of the body.

Steadiness of growth is likewise not the ordinary rule. Growth usually proceeds in spurts, with alternating phases of acceleration and retardation or even temporary arrest. If a stylus recording the ups and downs of temperature or barometric pressure writes on a moving tape, it leaves a tracing of the time course of fluctuations. Similarly the pattern of tree rings—the ornamental grain of wood—is a tracing of the seasonal variations in the growth history of the tree. And many patterns of rhythmic banding, striping, or segmentation in animals are likewise the residual traces of trains of pulsed production phases during development (Fig. 5). But in contrast to the tree-ring pattern, which is dictated by the outside climate, the latter patterns reside in an intrinsic periodicity as inherent in the law of growth itself as the beat is intrinsic to the heart. And just as the heart can function only if the actions of all its countless muscle elements are coordinated and synchronized so that by alternate contractions and relaxations they can jointly act as a pump, so the pleasing rhythms displayed in the designs of animals are evidence of the rule of order exercised by the system over its subordinate elements. A wave could not arise if each member of the group were to act on its own as independent agent. A wave front signifies that

... all points along the front are beating in unison and pass their rhythm on to the rest of the system. The system thus submits to coordination, in contrast to anarchic behavior, in which each element arbitrarily sets its own phase and its own pace of action unrelated to the others, the whole becoming a blur of randomness with no design whatever. On the other hand, we must not forget that even the regular wave, when viewed from close range, will at any one moment show capricious singularities that will never recur in quite the same form. In other words, order in the *gross* does not rule out uniqueness of *detail*, and vice versa.[3]

However, the mechanical wave produced by synchronous rhythmic excitation, as in the water wave or the acoustic sound, is not the only model of periodic pattern. At least two other types of different origin become conspicuous; in both the inducing agent itself is steady and continuous, but the excited system translates the steady action into a rhythmically discontinuous response, upgrading, as it were, the degree of order. For

190

brevity, we may refer to these two response mechanisms as "thresholds" and "nucleation."

The prototype of a threshold mechanism is the dripping faucet, where water feeds the drops continuously, but the drops break off only periodically as their weight overcomes cohesion. The same principle builds dunes in sand (Fig. 6): the steady wind piles sand as high as friction will hold it, which leaves a sheltered valley on the lee side, until at a certain distance past the shielded region the wind can become effective again, and so on down the plain. Mechanical determinacy is here replaced by the orderly result of probability, with evidently a wider latitude of expression—or, if one wishes to call it that, a higher content of uniqueness—but still not randomness.

Nucleation occurs whenever at a point in a material continuum there is initiated a change which spreads infectiously from point to point but which is of the kind that depletes the resources in its own neighborhood. An epidemic with immunity in its wake would be a fair analogy. The streaks of clouds on a mackerel sky (Fig. 7) are bands of condensed vapor which have starved the intervening clear zones of that commodity. As one will readily realize, this rhythm is the result of the competition of nucleated zones for limited supplies, the law of order being that no new center can survive too close to an existing one.

In the development of organisms we may expect such patterns to arise wherever local processes are in competition for something from their surroundings, so that another process of the same kind would have no chance to get started concurrently, except at a safe distance where it can assert its own competitive strength. As a result, there will remain blank no man's lands between the active centers, dividing the space continuum into harmonious patterns of rhythmically alternating properties.[4]

In Fig. 8 the types of ordered patterns resulting from such group dynamics are contrasted with those to be expected from sheer randomness. The lower quadrants show two patterns of continuous lines: the right one, of random dimensions and distribution; the left one, of more regular arrangement, the rule of order being that the line retains its average width and remains separated from a neighboring line by a standard margin. The top part of the diagram shows this same principle for discontinuous systems. The aesthetic superiority of the left over the right panels is immediately apparent. Although the lack of symmetry marks them as of a lower degree of order than that of our previous examples, they still contrast agreeably with the disordered randomness of their right-hand counterparts.

A few examples may illustrate how this principle of harmo-

191

nious space-filling has been implemented in organisms and their parts. A brain coral (Fig. 9) looks like a direct embodiment of the symbolic line pattern of the last diagram. Note how the sea-fan coral (Fig. 10) distributes its branches with the same average density throughout the structure, with no big holes nor overcrowding anywhere. The same pattern is found in the dendritic processes of a single nerve cell of the cerebellum (Fig. 11), or in the gastrovascular arborizations of the fluke (Fig. 12), or finally, perhaps the prettiest of them all, in the venation of a leaf (Fig. 13). All these are continuous line systems, branched with or without anastomoses, but always of regulated density.

Next is an example of harmonious but discontinuous filling of a given space. A cross section through a muscle (Fig. 14) shows the individual large muscle fibers set off in space, keeping their distance. If we single out one such fiber, we note that it is dotted with smaller discrete elements, the myofibrils appearing in cross section as black stippling. We may pick out one such black dot and magnify it enormously under the electron microscope (Fig. 15). A whole island here corresponds to one little dot of the preceding picture (the whole width of the illustration corresponds to approximately one micron). We observe now that each fibril is once more subdivided into a regular array of smaller units hexagonally packed and tentatively identified as the contractile protein chains of myosin and actin. Exemplified here is the identical principle of orderly packing repeated in three magnitudes, from the macroscopic down to the molecular.[5] If we view these same cylindrical units in profile instead of in cross section (Fig. 16), we note a regular lengthwise periodicity with bands and interbands, giving the muscle fiber in the aggregate its familiar cross-striated aspect. Now this rhythmic pattern owes its origin to yet another principle. It is produced by the stacking in tandem of molecular units of standard length, much like the coupling of coaches in making up a railroad train.

Such geometric stacking and spacing patterns along grids of varying degrees of regularity are the crux of organic form. Their elements may be molecules, as in Fig. 16, or single cells, as in the rows of scales covering the wings of butterflies (Fig. 17), or cell groups, as in the rasp on a snail's tongue (Fig. 18). But all of them are subject to a framework of supra-elemental order.

Thus the common element of appeal we have discovered in these manifold patterns is their nonrandomness—the presence of some rule of ordered distribution of units. It starts in the molecular realm and pervades the living structure all the way up to its harmonious total form. Yet, as I have tried to stress, the final harmony we visually admire is but the product of the rules of harmony that have governed its makings. In all these cases we have been dealing with the ordered reactions of orderly elements to an ordered set of conditions, and the result is order. It is this rule of order that we perceive as beauty.[6]

Yet, looking back over the whole series of our examples, we realize that this is order without minute precision, order within which there is scope. Therefore let us not confound rule with fixity, order with rigor, regularity with the concept of stereotypes. Each individual is a unique form of expression of general norms and laws. This uniqueness wants to be acknowledged and appreciated. It reveals the absolute stereotype as fiction, unnatural, unorganic, nonviable if it existed. Observation of nature thus justifies our instinctive rebellion against the stereotype, against a concept of order so mechanized and rigid as to make no allowance for some degree of latitude for the individual events within it. True organic order, as we know it, sets only the general frame and pattern, leaving the precise ways of execution adjustable and, to this extent, indeterminate. Aesthetically, the principle finds expression in the superiority of handicraft, with no two objects wholly congruous, over the monotony of serial machine production. Biologically, it manifests itself in the superiority of laws of development which prescribe only the mode of procedure but leave the actual execution free to adapt itself to the exigencies of a world whose details are themselves unpredictable.

If there is any lesson in the study of organic nature, it is that there is order in the gross with freedom of excursion in the small. Our sense of beauty only confirms it, for it combines pleasure in contemplating the gross, over-all order with appreciation of pleasing variations of detail. Let me show this once more in concrete form. Fig. 19 shows the two halves of the bivalve shell of a single animal. Our first impression is one of exquisite symmetry. Both patterns show, indeed, the very same character. Yet, if we try to compare the details, we promptly notice how greatly they diverge one from the other. Or take another case: the wing of the dragonfly (Fig. 20) shows meshes in its network which in their outlines and positions are individually as unique and arbitrary as the pattern of crackled enamel on a pot; only in general, one notes a gradient of density and numbers from the upper to the lower margin. I subdivided this wing into nine equal horizontal strips and counted the number of meshes within each. Plotted serially, these numbers closely fit a straight line (Fig. 21). This line then symbolizes the general law of distribution. But just as important as this standard course are the individual deviations of the actual values from the mean, which will be different in each individual case. It is these very differences that make for a diversity of individual

193

accomplishment within the rule; they make the individual organism unique, interesting, and, above all, viable.

There is a message, therefore, in the beauty of living things, a message I should like to summarize in a last diagram (Fig. 22). It represents two systems of order as two identical lattices of equidistant points defined by the centers of the stippled circles. The circles symbolize the range within which a black dot inside is free to roam—a range that is much wider in the right than in the left half. The black dots mark the station of individual items or events within the system—for instance, that of atoms in a crystal, cells in a tissue, or organisms in a group. I have let them assume random positions. Now note that in spite of this factor of uncertainty, or, if one wishes, of individual self-expression, the pattern as a whole is well preserved and stands out clearly in the left half; whereas in the right it is completely lost. Does not this spell out for us an organic design for living? Freedom within the law: responsible freedom to move within an orbit as wide as, but no wider than, what is compatible with the preservation of the over-all order that defines the harmony of relationships on which effective living and survival depend. To judge just what the right proportions are calls for a "sense of proportions," to borrow a term from aesthetics.[7]

In summary, this has been a very sketchy attempt to show that one can seek and find the roots of art and its philosophy in nature. Man with his powers of perception and aesthetic appreciation is one of nature's products, just as much as are the patterns of organic forms which he perceives in nature around him—the take-off points for his flights of artistic imagination; hence they are both of the same kind of origin and order. If in the limited space of a brief essay it has been impossible to present more than the seed of the idea, perhaps some future effort by one more competent to do so may bring it to germination.

REFERENCES

1 Paul Weiss, "Beauty and the Beast: Life and the Rule of Order," *Scientific Monthly*, 1955, *81*: 286-299.
2 *Loc. cit.*, pp. 288-289.
3 *Loc. cit.*, p. 293.
4 *Loc. cit.*, p. 294.
5 *Loc. cit.*, pp. 294-296.
6 *Loc. cit.*, pp. 296-297.
7 *Loc. cit.*, pp. 297-298.

ANDREAS SPEISER

Symmetry in Science and Art

Why Is Mathematics So Unpopular?

WHOEVER in his youth enjoyed musical instruction, as in playing the piano or the violin, will recall the course of such a lesson: it began with finger exercises, scales, and arpeggios, followed by an etude, then by a short composition, and at the end came the classical sonata. Thus each lesson became an adventure with an increasing content. The fact that the student was by no means capable of understanding the full import of the classical composition made no difference, and it became his permanent property, which he enjoyed again and again.

Instruction in mathematics, on the other hand, has for more than a century taken an entirely different course: often the student never passes beyond finger exercises and other boring, mindless gymnastics; while the same persons who enjoy card games, crossword puzzles, dancing, and drumming to the point of obsession regard mathematics merely as the very image of boredom. No subject of instruction in school is abused to such an extent as mathematics, and from this viewpoint it looks like a sterile desert.

It is quite understandable that no pleasure can ever be derived from this science when one is under such interminable torture. Its instruction is aimed entirely at practical applications—whereas the art is never mentioned. It cannot be denied, however, that most games enjoyed by human beings owe their laws, even their very existence, to mathematics, or that within man's soul there dwells a spiritual nature that derives enjoyment from these geometric and arithmetic structures themselves, quite apart from intellectuality. This teaching concerning the mathematical nature of our soul is very ancient: it was formulated by Kepler, who in turn took it over from Proclus.

How Symmetry Acts

Take a kaleidoscope, and put in it any arbitrary objects, such as several colored threads, several pieces of glass, or the like. Looking through the opening, one observes a beautiful structure, and new, charming figures constantly appear when the objects are displaced, to one's fascination. In this case it is clear that the effect is entirely created by the repetition of the object caused by reflection, in terms of a symmetry, without which there would be nothing interesting to see. Here we are dealing with a basic phenomenon of art. It is noteworthy that the intellect does not intervene, but that the effect arises directly. A fundamental law of our sensations is involved. There is no question of an explanation based on higher principles, since what we are dealing with is itself the highest within us.

Plato places at the head of science a structure with two identical sides, "The Existing Unity." Each of the two sides is again similar one to the other, and thus Plato obtained what nowadays is called a "structure," which extends to the infinite. Such superordinated and subordinated structures are encountered everywhere. Let us take, for example, the surface of the earth: It is divided into five continents, which in turn are divided into states, the states into communities, and so on. No matter how arbitrary these divisions are, they are nevertheless part of our thinking. Similarly, we have divided nature into genera and species; and no business enterprise exists that is not organized into such divisions and subdivisions. The same thing applies to art. For example, the outline of a Greek temple is repeated in its cornice and in smaller forms. It is from these similarities that the harmony of the building is derived. We encounter the same principle in music: the movement of a sonata presents a dominant form that is repeated on a smaller scale, and this small form is again divided into parts so that form is to be found in each measure. This structure can be demonstrated with surprising ease in every musical composition. We sense these symmetries directly, without exerting our intellect. A night club pianist, for example, can make such skillful use of them that we might think him to be constantly and creatively improvising.

Groups and the Visual Arts

Since antiquity, the basic forms of visual art have remained the same: rectangles, triangles, and regular hexagons. At the beginning of the Greek period, with the discovery of the Golden Section (*sectio aurea*), the regular pentagon was added. Mathematics was intimately connected with art, and served as a means of experiencing it. Thus the construction sheds when medieval domes were being built were simultaneously laboratories for research in geometry. We know that Brunelleschi revived the art of perspective, which had originated in antiquity, and that Piero della Francesca left a voluminous treatise on this science. The discoveries of Paolo Uccello are particularly notable: he used the antique perspective recently rediscovered by Alessandro Parronchi (see *Paragone*, Nos. 89 and 95, 1957), with which he has achieved surprising effects. Albrecht Dürer wrote three scientific works on geometry, on proportion, and the construction of fortifications. The art of the Renaissance and the Baroque periods as a whole was intimately associated with mathematics. Not until recent times has there appeared a theory that removes from the artist the need of using his intellect. The rising influence of historical thinking and of popular philosophy was responsible for the fact that mathematics fell into disuse, while terminologies previously reserved for the Deity came to be applied to the "divine" artist and his work—thus putting an end to discussion.

The artists themselves did not relish this, and many protested, well aware of how much intellectual exertion went into their acquiring knowledge and technique for the execution of a single work of art, nor did they ever appreciate the widespread notion that inspiration came to them in their sleep. In asserting that some work of art cannot be "calculated," one must certainly exclude music, since everything contributed by a composer is calculated: musical notation is a plane coordinate system in which a finite number of points has been entered, divided horizontally into measures, according to time, and fixed vertically, according to pitch. There can be no doubt as to the constructions of an artist being subject to law: his work is the most conscious in existence. If one asks a painter about a spot of color in his picture, one will be given a long explanation showing how profoundly the painting has been thought through. The very basis of art lies in its rationality. The irrational element is contributed by the spectator or the auditor, and is further compounded by the influence of mood, even of age. The German proverb, "There are as many interpretations as there are heads," certainly is borne out, but it is impossible to evaluate a work of art only on the basis of random and subjective impressions.

In the study of art the true task is to explore the spiritual world in which artists work. For this, a knowledge of mathematical thinking is indispensable, for the spiritual world is composed of the forces of mathematics. If art is approached from this viewpoint and with serious intent, the path is paved with gold: not only does the work of art now manifest itself, its secrets revealed, but it also becomes apparent how meticulously the artist works—how every tone, every spot of color is interrelated, even in the work of minor artists. Everything is symmetrical and proportionate, throughout. The work of art must "resolve," like a calculation. Only then does it deserve

197

the name of art. Certainly it is a miracle when this is achieved, as the laws of nature are miraculous. In both art and nature the miracle is a mathematical one—if the word be allowed its inclusive meaning. The spiritual world simply does not consist of fragments, it forms an entity, a whole structure, each part connected with every other. If we could reconstruct the image the artist himself has of his work, this would be immediately recognized. Unfortunately, however, we are still far from being able to do so.

New Proportions for Art

For some two hundred years, as we have suggested, the intimate relationship between art and active mathematics has been neglected. In this area artists have been limiting themselves to intuition, that is, to an unconscious imitation of time-honored proportions. It is just during these last two centuries that mathematics has made great discoveries. The beauty of these discoveries is apparent to every mathematician. It seems more than likely that these discoveries include structures that can be used in modern art.

The circular figures discovered about a century ago in function theory in connection with non-Euclidian geometry are of prime interest in this connection. These figures form the actual basis for the higher problems of the so-called automorphic functions, and they are associated with the names of the most eminent mathematicians of recent times: Hermann Amandus Schwarz, Felix Klein, Henri Poincaré. It may be appropriate to indicate the significance of these figures. The hyperbolic geometry worked out by Bolyai and Lobachevski simultaneously constructs an infinite plane that differs from the ordinary Euclidian plane, in that the sum of the angles of a triangle is smaller than two right angles. In its entirety this plane cannot be realized in our space, but it is possible to draw a map of it, one that fills the inside of a circle within the periphery exactly once. This map faithfully reproduces the angles, but the lengths are shortened; straight lines become circles perpendicular to the periphery; in the vicinity of the center, the distortion is small, but as soon as the edge is approached the images are progressively reduced in size.

Even our Euclidian geometry is best conceived by beginning with a square, then attaching a congruent square to each of the four sides, and continuing thus to infinity. Thus we can easily conceive of infinity, since each square in this figure is equally surrounded by all the others. In our new geometry there are no longer any rectangular squares, but there are squares with smaller angles. The same thing applies to the equilateral triangles: as soon as the angles at the corners become less than 60 degrees, such triangles exist.

Felix Klein discovered in this manner a circular figure that extends over the entire map with its repetitions, a figure in which seven triangles form a heptagon by whose aid the entire plane is paved. If this figure is systematically colored, a beautiful ornament results, one that represents the most symmetrical structure of this type discovered so far, and one that yields nothing to the exquisite structures in Oriental art. Nevertheless, in my opinion this figure is not yet suited to practical use because it is too complicated. There are simpler structures, however, that derive from modern mathematics and that could provide a new inspiration, particularly in architecture. The mathematical formula gives the artistic imagination the wings to take it to unknown lands and enable it to feel at home. Now, art cannot be pursued as a part-time occupation. Success comes only if one devotes his entire energy, his entire intellect. Therefore, the mathematician himself cannot produce the work of art, he can only draw the attention of the architects to his

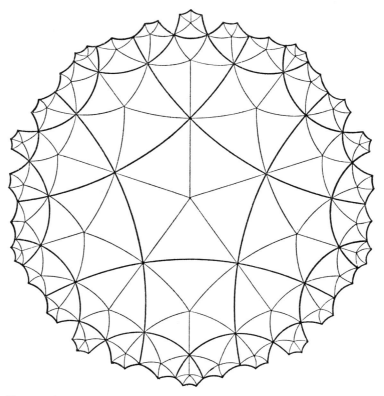

Figure 1.

world of thought. The architect himself must do the principal work. It is in precisely this sense that these remarks are written. While it is not for the mathematician to invade the realm of architecture, still the figure reproduced here may suggest something useful.

This figure (Fig. 1) shows a pentagon with right angles at its corners. At one corner four such pentagons abut; in the true plane they are all congruent; on our drawing they become progressively smaller toward the edge. Let us consider first the pentagon in the center: a new pentagon joins each of the five sides, and in our figure these pentagons are congruent. Between each two of the pentagons of the second kind we find another pentagon of the third kind, and so on. In view of the considerable reduction in size, the pentagons never pass beyond the periphery of the circle, but they do accumulate indefinitely within its neighborhood. In our figure the boundary circle has been omitted.

The Figure as a Plan for the Center of a City

Urban expansion today represents an important problem in architecture. Let our figure represent a new type of plan for a city. The central pentagon then represents the district at the center. The five circular arcs of its sides are the main boulevards leading from the center to the periphery. These are followed by five additional secondary sections, each of which is bounded by three main streets and two additional secondary streets. Within these secondary sections are located five additional tertiary sections, bounded by two main streets and three secondary streets. Up to this point the plan is effective, while the remaining smaller pentagons have no special interest.

I would suggest locating all the streets approximately ten feet lower, and using the sections only for pedestrians. Footbridges can lead over the streets and connect one section with another, as in Venice. The interior of the sections can be made accessible from the street by means of sunken paths, but in such a way that pedestrians and vehicles are separated. Since all the streets intersect at right angles, the traffic problem is easily solved. Architecturally, the plan has this advantage: there are no straight streets at all. Straight streets are known to be unattractive, and in all old cities—for example, Basel—the streets are slightly curved.

The Use of the Plan for a Church or a Secular Building

In the center of the first section an appreciable space must remain free so as to contain a principal building at its center. For this purpose, a single section of our plan can be used by taking only the central pentagon and the five adjacent ones. One enters at a corner and is immediately confronted by a symmetrical chamber. The five large circular arcs must be given a marked emphasis in height by balustrades, because they impart an impressive character. The total effect is in contrast to such interiors as those shaped like a Greek cross, for example, in which one never knows where to stand so as to gain a harmonious view of the whole (see Fig. 2).

Creative work by the architect is necessary for shaping the outer circumference. Probably the walls of the central chamber will have to protrude somewhat. The roof must have a shape concave to the outside, as with the Eiffel Tower, and must terminate at the top in a smaller pentagon. The five lateral transoms require ceilings of a new shape. Since one side is convex to the outside, while the four others are concave to the outside, one lateral surface must have a flat rising shape, while the four others at first fall off steeply, and then terminate in a gentler curve. The outline of the whole has a structure such as has never occurred in architecture before: it has the shape of a flower, perhaps a narcissus, with its five petals.

Although the general plan is now established, the develop-

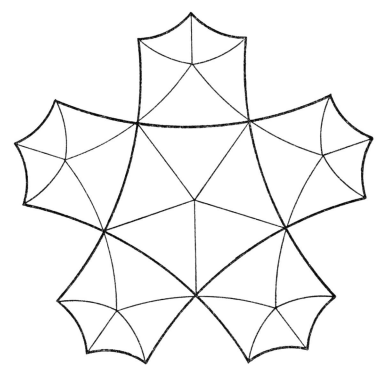

Figure 2.

ment of the elevation can be left to the imagination of the architect. Care must be taken only that unconscious work does not allow one of the old proportions—for example, the Golden Section *(sectio aurea)*—to creep into the shape of the building. It would be best to derive the proportions from the plan itself, since it contains new dimensional ratios never before used, and since it is desirable that the entire building have a unity of proportion so as to display its beauty properly.

This example shows how mathematics can stimulate artistic imagination. Here is a further illustration: the painter Braque once told me of having observed in his youth that pictures in perspective always draw attention to the background, away from the observer. He then had the idea of using perspective in the reverse direction, toward the observer. This effect can be seen in his pictures as early as 1905, and thus, through his collaboration with Picasso, arose the so-called Cubism, in which objects project out of the picture toward the foreground in planes. Now this is evidently a mathematical principle, and one that has proved extremely fruitful. It has been my aim in this discussion to call attention to precisely such relationships.

RUDOLF WITTKOWER

The Changing Concept of Proportion

PUBLICATIONS on proportion in the arts, searching, speculative, prophetic, assertive, and dogmatic, appear in a steady stream and in ever growing numbers.[1] Nobody today can claim to be fully informed about the subject, either on a world-wide scale or in all its ramifications. Nonetheless, I have accepted the invitation to take stock of the present position, for in spite of one's own shortcomings and unawareness of a good deal of the evidence, a general pattern seems perceptible in the more recent approaches to the concept of proportion in the arts.

1

To understand the problem of proportion in the visual arts today, we must hark back to the beginnings, at least in Europe.[2] It is one of the strangest chapters in the history of ideas that the real founder of theoretical geometry, Pythagoras, did not fight shy of applying his findings to non-mathematical phenomena. The extraordinary numerical relationships which he discovered led him to believe that the ultimate truth about the structure of the universe lay in certain ratios and proportions. He found that the musical consonances known to the Greeks could be produced by dividing a string of the lyre in the following invariably fixed ratios: 1:2 (octave); 2:3 (fifth); 3:4 (fourth); 1:4 (double octave). The discovery that the musical consonances were arithmetically expressible by the ratios of the first four integers (1:2:3:4), the discovery of the close interrelationship of sound, space (length of string), and numbers, must have left Pythagoras and his associates amazed and fascinated, for they seemed to hold the key to the unexplored regions of universal harmony.

By applying the Pythagorean theory of means to the ratios of the intervals of the Greek musical scale, the latter acquired a mathematical *raison d'être*. This statement calls for a brief explanation. The quantitative comparison of two magnitudes constitutes a ratio (e.g., 1:2), while a proportion is the equality of ratios between two pairs of quantities (e.g., 1:2=2:4). There must be at least three magnitudes in a true proportion —two extremes and a middle term, usually called the "mean." Now the three most important types of proportion, the properties of which were fully recognized by Pythagoras and his followers, determine the consonances of the Greek musical scale. A proportion is called "geometric" when the first term is to the second as the second is to the third (see the above example). Thus it is the geometric proportion that determines the octave and double octave. The second type of proportion is called "arithmetic." Here the second term exceeds the first by the same amount as the third term exceeds the second, as for instance in the proportion 2:3:4. In other words, the arithmetic proportion determines the division of the octave into fifth and fourth. The third type is called "harmonic proportion." Three terms are in harmonic proportion when the distance of the two extremes from the mean is the same fraction of their own quantity. Take 6:8:12: the mean 8 exceeds 6 by one-third of 6, and is exceeded by 12 by one-third of 12. This is an inversion of the previous case, for 6:8:12 divides the octave into fourth and fifth.

With Pythagoras and his school began the era of the mathematical approach to nature. Thus he opened the door to the specific Western view of the world. But such is the working of the human mind that, at the same time, two interpretative concepts of an entirely different character came into being, or rather acquired a new and long lease of life: number symbolism and number aesthetics. Number symbolism and number mysticism had seized a firm hold on people's minds long before the time of Pythagoras. It was the Pythagorean-Platonic number speculations, however, that figured strongly in the Western concept of macrocosm and microcosm, down to the eighteenth-century period of enlightenment. Moreover, the discovery of such relationships as those described above seemed convincing proof that certain ratios and proportions were intrinsically beautiful; it would appear to stand to reason that, if the invariable of all octaves is to be found in the ratio 1:2, it is this ratio that produces the musical consonances and is therefore beautiful. Once again, it was not until the eighteenth century that the logic of this reasoning was questioned.

In his *Timaeus* Plato employs two different kinds of Pythagorean mathematics. His explanation and division of the world-soul is based on the numerical ratios derived from the harmonic intervals of the Greek musical scale already discussed. When dealing with what might be called his atom theory (the ordering of Chaos), Plato reverts to the most perfect geometrical configurations—namely, tetrahedron, octahedron, cube, icosahedron, and dodecahedron, the only five solids that have equal sides, equal faces, and equal angles. Equilateral triangles are the basic element in the construction of tetrahedron, octahedron, and icosahedron. The square faces of the cube can also be broken down into triangles by the diagonal which divides each face into two right-angled isosceles triangles. Finally, a dodecahedron consists of twelve pentagons, and the pentagon is built up of isosceles triangles in which each of the angles at the base is double the vertical angle (72° and 36°). All these basic figures of plane geometry are charged by Plato with a deep significance. I think the emotional importance attached to them accounts for their extraordinary influence on European ideas of proportion.

The equilateral triangle, the right-angled isosceles triangle, the square, the pentagon, and derivative figures like the octagon and decagon formed the basis of medieval aesthetics. The evidence is overwhelming that many medieval churches were built *ad quadratum* or *ad triangulum*. Also, the doubling or halving of the area of a square which Plato explained in his *Meno* in order to exemplify the incommensurability of the sides of two such squares—a method discussed by Vitruvius in his ninth Book with reference to Plato—received a wide application during the Middle Ages, particularly in the construction of the tiers of Gothic spires.

On the other hand, numerical ratios were preferred to those derived from the Platonic bodies from the Renaissance onward. In the wake of the Platonic revival, interest now became focused on the theory of the means and the beauty of the "musical" proportions, which had never been entirely excluded from consideration. The *locus classicus* for this shift is Leon Battista Alberti's *Ten Books on Architecture* (c. 1450), in which he adduces Pythagoras' testimony for the statement that "the numbers by means of which the agreement of sounds affects our ears with delight, are the very same which please our eyes and our mind." And Alberti submits an arithmetical theory of proportion derived from the harmonic intervals of the Greek musical scale.

Thus two different classes of proportion, both derived from the Pythagorean-Platonic world of ideas, were used during the long history of European art: while the Middle Ages favored Pythagorean-Platonic geometry, the Renaissance and post-Renaissance periods preferred the arithmetical side of the same tradition. The reason for this can only be indicated here. Many of the geometrical proportions cannot be expressed by integral numbers or simple fractions, i.e., they are incommensurable or irrational. Thus the hypotenuse of the right-angled isosceles triangle is related to the shorter sides as $1 : \sqrt{2}$, and for the

205

construction of the pentagon lines must be "cut in extreme and mean ratio" (Euclid VI, 30), i.e., in the proportion of the Golden Section $\left(\frac{1+\sqrt{5}}{2}:1\right)$, which approximates 1.618:1. Irrational proportions would have presented a dilemma to Renaissance artists, for the Renaissance attitude to proportion was determined by a new organic approach to nature, which aimed at demonstrating that everything was related to everything by integral number. By contrast, the medieval quest for ultimate truth behind appearances was perfectly answered by geometrical configurations of a decisively fundamental nature. To put the problem differently: the medieval artist tends to impose a pre-established geometrical norm upon his imagery, while the Renaissance artist tends to extract a metrical norm from the natural phenomena that surround him (Fig. 1).

2

It was in the course of the eighteenth century that an attempt was made to separate mathematics from extra-scientific connotations. What mathematics gained as an abstract discipline from the seventeenth century on, it lost as a guiding principle in the field of aesthetics. When we turn the pages of Burke's *Enquiry into the Origin of our Ideas of the Sublime and the Beautiful* (first published in 1757), we find ourselves face to face with an emotional and subjective aesthetic theory. Burke categorically refutes the Pythagorean-Platonic notion, which the Renaissance had fully embraced, that beauty resides in certain fundamental and universally valid proportions—in other words, that mathematical ratios as such can be beautiful. He denies that beauty has "anything to do with calculation and geometry." Proportion, according to him, is only "the measure of relative quantity"—a matter solely of mathematical inquiry and "indifferent to the mind." Moreover, at the same historic moment aesthetics emerged as a separate field of study concerned with the problem of the autonomy of artistic creation. The reciprocal notions "proportion" and "beauty" were stripped of their metaphysical and universal character. They now appeared the result of an irrational creative urge; that is to say, they were turned from absolute truths into phenomena of subjective sensibility.

To accomplish the break of the arts away from mathematics, however, was no easy task. In actual fact, the "relapses" during the nineteenth century were countless. As a rule the artists, it is true, kept aloof. Romantic artists and their progeny clearly had no use for the shackles of intellectual number theories which would appear to endanger their hard-won freedom. And it may be said at once that we have not yet outlived the freedom for

Figure 1. Villard de Honnecourt: page from Notebook, *ca.* 1235.

which the eighteenth century prepared the way. The new
initiative came from scholars, historians, philosophers, and psychologists. These men approached the same problem from a
great variety of angles. Yet within the confusing mass of contradictory systems, one can discover definite trends that prepared
our present position.

To be sure, the most important single event was the sudden
prominence acquired by the Golden Section. Of course the
Golden Section had been known to the Greeks and to the
Egyptians before them.[3] Euclid had discussed it authoritatively
in Book VI of his *Elements* and elsewhere in the same work,
and the wonderful properties of this proportion were never forgotten. It is well to remember that, unlike any other true proportion, the Golden Section contains only two magnitudes and
that the two smaller members always equal the whole, thus:
$(a + b) : a = a : b$(i.e., 1.618:1 = 1:0.618). Mathematically
speaking, this is indeed a proportion of extraordinary beauty
and perfection. Leonardo da Pisa, called Fibonacci (1175-
1230), discovered that if a ladder of whole numbers is constructed as shown, so that each number on the right is the sum
of the pair on the preceding rung, the arithmetical ratio between
the two numbers on the same rung rapidly approaches the

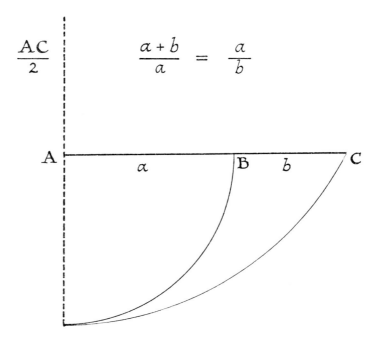

Figure 2. Construction of the Golden Section.

Golden Section. Thus for practical purposes the Golden Section, which can be constructed geometrically (Fig. 2), may be approximated by such arithmetical ratios as 5:8 or 13:21, etc.

1	1
1	2
2	3
3	5
5	8
8	13
13	21

Together with the Golden Section, the Fibonacci series became a treasured heirloom of Western mathematical thought. Renaissance artists were well aware of the exceptional properties of the Golden Section, and the mathematician Luca Pacioli in his famous treatise *De divina proportione* (1509), to which Leonardo himself contributed the designs of the five regular Platonic bodies, called it "divine." Nevertheless, as compared with the commensurable ratios of the small whole numbers, the incommensurable Golden Section played an insignificant part in Renaissance and post-Renaissance art, precisely because of its incommensurability.

It was Adolf Zeising who argued in a learned and persuasive treatise published in 1854[4] that the Golden Section was the central principle of proportion in macrocosm and microcosm. To him it was the perfect mean between absolute unity and absolute variety, between mere repetition and disorder. Zeising's fervent and mystic belief in the all-embracing property of the Golden Section was contagious, not only because of the learning and persuasiveness with which it was advocated, but also because the general trend was in the direction of an appreciation of irrational rather than rational proportions. And so a bridge can be constructed, leading from Zeising and his disciples to Hambidge's "dynamic symmetry" and on to Le Corbusier's "modulor."

Only recently M. Borissavliévitch[5] defined the beauty of the Golden Section:

It represents the balance between two unequal asymmetrical parts, which means that the dominant is neither too big nor too small, so that this ratio appears at once clear and of just measure. The perception of such a ratio is easy and rapid because of this clarity . . . and because it agrees with the hedonistic and aesthetic law, the law of least effort, hence the beauty of the Golden Section.

It will be noticed that the author bases his defense of the beauty of the Golden Section, not on grounds of mathematical perfection, but on those of a purported aesthetic law; as he further ex-

209

plains, it is our optico-physiological make-up that leads to the beatific sensory experience. Naturally, he gives high praise to Gustav Theodor Fechner's inductive aesthetic,[6] and he has full faith in the latter's experimental result, long since discredited, that "normal" people find the highest sensation of aesthetic delight in Golden-Section rectangles.

Hardly did Fechner's scientific method seem to have buttressed Zeising's findings than Theodor Lipps, the propagator of empathy, asserted that "it may now be looked upon as generally conceded that the ratio of the Golden Section, generally and in the case of the Golden Rectangle, is entirely without aesthetic significance in itself, and that the presence of this numerical ratio is nowhere the basis of any pleasant sensation."[7]

Yet before and after Lipps' assertion, the champions of the Golden Section encountered success after success. To name only a few, in Germany F. X. Pfeifer carried on Zeising's work (1885);[8] in France the Golden Section found advocates, from E. Henszlmann's *Théorie des proportions*[9] to Matila Ghyka's *Le Nombre d'or;*[10] while the pentagonal theory of F. M. Lund[11] no less than Ernst Moessel's "geometry of the circle"[12] are controlled by the Golden Section *Leitmotif.* The most enthusiastic partisan of the Golden Section, however, is Ch. Funck-Hellet, who since 1932 has published a steady stream of works expounding the mysterious qualities of an order which he summarized in the monumental sentence, *"Toute étude sur la proportion tourne autour du nombre d'or."*[13]

Funck-Hellet's investigations are too esoteric to be effective. It was Hambidge's suggestive "dynamic symmetry" that scored the greatest and most lasting success. Hambidge (1867-1924) read his first paper, entitled "Natural Basis of Form in Greek Art," in 1902, but his idea slowly developed in subsequent years. In 1916 he began to lecture on the subject, and from then on he had powerful patrons. In 1917 appeared his *Dynamic Symmetry,* which had the support of the influential Denman W. Ross at Harvard University. In 1919 he started the short-lived periodical *Diagonal,* financed by Yale University; 1920 saw the appearance of *Dynamic Symmetry: The Greek Vase,* again under the auspices of Yale University; in 1923 he published *Dynamic Symmetry as Used by Artists;* and in 1924, the year of his death, appeared his well-known work, *The Parthenon and Other Greek Temples.*

These titles reveal part of the secret of Hambidge's success: he bridged the gap between Greek art—still the ideal of the older generation of modern artists (Picasso, Le Corbusier)— and modern aspirations. Briefly, his theory was based on the following appealing assumption: what the logarithmic spiral means for the structural understanding of growth in botany, as in shell formations, etc., the incommensurable root rectangles (with their sides of $1 : \sqrt{2}$, $1 : \sqrt{3}$, $1 : \sqrt{5}$) mean for the structural understanding of Greek art and architecture.[14]

Although the interest of mathematicians in the logarithmic spiral dates back to the seventeenth century, it was only with T. A. Cook's *The Curves of Life* (New York, 1914) and D'Arcy W. Thompson's classic *Growth and Form* (Cambridge, 1917) that the importance of the logarithmic spiral for the morphology of natural phenomena was fully explored. What could be more appealing than the discovery that the Greeks had worked according to the law of dynamic growth found in nature? Moreover, Hambidge has the simple and strong diction of a man with deep convictions: he disarms even before a potential opponent collects his wits. "The Greek artist," he tells us, "was always virile in his creations, because he adopted nature's ideal" —namely, to base his work on root rectangles. And what modern artist, one is tempted to ask, can resist the challenge that the "realization of nature's ideal and understanding of the significance of structural form should enable him to anticipate nature, to attain the ideal toward which she is tending, but which she can never reach"?[15]

Some archeologists accepted Hambidge's theories with enthusiasm. L. D. Caskey of the Museum of Fine Arts in Boston followed him;[16] Gisela Richter, then the Curator of Greek and Roman Art at the Metropolitan Museum of Art, was in sympathy. Artists began to work in accordance with Hambidge's ideas. Architects like Walter Dorwin Teague[17] were fascinated. In fact, even *ante festum* Samuel Colman's *Nature's Harmonic Unity: A Treatise on Its Relation to Proportional Form*[18] professedly made use of Hambidge's theories.

After 1945 the circle of followers expanded. George Jouven, *Architecte en Chef des Monuments Historiques*, makes Hambidge's dynamic rectangles the core of his investigation of seventeenth- and eighteenth-century French architecture.[19] One can confidently maintain, however, that at this period architects worked almost without exception with a commensurable module system derived via the Italian Renaissance from Vitruvius. Hambidge had proved (in any case to the satisfaction of many) that the use of commensurable proportions leads to "static symmetry"; by contrast, the incommensurable ratios recommended by him lead to "dynamic symmetry" with its infinitely superior vitality and flexibility. According to him, few periods in history were aware of the secret of dynamic symmetry. By demonstrating that French architects of the Baroque were so initiated, Jouven implicitly pleaded the superior quality of their work.[20] In a much more rational book than Jouven's, the Italian architect, Cesare Bairati[21] made an equally unfortunate attempt to trace the use of root rectangles in the Italian architecture of the sixteenth and seventeenth centuries. Dynamic symmetry inspired others to new ventures. Irma A. Richter[22] modified Hambidge by replacing his root rectangles with concentric circles which had a Golden-Section relationship to one another. She claimed her method to have been the guiding principle in great works of art from Chartres to Piero della Francesca and from Raphael to Cézanne.

Hambidge seemed to carry everything before him. Had he really solved the problem of proportion for Greek art and shown the road to salvation for modern artists? He was biased—and in this lay his strength. Surely, by exalting dynamic symmetry at the expense of static symmetry, Hambidge was advocating his own creed and that of his time. While he developed his theory at Yale, we find some of the most advanced artists in Paris groping in the same direction. The year 1912 saw the first exhibition of the *Section d'Or* group, to which, among others, Léger, Gleizes, Delaunay, Metzinger, Marcel Duchamp, Duchamp-Villon, and Gris belonged. But in 1925 the activity of the group came to an end without a clear theoretical statement, apart from the suggestive name.

Not everything was sweet harmony, and not everyone was converted. Sober-minded archeologists like W. B. Dinsmoor[23] had nothing but derision for Hambidge's ideas. Others prepared for a counter-attack. It came with a vengeance as early as 1922 from the pen of Theodore A. Cook, whose work as a scientist paved the way for dynamic symmetry. In an article entitled "A New Disease in Architecture,"[24] he ridiculed interest in the Golden Section as a sudden and devastating malady that showed no sign of stopping. His attack was concentrated on the works by Lund and Colman and above all on Hambidge, who "has an especially virulent form of the disease." His main counter-argument was that "the excessively delicate phenomena of beauty can never be either defined or reproduced by such ancient and childlike simplicities as the Golden Measure, the Root-five Rectangle, or the Square." To him the beauty lay not in the "unabashed and platitudinous rectangles" but in the delicate divergencies, in the variations from dull exactitude. Cook must have written this under the influence of W. H. Goodyear's persuasive publications on "optical refinements" in classical and post-classical architecture. The terms of reference Cook used for his condemnation of Hambidge were therefore hardly less doubtful than was Hambidge's own theory.

In his important work *Aesthetic Measure* the mathematician George D. Birkhoff[25] discusses Hambidge in two sentences: "The theory of Hambidge concerns itself mainly with geometric ratios derived from irrational numbers. . . . Such ratios cannot be appreciated by the eye." Thus he dealt a blow at the very essence of dynamic symmetry. But can irrational ratios really not be appreciated? Fechner and Borissavliévitch gave positive answers from a psychological and physiological point of view. Or, perhaps, is the whole question of the visual appreciation of one type of proportion as against another basically wrong? I shall attempt an answer in the next section of this paper.

Hambidge's critics, of course, were also recruited from among freedom-loving artists and architects. For Percy E. Nobbs[26] Hambidge is simply one of the architectural astrologers "who have achieved fame through exploiting that mystic faith in perfect numbers which has impelled them—all for the supposed benefit of future designers—to spin webs of circles, diagonals, triangles, squares, and parallelograms over the elevations of ancient buildings." After the war Eliel Saarinen[27] asserted that dynamic symmetry was a diagrammatic method arbitrarily superimposed upon a piece of architecture.

It appears that in spite of the enthusiasm built up for the Golden Section and the allied root rectangles during the last hundred years, opinions regarding the use and usefulness, the efficacy, the perceptibility, and the beauty of these proportions differ widely, and more material to demonstrate this fact could easily be adduced.[28] Nor has dynamic symmetry helped to "explain" the miracle of the Greek achievement. If one takes the trouble to delve into some of the proportional analyses of the "poor old Parthenon" (to quote Theodore A. Cook) published from Penrose's days on (1851), it will be seen that almost anything under the sun can be proved: that the design was based on the Golden Section (Zeising, 1854), on commensurable ratios (Pennethorne, 1878), on triangulation (Dehio, 1895), on the ratios of small whole numbers (Raymond, 1899),[29] on root-five rectangles (Hambidge, 1924), on Greek modules (Moe, 1945),[30] and so forth.

Can one blame skeptics if they brush aside the whole quest for proportion as a silly pastime, unrecorded in J. Huizinga's *Homo Ludens?* On the other hand, the very fact that so many able and highly intelligent men of the past and present devoted and still devote years of their lives to the investigation of this problem should make us careful, and should lead us at least to concede that we are after all facing a serious concern of *Homo sapiens.*

3

Evidently, reflections of this kind led to the First International Congress on Proportion in the Arts, held in Milan, 27 to 29 September 1951.[31] The urge to discuss a problem keenly felt in the early post-war years brought together philosophers, painters, architects, musical historians, art historians, engineers, and critics from many countries. They had gathered because they agreed on the one point: that some kind of controlling or regulative system of proportion was desirable. But although the Milan Congress had repercussions down to Le Corbusier's *Modulor 2*, which appeared in English in 1958, it nevertheless fizzled out without making an appreciable impact on the younger generation.

The bankruptcy of the Milan meeting was publicly sealed at a historic meeting of the Royal Institute of British Architects in London on 18 June 1957, where a debate took place on the motion "that systems of proportion make good design easier and bad design more difficult"—a motion that was defeated with forty-eight voting for and sixty voting against.[32] One of the leading Italian architectural periodicals, *L'Architettura*, directed by the versatile Bruno Zevi, who had actively participated in the Milan Congress, acclaimed the wisdom and courage shown in refusing to support the motion and declared that "no one really believes any longer in the proportional system."[33]

This is very nearly a correct statement, for even many of the supporters of the motion had their reservations. Nor is it possible to prove that one system of proportion is better than another or that certain proportions are agreeable and others not. Such aspects appeared central when the problem lost its universality and shifted to the level of empiricism. In most periods of history artists were convinced that their specific system of proportion had universal validity. These systems derived their all-embracing character from thought processes rather than from sensations. It is now two hundred years since the belief in absolute values was shaken, perhaps for all time; it can surely not be won back by an act of majority decision. As long as a broad foundation for a resurrection of universal values is lacking, one cannot easily predict how the present dilemma can be resolved. The very formulation of the motion put before the R.I.B.A. meeting shows that we have left far behind the realm of the absolute, and are submitting to pragmatic and opportunistic motivations.

In attempting to pin-point the position of today, one has to admit that the majority decision at the R.I.B.A. reflects the current reaction of artists, architects, and critics, and that a definite shift of response to the problem of proportion had taken place between the Milan and London meetings. The reason seems obvious. We have all witnessed the quick rise and the easy victory of abstract expressionism, the almost general acceptance of an art based on the hardly controlled incident.[34] As far as painting is concerned, one may talk of the "splash-and-dribble

214

style." No wonder that the *objet trouvé* is adulated as a work of art, and the piece of driftwood is often preferred to manmade sculpture. At such a moment of absolute subjectivism any interest in systems of proportion would be out of order. And clearly, to a large sector of the most serious young artists, the word "proportion" is anathema.

Is this, then, the end of a process that began in the Romantic era? Will future generations of artists also regard systems of proportion as incompatible with creative processes? In a fascinating paper Sir John Summerson seems to argue[35] that, as far as architecture is concerned, the old systems of proportion that belonged to a formal order are indeed dead and buried at a time when "the source of unity in modern architecture is in the social sphere, in other words in the architect's programme." But is it not a fact that the architects of the past were faced with similar problems on a different level? The formal order was not a superimposed discipline, but an integral part of their planning. It seems to me that Summerson's *quid pro quo* implicitly affirms the subjective standpoint of architects and artists, which may be summarized in Eliel Saarinen's words, "To lean upon theoretical formulas . . . is a sign of weakness that produces weak art."[36]

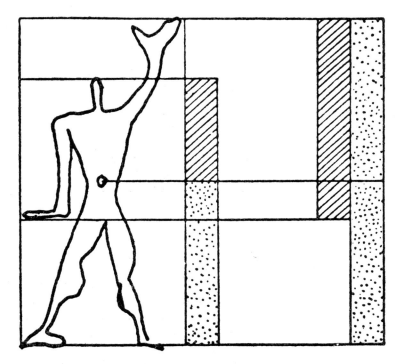

Figure 3. Le Corbusier's Modulor.

It is well known that Le Corbusier's answer is quite different. He distinctly believes in the older systems of proportion, newly dressed up by him and his team. The elements of his Modulor are traditional and extremely simple: square, double square, and divisions into extreme and mean ratios. These elements are blended into a system of geometrical and numerical ratios: the principle of symmetry is combined with two divergent series of irrational numbers derived from the Golden Section (Fig. 2). In contrast to the older "one-track" systems of proportion, Le Corbusier's is a composite system, and—in spite of its ultimate derivation from Pythagorean-Platonic thought—its vacillating quality seems to reflect the spirit of our non-Euclidian age. What is even more important, by taking man in his environment, instead of universals, as his starting point, Le Corbusier has accepted the shift from absolute to relative standards. His Modulor lacks the metaphysical connotations of the old systems. Today an attempt at reviving them would only smack of quackery.

The next step on the way adumbrated by Le Corbusier is to regard the whole question as one concerning technology. Modulor societies advocate issuing building components of a fixed size, and at this level the quest for proportion is sufficiently characterized by the phrase, "Standardization takes command." One of the best studies of this kind is by Ezra D. Ehrenkrantz,[37] whose ideas partly reflect the work on modular coordination undertaken by the Building Research Station at Watford, England. The author also surveys the many similar attempts launched on a national and international level during recent years.[38] So it would seem that practitioners are all agreed in giving systems of proportion a new lease of life, if such systems can increase the industrial potential, allow quicker and more economic construction, and thus help to raise the living standard of the masses. We may say, therefore—too pointedly perhaps—that the belief in systems of proportion in modern society is proportionate to the amount of industrial energy they generate.

4

I considered ending my paper at this point, but too many aspects of the problem of proportion would have remained unmentioned. The few scattered remarks that follow may perhaps help to show the question in broader perspective.

It is a fact of considerable interest that outside the realm of art scientists and philosophers keep alive the quest for the great order in macrocosm and microcosm. Whitehead's well-known Platonism may be recalled: "The Platonic doctrine of the interweaving of Harmony with mathematical relations has been triumphantly vindicated." Einstein's prophetic words that "human nature always has tried to form for itself a simple and synoptic image of the surrounding world" are fully supported by the whole history of human thought and endeavor. Such behavior may be biologically conditioned. As Lancelot Law Whyte has expressed it: "If biology comes to recognise that all organic processes are ordering processes, then thought itself may be understood as a special kind of ordering process."[39] Gestalt psychology bears out such hypotheses. It has been found that in animal as well as human behavior symmetrical and regular forms—forms, in other words, which can be expressed in terms of simple mathematical relations—are seized upon. The human brain is capable of ordering the most complex sensory stimuli and shows a clear preference for the perception of simple mathematical patterns.

In his Princeton lectures Hermann Weyl[40] discussed the many types of symmetry that prevail in crystals and in plant and animal life, and for which man has shown an unflagging enthusiasm in his artistic productions over thousands of years. Symmetry, as the balance of parts between themselves and the whole, is a primary aspect of proportion. Bilateral symmetry is only one of seventeen species of symmetry. It is the symmetry of the human body, and for that reason of towering importance to mankind. Again the concordance of the two halves of the body can be expressed in terms of ratios and proportions, and it is these in fact which we perceive without fail. Every disturbance of the balance of parts (e.g., a short leg, a crippled hand) evokes reactions such as pity, irritation, or repulsion.

When all is said and done, it must be agreed that the quest for symmetry, balance, and proportional relationships lies deep in human nature. It can confidently be predicted that today's "organic chaos" is a passing phase, and that the search for systems of proportion in the arts will continue as long as art remains an endeavor of man.

REFERENCES

1 Hermann Graf, *Bibliographie zum Problem der Proportionen* (Speyer, Landesbibliothek, 1958), contains nine hundred items but is far from complete.

2 The first part of the present essay relies to a large extent on my paper "Systems of Proportion" (*Architects' Year Book*, 1955, 5: 9-18), where a fuller statement of the problem in its historical aspect is to be found.

3 André Fournier des Corats, *La Proportion égyptienne et les rapports de divine harmonie*. Paris, Editions Véga, 1957.

4 Adolf Zeising, *Neue Lehre von den Proportionen des menschlichen Körpers*. Leipzig, R. Weigel, 1854.

5 Miloutine Borissavliévitch, *The Golden Number and the Scientific*

Aesthetics of Architecture (London, Tiranti, 1958; first French edn., Paris, Imprimerie des Orphelins, 1952), pp. 37 ff.

6 Gustav Theodor Fechner, *Vorschule der Aesthetik*. Leipzig, Breitkopf & Härtel, 1876.

7 Theodor Lipps, *Aesthetik, Psychologie des Schönen und der Kunst* (Hamburg and Leipzig, L. Voss, 1903), I, pp. 66 ff.

8 F. X. Pfeifer, *Der goldene Schnitt und dessen Erscheinungsformen in Mathematik, Natur und Kunst*. Augsburg, M. Huttler, 1885. For further material see R. C. Archibald, "Notes on the Logarithmic Spiral, Golden Section and the Fibonacci Series" in Jay Hambidge, *Dynamic Symmetry: The Greek Vase* (New Haven, Yale University Press, 1920), pp. 152 ff.

9 E. Henszlmann, *Théorie des proportions. . . .* Paris, A. Bertrand, 1860.

10 Matila Ghyka, *Le Nombre d'or*. Paris, Gallimard, 1931.

11 F. M. Lund, *Ad Quadratum*. London, B. T. Batsford, 1921.

12 Ernst Moessel, *Die Proportion in Antike und Mittelalter*. Munich, C. H. Beck, 1926.

13 Ch. Funck-Hellet, *De la proportion. L'équerre des maîtres d'oeuvre* (Paris, Vincent, Fréal, 1951), p. 13.

14 Hambidge demonstrates how the curve of the logarithmic spiral can be transformed into a right-angle spiral.

15 Jay Hambidge, *op. cit.* (note 8), p. 142.

16 L. D. Caskey, *The Geometry of Greek Vases*. Boston, The Museum of Fine Arts, 1922.

17 Walter Dorwin Teague, *Design This Day*. New York, Harcourt, Brace, 1940.

18 Samuel Colman, *Nature's Harmonic Unity: A Treatise on Its Relation to Proportional Form*, edited by C. A. Coan. New York and London, G. P. Putnam's Sons, 1912.

19 George Jouven, *Rythme et architecture: Les tracés harmoniques*. Paris, Vincent, Fréal, 1951.

20 How wayward the thinking of rational beings can become when they get involved in the mystique of proportion is shown by Jouven's belief that Dürer in his *Melancholia* engraving arranged that the sum of numbers of the magic square should be thirty-four, because this was *"l'âge où Dürer dut être initié à la Divine Proportion par Pacioli."*

21 Cesare Bairati, *La simmetria dinamica. Scienza ed arte nell'architettura classica*. Milan, Libreria Editrice Politecnica Tamburini, 1952.

22 Irma A. Richter, *Rhythmic Form in Art*. London, John Lane, 1932.

23 W. B. Dinsmoor, in a carefully argued review of Jean Bousquet's *Le Trésor de Cyrène* (*American Journal of Archaeology*, 1957; 61: 402-411) calls the author's method an offshoot of Hambidgian dynamic symmetry, and expresses the hope to have killed it "before it becomes an integral part of our archaeological vocabulary."

24 Theodore A. Cook, "A New Disease in Architecture," *The Nineteenth Century*, 1922, 91: 521 ff.

25 George D. Birkhoff, *Aesthetic Measure* (Cambridge, Harvard University Press, 1933), p. 72. For a criticism of Birkhoff's work, see H. J. Eysenck, *Sense and Nonsense in Psychology* (Harmondsworth, England, Penguin Books, 1957), pp. 326 ff.

26 Percy E. Nobbs, *Design: A Treatise on the Discovery of Form* (London, Oxford University Press, 1937), p. 123.

27 Eliel Saarinen, *Search for Form* (New York, Reinhold Publishing Company, 1948), p. 259.

28 See Katharine E. Gilbert and Helmut Kuhn, *A History of Aesthetics* (Bloomington, Indiana University Press, 1953), pp. 531 ff.

29 George Lansing Raymond, *Proportion and Harmony of Line and*

Color in Painting, Sculpture, and Architecture (New York and London, G. P. Putnam's Sons, 1899), pp. 201 and *passim*.

30 C. J. Moe, *Numeri di Vitruvio*. Milan, Edizioni del Milione, 1945.

31 The papers read at the Congress were unfortunately not published together. A good report appeared in the *Neue Züricher Zeitung*, 11 October 1951; for summaries of all the papers, see *Atti e Rassegna tecnica* (Società degli Ingegneri e degli Architetti in Torino), 1952, 6: 119-135.

32 The full report is in the *Journal of the Royal Institute of British Architects*, 1957, *64:* 456-463. The motion was introduced by Nikolaus Pevsner, while Maxwell Fry, Misha Black, W. E. Tatton Brown, Peter D. Smithson, Sir John Summerson, and others shared in the discussion.

33 *L'Architettura*, 1957, *3:* 508 f.

34 Years ago the Parisian Jean Fautrier coined the motto for the whole trend when he said that art is *"un moyen fou sans règles ni calculs."*

35 Sir John Summerson, "The Case for a Theory of Modern Architecture," *Journal R.I.B.A.*, 1957, *64:* 307-313.

36 Saarinen, *op. cit.*, p. 261.

37 Ezra D. Ehrenkrantz, *The Modular Number Pattern: Flexibility through Standardisation.* London, Tiranti, 1956.

38 Ehrenkrantz does not mention, however, *Modulor Coordination in Building. Project 174.* Paris, European Productivity Agency of the Organization for European Economic Cooperation, 1956.

39 Lancelot Law Whyte, "The Growth of Ideas," *Eranos Jahrbuch*, 1955, *23:* 367-388.

40 Hermann Weyl, *Symmetry*. Princeton, Princeton University Press, 1951.

JAMES J. GIBSON

Pictures, Perspective, and Perception

THE WRITER of this essay is an experimental psychologist with a long-standing interest in the problem of how we see. As concerns vision, a perceptual psychologist like myself stands somewhere between the physicists and the physiologists on the one hand, and the critics and philosophers on the other.

It seems to me that a great deal of the current discussion about pictorial communication and pictorial art is confused. We often use the same word for different things. One of the worst sources of misunderstanding is the nature of perspective representation. Another is the nature of the perceptual process itself. If we could agree on what the facts of perspective are for ordinary vision, we should be better able to discuss its validity for painting. And if we could get rid of certain historical prejudices about the act of perception in everyday life, we could consider more clearly the special kind of perception aroused by a picture.

Perspective

The fundamental problems in pictorial communication, as I understand it, are first, the relation of the picture to the world, and second, the effect it will have on the perceiver.

The term "perspective" has several different meanings. It can refer to the various techniques of painting or drawing which give the illusion of a scene in depth. This is what it usually means to artists and architects. It can refer to the geometrical projection of a form on one plane to a form on another plane by a bundle of lines intersecting at one point. This is what it means to a mathematician. Or it can refer to a certain way of seeing a natural scene as a patchwork of colors; that is, to "seeing in perspective." This is what it has meant to philosophers and psychologists who believed it important to analyze visual sensations. These various meanings often get mixed up in discussions of perspective.

There is, however, a single fact which underlies them all and makes them intelligible—the fact of the behavior of light in the world of animals and men.

The Fact of Ambient Light. If we forget about abstract empty space and consider the concrete world, the important thing about light is that it fills the air and surrounds the individual on all sides. Light that has been reflected and scattered by surfaces is the light by which things are seen. Ambient light carries information, which can be observed simply by looking around. Illumination consists of a reverberating flux, echoing in straight lines throughout the open spaces of a terrestrial environment. During the day it is as much a part of the environment as are the reflecting surfaces themselves. It can be registered anywhere the individual may go. In fact the changes of light from moment to moment are the principal controls that govern his locomotion.

The Optic Array at a Station Point. The rectilinear propagation of light means this: that the echoing light flux consists of interlocking bundles of rays. Each bundle consists of rays intersecting at a common point, and there is one such bundle for every point in the open air. Every such point is a potential station point for an eye—a place where an eye might be stationed. Rays are not only projected from a source; they are also introjected, as it were, to a point. We are concerned only with the converging bundles of rays. Each of these may be termed an optic array.

We need not think of an optic array as composed of lines, however. At the station point, it consists of differences in the intensity and frequency of light in different directions. The reason for this is that light is altered in energy and wave-length composition when it is reflected; and different surfaces, or parts of a surface, alter it in different amounts. A given pencil of light in an optic array will have imposed on it a certain relative intensity and a certain relative "color" with respect to other pencils of the array. An optic array, therefore, is a matter of transitions from one adjacent pencil to another—not of rays. The rays are useful fictions. The absolute intensity and the absolute color of a pencil do not matter to the eye; what matters is the structure and the relative composition of an optic array. These relational properties are constant under all conditions of illumination. In short, the mathematical structure of an optic array corresponds to the light-reflecting capacities of the surfaces surrounding the station point. It carries information about the world. For example, wherever the array is textured, there are surfaces in the world; wherever the array is homogeneous or untextured, there is only sky.

The structure of an optic array can be analyzed, for example, by angular coordinates. Or it can be treated topologically in terms of the contours between regions of different intensity. A complete optic array can be projected only on a sphere. A

221

part of an optic array—one sector of the total pie, as it were—can be projected on a plane. At best, this can represent less than half the array. If the plane is small, with rectangular edges, the projection begins to resemble that of a window or an ordinary picture. The familiar meanings of the term "perspective" begin to apply. But note that the principles which underlie all varieties of perspective, which make them intelligible and can reconcile the riddles they pose, are the fact of the optic array itself, and the further fact of different optic arrays at different station points.

An optic array is something external to and independent of an eye. It is quite different from a retinal image. The latter will be considered separately.

A Generalized Geometry of Perspective. It is possible, therefore, to think of perspective as a more general science than the rules of representative drawing, or the description of visual sensations, or even the transformations of forms on one abstract plane to forms on another plane. It would be the geometry of the ways in which light specifies the world of surfaces from which the light is reflected. Linear perspective of the classical sort would only be a small part of it, for that is merely the perspective of the edges of rectangular objects. There is also the perspective of the textures of inclined surfaces, the gradients of texture-density, the steps of density at the edges of objects, the ratios of densities in different directions, and still other variables of higher order.

Above all, there is the perspective of change of position, as distinguished from the perspective of position. When the station point moves, the whole structure of the optic array undergoes transformation. A new set of variables arises to confirm the information in static perspective. The parameters of transformation are specific to the motion of the station point; the invariants under transformation are specific to the permanent properties of the environment. The optic array has a unique structure for every station point in the world. And the change in structure of the array is unique for every change of station point in the world. This is essentially what is meant by saying that ambient light carries information about the world.

Images. It will have been noted that nothing whatever, so far, has been said about images, retinal, photographic, or other. Environmental optics, unlike physical or physiological optics, is not concerned with images but with the fundamental conditions which make images possible. A differentiated optic array depends on two things: a source of light to illuminate the surfaces, and a medium free of dust or fog which would veil the contours; but it does not depend on the formation of an image. The structure of an optic array may or may not be

222

registered by an animal with eyes; it exists, whether or not an animal occupies the station point.

The common belief that vision necessarily depends on a retinal image is incorrect, since the eye of a bee, for example, does not have a retinal image. What eyes do is to pick up all the useful information in light of which they are capable; retinal images are merely incidental in the process. The human eye explores an optic array by taking in cones of the array in succession. The process could be compared to the way a searchlight beam is moved around a dark environment, with the difference that the light is being absorbed instead of being emitted.

The Fallacy of Comparing a Retinal Image to a Picture. We can now clear up a misunderstanding which has persisted for centuries: the notion that a retinal image is like a picture. However a picture may be defined, everyone would agree that it is something to be looked at by an observer. A retinal image is not something to be looked at by an observer. It is therefore profoundly unlike a picture. There is a distribution of energy on a sensory mosaic, but it is not a replica, or a copy, or a model, or a record. It is a continuous "input," as computer theorists say. It starts impulses in the optic nerve. The retinal image is easily visualized, but one should do so only at one's peril, for it encourages the fallacy of assuming a little man in the brain who looks at the retinal image. Whenever one is tempted to think in this way, one should remember the eye of the bee. A retinal image is no more like a picture in the eye than an auditory stimulus is like a phonograph record in the ear.

The designers of lenses and optical instruments are as badly mixed up about their so-called images as anyone else. What they do is to manipulate light in ways which enable us to get more information out of it than we ordinarily would. To magnify a cone of an optic array, as by a telescope or a microscope, is to alter the light entering an eye so that its fine structure becomes big and bright enough for the eye to pick up. Magnification can be accomplished either by producing a large picture on a screen to be looked at, or by applying an instrument directly to an eye and pointing it at the light coming from the real thing. In either case, it is the light to the eye that counts.

The human retinal image is only one stage in the human process of seeing. What the instrument makers, the photographers, the visual educators, and the artists in their own way are trying to do is to aid or enhance the process of seeing. By "seeing" I mean understanding, not the special process of considering one's sensations or the special act of seeing in perspective.

223

Perception

Perception is the having and achieving of knowledge about the world, and visual perception is the most exact kind of perception. The process depends on the stimulating of receptors, but receptors are combined into whole input systems with harmonious functions. The ocular system of man is the most elaborate input system of all. It responds to the optic array of the moment and to the changes of the array over time. Such is its stimulus—or, more correctly, such is the flowing array of potential stimulation to which it responds. The eyes react by exploring the array, fixing and converging on certain details, sharpening the contours by focusing the lens, and pursuing a moving bit of detail. The sequence of fleeting retinal images is scarcely detectible in perception; what emerges is a phenomenal scene together with its interesting features.

The essence of perception is selective attention to something important. The receptive system "tunes itself" by adjusting the apparatus for clear reception. The lens-retina-nerve-muscle system is not passive but active. It continually creates new stimuli for itself, searching out in an optic array the relations, ratios, grades, and invariants of pattern which specify facts of the world. The amount of potential information in the light reaching the eyes is unlimited.

As a consequence of the unlimited possibilities for informative stimulation, and of the exploring and selecting activity, two conclusions follow with regard to perception: first, it depends on stimulation; and second, it depends on the interests of the individual observer. These conclusions have appeared contradictory in the past, and the horns of a dilemma seemed inescapable: the perceiver can only mirror the world, or else he creates the world for himself. But this is a false issue.

The perceiver who has observed the world from many points of view, as we say, is literally one who has traveled about and used his eyes. That is, he has looked at the furniture of the earth from many station points. The more he has done so, the more likely it is that he has isolated the invariant properties of things—the permanent residue of the changing perspectives. Only because of the perspective transformations do the permanent properties emerge in perception. And only thus can he see the world as a whole, with every part connected to every other. The artist is a perceiver who pays special attention to the points of view from which the world can be seen, and one who catches and records for the rest of us the most revealing perspectives on things.

Perceiving, I have suggested, is the having or achieving of knowledge about the world. But visual perceiving often enough does not feel like knowing; instead, it feels like an immediate acquaintance or a direct contact. To see a thing, a place, an event, an animal, or a person means to be in touch with it. What is to be said about this difference between immediate and mediated perception?

There are different degrees of mediation for different kinds of perception, all the way from the direct impression to the roundabout inference. One dimension varies between certainty and uncertainty; this depends, for example, on good illumination or poor illumination—that is, on the amount of potential information in the existing conditions of stimulus. Another dimension is between first-hand acquaintance at one extreme and hearsay at the other. This is a kind of mediation we should now consider—perception at second hand—that is, perception through the eyes of another person.

The Nature of Pictures

The above discussion of perspective and the further discussion of the perceptual process are intended to make possible an explicit statement of what a picture is and what it does. Whether or not the formula I suggest is acceptable, it will have at least the virtue of being clear: in general, a picture is a human artifact which enables another person to perceive some aspect of the visible world in the same way that the artist, the maker of the artifact, has perceived it. This definition is intended to apply to any picture—any drawing, painting, photograph, motion picture, or television image, whether representational or not—so long as it is intended to be looked at.

Concretely, a picture is always a physical surface, whether of canvas, paper, glass, or some other substance, which either reflects light or transmits it. It is an object, in short, commonly a flat rectangular one, but what is unique about it is the light coming from it. The surface has been treated or processed or acted upon in such a way that the light causes a perception of something other than the surface itself. It delivers a sheaf of light rays to a station point in front of the surface, rays that contain information about quite another part of the world, perhaps a distant world, a past world, a future world, or a wished-for world; a delicious world or a horrifying world; but at any rate some part or aspect of a world which is not literally present at the station point. If an eye is actually stationed in front of the picture, and if its possessor can register the information contained in the sheaf of rays, then the picture has served its fundamental purpose. There has occurred a perception at second hand—a vicarious acquaintance with an absent scene.

The Ways of Making Pictures. A picture is not only a surface

225

but also, and more truly, an artificial optic array. The surface must have been treated or processed or acted upon in such a way as to determine the texture and structure and wave-length composition of the light to the station point. Many ways of doing this have been invented over the thousands of years of human history. But fundamentally they are of two types: a picture can be made by hand and eye, or it can be made by some adaptation of the photographic camera. The virtues of each method need to be considered objectively.

The Fidelity of a Picture. It is theoretically possible to construct a dense sheaf of light rays to a certain point in a gallery or a laboratory, one identical in all respects to another dense sheaf of light rays to a unique station point thousands of miles away on the surface of the earth. If each of the two pyramids of light were isolated from the surrounding optic array by an aperture or peephole, an eye could not detect any difference between them: the perceiver would be unable to say which was the artificial and which the natural scene. This follows from an elementary principle of psychology which says that, other things being equal, two identical instances of stimulation must arouse the same percept. Vision depends on the structure of the optic array, however this may have been caused.

The complete identity of two ray sheaves, point for point, with respect to intensity and wave-length composition, is in practice impossible. For one thing, the density of rays in a natural array is infinite; the texture of ordinary light is informative, no matter how finely it is analyzed microscopically, whereas the texture of an artificial array begins to show only the grain of the photograph or the pigment when it is analyzed. For another thing, the range of intensities in a natural array with good illumination exceeds the range of intensities coming from the best photographic transparency, and far exceeds that from the most meticulous painting. Still further, the wave-length composition of artificial dyes or pigments on a film or a canvas cannot be made to match exactly the spectral composition of the light from natural surfaces.

But this simple physical identity of the ray sheaves is not necessary for the success of the experiment described above. An eye responds primarily to the transitions and relations of an array—the relative variables instead of the absolute magnitudes of physical radiation. The texture of a pictorial array at a station point need be no finer than the acuity of the eye; the intensities are unimportant compared to the contours and gradients of intensity; and the "colors" of a pictorial array need be preserved only in relation to one another and to the prevailing illumination in order to specify quite well the main classes of surface pigmentation. Consequently, two pyramids of light to a station point may be functionally identical as stimuli without being physically identical as energy inputs.

The experiment of constructing a picture indistinguishable from the original scene has been carried out, although it is not fashionable nowadays. In the centuries prior to photography, painters were often fascinated with the type of picture called "trompe l'oeil"—that is, a painting which could be illuminated and arranged so as to deceive the eye with a perception of a room, a relief, a doorway, or a still life in full three-dimensional reality. The experiment can be done within certain limits with a photographic transparency or a photomural, and it is successful even when the pictorial scene is arranged side by side with the original scene pictured.

The fidelity of a picture can be defined as the degree to which its surface sends the same sheaf of rays to its station point that is sent to a certain fixed station point at the scene represented. But a picture's *functional* fidelity to the scene represented is simply the degree to which the variables to which the eye is sensitive are the same in one array as the other. Complete fidelity of the latter sort is achievable.

An eye is particularly sensitive to contours—that is, to abrupt transitions of intensity in light. A line specifies a contour to an eye without replicating the different brightness on either side of the contour. This is why a line drawing can have a considerable fidelity to an original scene without any matching of brightness or color. An eye is also particularly sensitive to the straightness of contours and the alignment of details in light. Straight contours in a projection mean straight edges in the world. Hence it is, probably, that linear perspective in a picture is so compelling for most people. It is only one feature of the general geometry of perspective, as I argued above, but it is one to which the human eye is particularly sensitive. Man lives in an environment of buildings and pavements whose edges he has generally made rectilinear.

Fidelity of form and proportion in a static picture entails that the perspective be "correct." It is automatically so in a photograph taken with a camera having a well-designed lens system, where the print is viewed with a single eye at a perpendicular distance equal to the focal length of the lens. It is also correct for a representative painting made in accordance with the techniques discovered by the Renaissance painters when viewed from the station point. They come to the same thing, since both derive from the theory of rays intersecting a picture plane and from the fundamental experiment of the pinhole camera.

The faithful representing of solid objects with respect to form and proportion is not to be scorned, although it may be

227

pedestrian work for an artist. It permits the vicarious experiencing of an absent thing or the mediated perception of a distant place. It is perception at second hand, to be sure, but the greater the fidelity of the picture, the more it resembles perception at first hand. It may be only a fixed window on the part of the world in question, a mere peephole on reality, but with all its limitations it is a kind of visual education. Anatomical drawings, scientific records, documentary pictures, and even travel snapshots of distant places are all ways of getting knowledge about the shapes of things, and this is important knowledge.

The Illusion of Reality from Pictures. The optic stimulus provided by an ordinary picture may be indistinguishable from that provided by the scene represented, when the latter is viewed with one eye through a window. The viewer is transported to the scene in question. But at best the perception aroused fails in three respects to be lifelike. First, the viewer cannot look around the scene. Second, he cannot move around in the scene nor can he observe anything moving in it. Third, he cannot obtain the binocular parallax resulting from the use of both eyes. The illusion of reality is incomplete, and no observer of an ordinary picture would ever suppose that he had literally been transported to the scene.

The makers of pictures, at least those with commercial ambitions, have generally wanted to remedy these defects in the lifelike quality of pictorial perception. They would like, if possible, to create a complete illusion of reality. In the effort to do so, they have tried to extend the scope of a pictorial array, to give it progression in time, and to make different arrays to each eye.

1. *The Scope of a Pictorial Array.* The scope of a picture may be defined as the angular size of its sheaf of rays at the proper station point. The field of view embraced by a picture determines to a considerable extent the illusion of being at the scene pictured. The easel painter and the photographer are limited in the size of the field they can represent. The flat canvas and the photographic print are of fixed dimensions, and the taking in of any larger field than about 45 degrees each way is extremely difficult.

The ordinary picture is a selection from the total scene—a choice of a certain angular sector which the viewer is permitted to observe. The situation is not like "life," in which every viewer can choose for himself what to observe. The alternative to an ordinary picture is a panoramic picture—that is, an array of increased scope.

Panoramas of battle scenes or historic events used to be very popular. Such a picture must be painted on a curved surface, cylindrical or spherical. It can be designed to fill the field of view of an observer who does not move his head, a hemispherical array—or it can be designed to fill the whole environment of an observer who turns around, a roughly spherical array. There are still a few circular buildings in various countries which house complete panoramas. The constructing of panoramic arrays by photographic projection methods is difficult. The semipanoramic motion picture, in the form of "Cinerama," is full of optical compromises, but most movie-goers agree that it nevertheless yields a strong illusion of reality. It is being employed, apparently, to satisfy the urge of people to see the world—that is, to witness strange events and popular spectacles.

2. *Progression in Time.* The greatest achievement in the pursuit of the illusion of reality was the invention of the motion picture. It is poorly named, for the picture does more than represent motion or physical movement; it imitates time. The light surrounding a living person is a continuous flow of transformations and changes which specify the sequence of events in the neighborhood. This is what cinematography succeeds to some extent in representing.

The static picture can represent, it is true, a critical moment in time. The artist can choose the significant cross section in a continuous process or the high point of an event. But the pictorial array is itself unchanging, and the picture inevitably gives some suggestion of a dead and frozen world.

A camera which records a pictorial array over time, a cinematic or kinescopic camera, can "pan," or "dolly," or "cut," or "fade." This is to say, in effect, that it can look around after a fashion, can perform locomotion, can shift attention from one place to another, and can indicate the passage of time. It does all this in addition to recording simple motions. These are some of the perceptual capacities of the living observer, and hence the cinematic screen picture can imitate natural perception.

3. *Different Arrays to Each Eye.* More than one hundred years ago it was proved by Wheatstone that the slight discrepancy between the inputs to the right and left eyes explains in part how we see the depth of a scene. This disparity of pattern, when artificially produced by a device called the stereoscope, yielded an illusion of depth.

With any such device, each eye must be located close to the proper station point of its corresponding picture. A stereoscopic panorama, therefore, is almost inconceivable. For the same reason, stereoscopic motion pictures are unsatisfactory to those viewers in a large group whose position relative to the screen is not optimal. The idea of combining all the inventions for improving the realism of a picture into one grand display—

the panoramic, stereoscopic, colored motion picture—is probably impractical.

What can be said about these technical achievements as to the fidelity of pictorial representation and the lifelike quality of pictorial presentation? They help to satisfy men's curiosity about the world. They convey knowledge of a sort. They make perception effortless by approximating the natural kind of perception. They permit an almost direct acquaintance with things, events, places, and people. But they leave nothing to the imagination; perhaps they stultify it. They might be said to encourage in the observer passivity rather than activity. They do not impose the emphasis of the artist on the perception of the viewer.

The Education of Attention

A picture, I have suggested, conveys an aspect of the world as the maker of the picture has seen it. The "world" should be in some sense real, but it is not necessarily the literal existing world, and the "aspect" need not be a literal perspective from an existing station point.

If there is actually information in light, and if it is unlimited in amount, then each perceiver must select that part of the potential information he needs. When perceiving is mediated by a picture, some part of the selecting has already been done. Even a photograph is selective in its own way; but a painting is more selective, and in a different way. Each painter has his own habits and skills of selecting information from light. Each age of painting and each culture has its way of selecting what is important to see. If the artist emphasizes the information about the world that people need, he has done them a service. If they can register such information, he has made their vision more acute. Their eyes will become more sensitive, not at the level of anatomy or physiology, to be sure, but at the level of psychology. At this level, the subtleties and complexities of light are enormous. And hence the different ways of seeing the world are equally variable, though all may be valid.

Under this theory, selection and abstraction in painting are understandable. But what about "distortion" in nonrepresentative painting as the ordinary person thinks of it—that is, departures from fidelity to form and proportion? Why are people and places so often represented by modern painters as literally deformed, in the geometrical sense of the term? The answer, perhaps, is that only certain departures from literal representation are genuinely informative. Consider the representation of a human face. The caricaturist who has real insight into personality departs from an exact portrait in a single direction. The deformation is just that which shows the differences between this individual and all other individuals—the real differences, the traits of the person. In this case the deformation is not false but, in a paradoxical sense, true.

From what I know of the perceptual process, it does not seem reasonable to assert that the use of perspective in paintings is merely a convention, to be used or discarded by the painter as he chooses. Nor is it possible that new laws of geometrical perspective will be discovered, to overthrow the old ones. It is true that the varieties of painting at different times in history, and among different peoples, prove the existence of different ways of seeing, in some sense of the term. But there are no differences among people in the basic way of seeing—that is, by means of light, and by way of the rectilinear propagation of light. When the artist transcribes what he sees upon a two-dimensional surface, he uses perspective geometry, of necessity. Human visual perception is learned, but not in the same way that we learn a language. It can be acquired by education, but not by the kind of education that consists in memorizing a new set of symbols. What the artist can do is not to create a new kind of vision, but to educate our attention.

E. H. GOMBRICH

On Physiognomic Perception

AN APOLOGY is needed for introducing a discussion of the visual arts today with extracts from a lighthearted skit published by the Goettingen physicist, Georg Christoph Lichtenberg, in 1783.[1] If the reader glances at the illustrations, the general direction of the argument should become apparent: they come as near as the eighteenth century ever did to experiments with "abstract" shapes. It is true that they are intended as representations depicting various forms of tails, tails of dogs and of pigs, and "pigtails" of men, but they are shown for their physiognomic, or as we would say today, for their "expressive" qualities. The target of the satire was the method of Johann Caspar Lavater, who had started a vogue for reading people's characters from their portrait silhouettes.[2] What provoked Lichtenberg was not only the matter but also the manner of Lavater's effusions, his pretentious and exaggerated language, his rapturous intuitionism—a style, by the way, that betrays the influence of art criticism, the famous purple passages in which Winckelmann tried to convey his admiration for the masterpieces of Greek sculpture.[3] A few samples from Lichtenberg's parody must suffice to establish my point that there is still something to be learned from his implicit criticism of this "physiognomic" approach to shapes and forms.

A Dog's Tail [Fig. 1]

With a warm heart embracing the whole of nature and with pious awe contemplating every one of her creations, dearest reader, beloved friend of my soul, behold this tail of a dog and declare if Alexander, had he wished to sport a tail, need have been ashamed of such a one. There is nothing namby-pamby ladyship's-pet-lap-doggie sweetie mousie nibbling tiny creature here. All is manliness, forward urge, a high sublime sweep and a thrust, calm, pensive, charged with dynamic power, as far removed from servile slinking between the legs as from the pointer's game-scenting worried and indecisive horizontality. Were man to perish, in truth the sceptre of this earth would go to tails like this. Who does not feel a sublime caninity bordering on humanity in the curve near a.? In position,

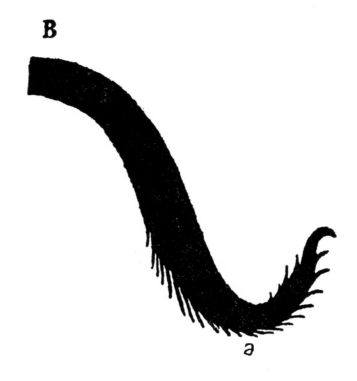

B

a

Figure 1 (after Lichtenberg, 1783).

how near to the earth, in significance, how close to the heavens!
Beloved Nature, darling of my heart, if ever you may desire to grace
your masterpiece with a tail, listen to the fervent prayers of your
doting servant and bestow on him such a one as B.

This tail belonged to the favourite dog of King Henry VIII.
Caesar he was called and Caesar he was. On his collar one read the
motto: *aut Caesar, aut nihil* in golden letters and more clearly yet,
and more firerily his eyes declared the same. His death was caused
by a fight with a lion; but the lion died five minutes before Caesar.
When they called out to him "Marx, the lion is dead" he wagged
this eternalised tail three times, and died, a hero avenged . . . .

*Eight silhouettes of students' pigtails as an exercise:** [Fig. 2]

1. Almost the ideal pigtail. The shaft teutonic, steel-like, the flag
noble, the rose of aggressively loving tenderness. It snarls death
to the philistine and to the unpaid bill. Certainly more power than
prudence.

*Another apology to historians of costume for the inaccuracy of my
terminology.

233

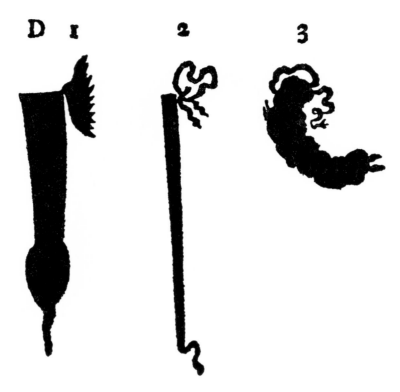

Figure 2(a).

2. Here everywhere more prudence than power. Timidly straight, nothing highminded, no surges of temper, neither a Newton nor a Jack the Ripper. A sweet dandyish whip of a pigtail, not for discipline but for decoration, a tender marzipan heart lacking the pulse of fire. Its highest flight a little song, its boldest wish a little kiss.

3. Dammed-up dynamism. A powderkeg forgotten under a brazier, if it explodes it fills the world. Oh noble, excellent pigtail. *Angli et angeli*. A pity only that you depend on a mere mortal neck; if you flew through the heavens the comets would say: which of us could vie with you? Studies medicine.

[4 and 5 omitted]

6. Assuredly either a young tomcat or a young tiger, a hairsbreadth closer to the latter.

7. An abomination. Fie, fie, indeed! How can you have sat on a head consecrated to the Muses. Maybe you were once torn in a drunken brawl from the wig of a barber's apprentice or a strolling musician, and tied as a trophy to the student's hair. Wretched botchery, not nature's work, but a ropemaker's. Hemp thou art and hemp should rather have strung up the neck of thy tasteless possessor to the gallows.

Figure 2(b).

8. Hail to thee and eternal sunshine to the blessed head that wears thee. If ever reward accorded with merit it is thou who wouldst be the head, thou excellent pigtail, and thou the appendage, blessed head. What kindliness in the silky tender slope, effective without any masking hemp-hiding ribbon, and yet smiling bliss like plaited sunbeams. Soaring as far above even crowned heads as a saint's halo over a nightcap. . . .

Questions for further exercise:
   Which is the most powerful?
   Which is most charged with creative energy?
   Which is the lawyer, the medical student, the theologian?
   Who is most in love?
   Who has a scholarship?
   Which of them might have been worn by Goethe?
   Which of them would Homer select were he to return to earth?

There is no surer way of killing a joke than explaining it. I shall certainly leave it to the reader to draw the parallel between Lichtenberg's butt and those effusions of modern critics that may come to his mind. My purpose is not so much to attack nonsense as to discuss the validity and the limits of the physiognomic approach. For clearly there is some residue of sense in his commentaries. They could not be swapped round among the illustrations without losing in conviction. And this conviction is not only strong but lasting. To me the dog's tail has become "charged" with that expression of heroic poise that Lichtenberg manages so brilliantly to read into it.

For there is indeed such a thing as "physiognomic perception" which carries strong and immediate conviction. We all experience this immediacy when we look into a human face. We see its cheerfulness or gloom, its kindliness or harshness, without being aware of reading "signs." Psychologists such as Heinz Werner[4] have emphasized that this type of "global" and immediate reaction to expression is not confined to the reading of human faces or gestures. We all know how easily a similar response is evoked by other creatures, how the penguin will strike us as grave, the camel as supercilious and the marabou as wise—needless to say, without warrant from the "behavioral sciences." Moreover, the metaphors of our speech testify to the ease with which we carry this physiognomic perception into fields even further removed from rational inference; we speak of cheerful colors or melancholy sounds. Any poem, good or bad, will furnish examples of this extension of physiognomic perception, also known as the pathetic fallacy, telling of smiling skies and menacing clouds, the caress of the wind and the soothing murmur of the brook. These reactions testify to the constant scrutiny with which we scan our environment with the one vital question: are you friendly or hostile, a "good thing" or a "bad thing"? It may be argued that the answer to this question is as basic to the survival of any organism as are the answers to the questions of other perceptual probings, such questions as "What is this?", "Where am I now?", "How do I get from here to there without bumping into things?" Indeed if we follow Bruner[5] and others in regarding perception as a process of categorizing, we may argue that the physiognomic categories of "smiling" or "menacing" are among our earliest and most basic responses.

What speaks in favor of this view is the "regressive" character of these experiences. There is something basic and compulsive, as Lorenz has shown,[6] in our reading of animal physiognomies which suggests the proximity of unlearned layers. Even the poet's metaphor of the smiling sky suggests, as do all metaphors, a looser network of categories than do the tighter meshes of literal and rational language: the poet lives in a world where all things can still be divided into those that smile and those that frown, he has preserved the child's capacity to probe and question anything in nature—and anything in nature will answer him clearly enough to allow him to "sort" the world into these "physiognomic" categories.

From this point of view, metaphors are not necessarily "transferred" meanings, linkages established, as the classical theory of metaphorical expression has it. They are rather indicators of linkages not yet broken, of pigeonholes sufficiently wide to encompass both the blueness of a spring sky and a mother's smile.[7] It adds to the interest of these categories that they are

236

so often intrasensory: the smile belongs to the category of warm, bright, sweet experiences; the frown is cold, dark, and bitter in this primeval world where all things hostile or unpleasant strike us as similar or at least equivalent.

How far are these reactions subjective or culturally conditioned? Not entirely, it seems. Even though language and cultural habits may contribute much to the currency of individual metaphors and poetic clichés, we still do not expect any people to call their sweethearts "bitter" or to sing of the cold and dark smile of a mother fondling her baby. Osgood's experiments in his much discussed book, the *Measurement of Meaning*,[8] seem to point in a similar direction: his team asked subjects to classify a number of random words in terms of the most unexpected qualities, e.g., are fathers more heavy than light, are boulders more serious than gay? Whatever criticism of Osgood's methodology may be possible, one thing emerges from these curious questionnaires: we are ready to categorize any notion in terms of any contrasting quality, and our response, so it seems, will not be entirely random. Boulders, it may be, belong to the world of potential obstacles, and so, by the way, do fathers, if compared to feathers. What wonder that they are both found on the harsher side?

It is obvious that not only poetry but all the arts rely on these responses for some of their effects. What we call the "expressive" character of sounds, colors or shapes, is after all nothing else but this capacity to evoke "physiognomic" reactions. There is no theory of art, old or new, which ignores this element altogether. The ancient theory of music, for instance, elaborated the "expressive" character of modes and keys, orators discussed the physiognomy of words, rhythms, and sounds, and architects had something to say about the physiognomy of the various "orders" in architecture. Even in the visual arts, the expressive possibilities of shapes and forms as such were by no means neglected by the writers of the academic tradition.[9] It was only with the rise of Expressionism, however, that the artist's and critic's attention was almost exclusively focused on this elementary effect. The first thing that teachers of art and art appreciation try to impress on their students nowadays is to look out for the expressive character of shapes, textures, and colors. This shift of emphasis may well be a necessary reaction to the increased demands by our technological civilization on the rational faculties. To those who fear that the rush of mechanized living deadens our immediate response to the voice of things and kills the child within us, it is a source of comfort that artists and critics remind us of these pristine layers of experience. There is thus a good deal to be said for exploring and developing these sensitivities, but only on one condition:

237

we must not confuse response with understanding, expression with communication.

It was this confusion, I contend, that Lichtenberg found in Lavater. Not that he denied the possibility of understanding and interpreting physiognomic expression. He was himself the author of the most detailed commentary on Hogarth's satirical sequences ever to appear. But here, he would have argued, the context of the story, together with all the emblematic allusions introduced by the artist, guided the interpreter and controlled his flights of fancy. The reason why Lavater's method of physiognomic intuition results in nonsense is not that he explores his own response, but that he treats it like an infallible oracle that is in no need of corroboration.

The scientist Lichtenberg, on the other hand, knew that the intensity of a personal intuition is no measure of its correctness. He had experimented with physiognomic impressions and found them wanting. He had tried, for instance, to picture to himself the face of the night watchman from the way he heard him call the hours during his nightly round, and then he sought him out to sketch his portrait. There was no similarity.

Popular wisdom, of course, has always warned us against relying on "first impressions." Why, then, are we so rarely aware of the extent of their fallibility? All cognitive processes, I believe, demand above all a flexibility and elasticity of mind. There is no advantage in our remembering the early stages of our probings that have been superseded by a better fit. Unless we fix them deliberately, as Lichtenberg did, they are conveniently discarded and forgotten. It is a worthwhile and humbling exercise to follow his example and (in the absence of night watchmen) to listen to a conversation behind you on a bus, trying to figure out the appearance and social status of the speakers before turning round and checking your intuitions, or consciously to anticipate the voice of a person who is just being introduced to you. Only by such introspective experiments can we learn how we actually build up the image of a person in real life. We always try to make as much sense as we can by such clues as are given us. But we are flexible enough to amend this guess as other clues become available.

The person with a gloomy face will alert us to the possibility of other gloomy utterances; but as soon as his voice or his smile refutes this expectation we forget or ignore our first impression and adjust the category in which we place the person. We may see his handwriting, and if we are responsive to those signs, we may enter its surprising boldness on our image of the man. Should we then hear of other traits, his heroic war record or his fondness for Verdi, we will always add the information to rectify our former image (which we quickly forget). Every

238

time we will instinctively conceive it as our task to fit the mosaic stones into one unified impression, our picture of the man as we form it through our efforts to "make sense" of all his traits.[10] It would need a very severe jolt for us to abandon this basic physiognomic hypothesis of a unified character behind all the manifestations we register. The "split personality" is something we may be able to grasp intellectually, but hardly emotionally.

What should emerge from this discussion is both the value and the fallibility of physiognomic intuition. Without its initial response we could never arrive at a hypothesis which we could subsequently modify and adjust to the evidence provided by life or by history. But we destroy the value of this instrument if we overrate that initial groping, our first move in the effort to make sense.

The role of such initial probings for any act of understanding, any hypothesis, has been stressed with particular force in K. R. Popper's epistemology.[11] We could not find our way through the world if we did not use the stream of incoming stimuli to answer specific questions that help us to decide between given alternatives. Where we lack all other clues, we must venture on a random guess that subsequent observations will have to confirm or refute.

I believe that the physiognomic reactions that Osgood and others have investigated are of a similar character. In normal conditions we would not operate with them any longer than necessary to perform the first unstable act of categorization which serves as a starting point for subsequent probes. Lichtenberg's "further questions for exercise" illustrate the same effect of a choice situation when we are asked to decide which of the wigs might have been worn by Goethe.

No one has more reason to interest himself in this type of situation than the historian, who tries to build up a picture of the past by asking it questions of a similar kind. There is a charming sketch by Max Beerbohm which happens to take us into the same milieu as did Lichtenberg's skit. It is entitled "A Clergyman," and it deals with a scene reported in Boswell's *Life of Samuel Johnson*.[12] A simple question interjected by an anonymous clergyman provoked one of the Doctor's characteristic outbursts. Beerbohm fills in the details of the scene from his imagination, he convinces us that the interjection must have been made in a high-pitched voice, and he gradually builds up the image, and indeed the whole melancholy life-story, of the unfortunate vicar whose fate it was to be crushed by the great bear.

In a sense, Beerbohm provides a model of how every historian should and does react to the stray pieces of evidence that

239

reach him from the past. But remembering the warnings of the satirist, he will always be ready to abandon or modify his imaginative reaction as soon as more clues become available. Who knows? He may after all be able to identify the clergyman present at Mrs. Thrale's party, and even to find his portrait or description. The very intensity of his vision will spur him on to test it against fresh evidence. His training has made him aware of the subtle difference between the ability to make sense and the possibility of understanding.

Here, at last, we come back to the problems of art and understanding which are the real concern of this essay. I have drawn attention in a different context to what I have called the "physiognomic fallacy" in the history of art.[13] It is first exemplified by Winckelmann, who professed to divine the "noble simplicity and quiet grandeur" of the Greek soul behind the impassive marble front of classical statues. The misleading character of such impressions has been commented on by critics as diverse as Meyer Schapiro[14] and André Malraux.[15] And yet the illusion of a "spirit of the age" persists. We may now understand a little more clearly how this illusion of unity arises and what its function may be in the historian's work.

Whenever an ancient cult image, the pattern on a brooch, a broken column or a painted potsherd asks to be interpreted, any historian worth his salt will try to make sense of it in such terms as his creative imagination suggests. But a critical mind will not rest content with this vision. He will watch for further evidence to fit it into the image of the lost culture. Usually, of course, such further evidence is available in one form or another, and the historian's task is precisely to fit it all together into a context that "makes sense." And so intensely does his imagination become engaged that he begins to people the past with the men who might have created those very brooches and done those very deeds of which the sources tell us. There is much to be admired in this effort of the imaginative historian to "wake the dead" and to unriddle the mute language of the monuments. But he should never conceal from himself that his method is circular. The physiognomic unity of past ages which he reads from their various manifestations is precisely the unity to which the rules of his game have committed him. It was he who unified the clues in order to make sense of them.

There is a natural transition between these techniques and compulsions of the historian to make sense of the unintelligible, and the problems confronting the critic of contemporary art. Much of this art demands to be interpreted in historical terms: it is said to represent the spirit of this age (except, of course, where it expresses that of the future!). No wonder that art criticism has largely been replaced by what theologians used to call "apologetics," the teacher or preacher expounding the esoteric mysteries of the oracle *in partibus infidelium.* Whenever the public fails to understand, this must be due to their incapacity to respond, and so he demonstrates that it is possible to "make sense" of those bewildering configurations on the museum walls or the lecturer's screen.

But, I fear, no more is needed for this demonstration than that skill of verbalizing our physiognomic responses that is so successfully parodied by Lichtenberg. We can all train ourselves to do a Lichtenberg for almost any lump or blot. By virtue of their mere existence they must have a physiognomy, some kind of expressive character, if only we dig deep enough into the layers of our mind that respond to the voice of things. The only trouble is, that the way of regression is not the way of understanding. In the unified physiognomic world of the child no differentiation has yet occurred between the inanimate and the animate, let alone between things and symbols. Can we be surprised that art, having embarked on the road of systematic regression, seems also on the way to abolishing these distinctions and to exploring the expressive voice of accidental shapes and random movements? If we train the public to share in this game, Burri's framed piece of old sacking can soon be trumped by any old sack. In one way, of course, art has always had this function of teaching regression. It is the poet and the landscape painter who have kept alive the voice of nature for an urbanized civilization. But regression alone is not art. Where it reigns supreme, everything becomes charged with meaning, as in a dream, and there can be no difference between sense and nonsense. The physiognomic approach may lead to the suicide of criticism.

I believe that this sad event will be the outcome of a real moral dilemma which does honor to our age. We have learned that *tout comprendre c'est tout pardonner,* but we tend to forget that this admirable maxim befits the psychiatrist rather than the critic. True, the critic too must widen his sympathies and cultivate his capacity to respond, but he must still keep his will to understand sufficiently under control to distinguish between Goethe's pigtail and Goethe's *Faust.*

I have no ready solution for this dilemma. But I would contend that the first step will be made when the critic again regards it as his duty to understand *and* to criticize. He need not surrender his new tolerance to do so. He need not even criticize the shapes and configurations offered for his response any more than he would criticize the shapes of the mountains in Switzerland. You cannot argue with shapes, but you can argue with painters and those philosophies of art that have resulted in a situation that is as torturing to the artist[16] as it is

241

stultifying to the critic. What we need above all, I believe, is a fresh analysis of fundamentals. Having seen where the identification of art with expression leads us, we must claim the right to examine its credentials.

In conclusion, therefore, I should like to glance at one characteristic passage in Dewey's *Art as Experience* which illustrates, to my mind, the weaknesses of this approach.[17] It is all the more interesting, as Dewey here argues against Roger Fry's rejection of all content in painting.

A person with a knack can easily jot down lines that suggest fear, rage, amusement, and so on. He indicates elation by lines curved in one direction, sorrow by curves in the opposite direction. But the result is not an object of *perception*. What is seen passes at once over into the thing suggested. . . . The meaning of an expressive object, on the contrary, is individualized. The diagrammatic drawing that suggests grief does not convey the grief of an individual person. . . . The esthetic portrayal of grief manifests the grief of a particular individual in connection with a particular event. It is *that* state of sorrow which is depicted, not depression unattached. It has a *local* habitation.

One feels the validity of Dewey's strictures, but their formulation is open to doubt. We remember that the meaning of his contrasting lines will indeed be obvious, but only on one condition, the condition of Osgood's experiment: if we ask any beholder which of the lines are more sad than gay, the answer will be not only easy but trivial. Without some such context it will not only be hard but impossible to find their "meaning." Not only might the same pair of lines be used to suggest the contrast between youth and age, dark and light, earth and air,[18] but if we encountered them among geological diagrams or statistical graphs, their expressive character would cease altogether to be perceived. If, on the other hand, we were determined to individualize their expression, there would be nothing to stop us, as Lichtenberg's skit proves. Why should we not ask those "diagrammatic lines" if they represent the grief of a man or a woman? if of a woman, whether that of an old or a young woman? if of a young woman, whether that of a fair or a dark girl? What can prevent us, in the end, from charging those lines with as much meaning as Lichtenberg projected into the tail of his dog Caesar? Is it not precisely the point that we can always give any utterance a local habitation if there is nothing to contradict our projections?

No line as such, whether drawn by an artist or merely by a "person with a knack," can alone and unaided "convey the grief of an individual person." Communication, as engineers have been reminding us in the last few years, always presupposes a

242

selection between possible alternatives, a tuned receiver ready to be switched from one state to another by some impulse traveling along a channel.

Those who subscribe to the theory of art as communication have not helped their case by calling any mark the artist makes on the canvas a "statement." They forget (if they ever knew) that this description should be reserved for propositions that can be true or false. A patch of red is no more a statement than the word "fire." True, we may use either of the two for a communication, but only on one condition: that the context is clear enough to allow of only one answer. The red light will serve as a traffic signal, because it is neither green nor yellow. The word "fire" will serve the platoon commander because his soldiers are set for this message. If we twiddle the knob of our radio and hear only a shout of "fire," we cannot know whether it was part of a message to the police, part of a battle scene, a conductor imploring his orchestra to play with more verve, or an angry boss demanding the dismissal of a stupid employee. Here, as always, we can narrow down our guesses by sampling the broadcast again, but such efforts at making sense should not be confused with understanding the meaning of the statement that a fire has broken out at a given place and time, a message which the fire brigade may find true or false.

It is the problem of the artist that he must, in the nature of things, know the meaning the red patch has for him within the physiognomic context of his private world. The idea that all he need do is to transform his emotion into an "expressive" configuration and send it across to the sensitive beholder, who will unwrap the parcel and take out the emotion, is responsible for much confusion in these matters. If the rise and fashion of information theory has done any good, it is to have disposed of this primitive "parcel post model."

I am by no means sure that art can be wholly described as "communication" in this or any other sense. But I am convinced that those who desire it to communicate anything must narrow down the vagueness of that first physiognomic guess, which is too often identified with the aesthetic response. Here is the reason why every contextual aid is of so much value—the captions provided by Klee, for instance, or the traditions of certain forms. Here, I believe, is also the reason why we find it so much easier nowadays to cope with paintings by artists we know personally or who, at least, have long been familiar to us through their work. Without some framework against which to test and modify our first impressions, we are left to the tender mercies of our initial projections.

Dewey may be right when he implies in the context of his passage quoted that the content of the picture will often provide

243

the additional dimension needed to question the line for its "expressive" meaning. This was the traditional solution that certainly proved its worth in the theories of the past. It demanded that the various elements of a work of art be harmonized so as to form a "whole": the tune of the song had to be fitted to the mood and meaning of its words, the character of a landscape background to the import of the scene represented. To continue with Dewey's example, the grief of the Madonna would be accompanied by lines different from those that might fit the grief of a jilted girl.

I do not wish to imply that Dewey's argument disposes of all attempts to build up an art of expressive forms alone. Instrumental music is always there to remind us of the possibility of such an art, but music does not rely on the physiognomic impact of one intuitive response. The opening chords of Beethoven's *Eroica* are certainly expressive, they put us in a frame of mind, but they alone are not the symphony. The symphony, it seems to me, takes shape precisely as we follow the anticipations of these chords and find them modified, confirmed and transformed by the subsequent development. Understanding the *Eroica*, in other words, may have some features in common with those other processes of understanding that I have described before. To be sure, it needs that state of responsiveness that goes with regression, but it also needs that willingness to revise, that alertness to further clues, that we associate with other faculties.[19] Only the future can show whether similar modes of apprehension can also be developed for combinations of pure shapes and colors in painting and sculpture. Given certain standards and traditions, this might still happen. But if we do not want to kill these arts with kindness, we must help the artist to find a valid theory of articulation that does justice not only to the expressive character of his elements but also to the mystery of ordered form.

REFERENCES

1 Georg Christoph Lichtenberg, "Fragment von Schwänzen," *Baldingers Neues Magazin für Aerzte*, 1783, 5. I am quoting from the reprint in Lichtenberg's *Vermischte Schriften*. Göttingen, Dieterichsche Buchhandlung, 1867.

2 Johann Caspar Lavater, *Physiognomische Fragmente*. Leipzig and Winterthur, 1775-1778.

3 Charlotte Steinbrucker, *Lavaters Physiognomische Fragmente in ihrem Verhältnis zur bildenden Kunst*. Berlin, Wilhelm Borngraber, 1915.

4 Heinz Werner, *Einführung in die Entwicklungspsychologie*. Leipzig, Ambrosius Barth, 1926.

5 Jerome S. Bruner, "On Perceptual Readiness," *Psychological Review*, 1957, 64.

6 Konrad Lorenz, "Die angeborenen Formen möglicher Erfahrung," *Zeitschrift für Tierpsychologie,* 1943, 5.

7 See also my paper, "Visual Metaphors of Value in Art," in *Symbols and Values: An Initial Study,* Thirteenth Symposium of the Conference on Science, Philosophy, and Religion. Ed. Lyman Bryson and others. New York, Harper and Brothers, 1954.

8 Charles E. Osgood, George J. Suci, Percy H. Tannenbaum, *The Measurement of Meaning.* Urbana, University of Illinois Press, 1957.

9 See my forthcoming book, *Art and Illusion* (The A. W. Mellon Lectures in the Fine Arts). New York, Bollingen Series, 1959.

10 I wish to acknowledge my indebtedness to Mr. Donald Hope, with whom I discussed these matters.

11 K. R. Popper, *The Logic of Scientific Discovery,* New York, Basic Books, 1959; and the same author's "The Philosophy of Science: A Personal Report," in *British Philosophy in the Mid-Century,* ed. Cecil A. Mace, London, Allen and Unwin, 1957.

12 Max Beerbohm, "A Clergyman," in *And Even Now.* London, William Heinemann Ltd., 1920.

13 See my lecture on "Art and Scholarship," London, University College, 1957, reprinted in *College Art Journal,* 1958, 17.

14 Meyer Schapiro, "Style," in *Anthropology Today* (ed. A. L. Kroeber. Chicago, University of Chicago Press, 1953), p. 302.

15 André Malraux, *The Psychology of Art.* New York, Bollingen Series, 1949-1951. See also my review, "André Malraux and the Crisis of Expressionism," *The Burlington Magazine,* December, 1954.

16 See my article, "The Tyranny of Abstract Art," *Atlantic Monthly,* April 1958. (The title was the Editor's; my own was "The Vogue of Abstract Art.")

17 John Dewey, *Art as Experience* (New York, G. P. Putnam, 1958), p. 90.

18 For similar experiments (emerging from the school of Heinz Werner) see Reinhard Krauss, "Ueber den graphischen Ausdruck," *Beihefte zur Zeitschrift für angewandte Psychologie,* 1930, 48.

19 Such a theory of the aesthetic response would run parallel to the theory of artistic creation adumbrated by Ernst Kris, *Psychoanalytic Explorations in Art,* New York, International Universities Press, 1952.

SUZANNE K. LANGER

On Artistic Sensibility

THERE IS A STRONG tendency today to treat art as a *significant* phenomenon rather than as a pleasurable experience, a gratification of the senses. This is probably due to the free use of dissonance and so-called "ugliness" by our leading artists in all fields—in literature, music, and the plastic arts. It may also be due in some measure to the striking indifference of the uneducated masses to artistic values. In past ages, these masses had no access to great works of art; music and painting and even books were the pleasures of the wealthy; it could be assumed that the poor and vulgar would enjoy art if they could have it. But now, since everybody can read, visit museums, and hear great music at least over the radio, the judgment of the masses on these things has become a reality, and has made it quite obvious that *great art is not a direct sensuous pleasure.* If it were, it would appeal—like cake or cocktails—to the untutored as well as to the cultured taste. This fact, together with the intrinsic "unpleasantness" of much contemporary art, would naturally weaken any theory that treated art as pure pleasure. Add to this the current logical and psychological interest in symbolism, in expressive media and the articulation of ideas, and we need not look far afield for a new philosophy of art, based upon the concept of "significant form."

But if forms in and of themselves be significant, and indeed must be so to be classed as artistic, then certainly the kind of significance that belongs to them constitutes a very special problem in semantics. What is artistic significance? what sort of meaning do "expressive forms" express?

Clearly they do not convey propositions, as literal symbols do. We all know that a seascape (say) represents water and rocks, boats and fish-piers; that a still-life represents oranges and apples, a vase of flowers, dead game or fish, etc. But such a content is not what makes the paint-patterns on the canvas "expressive forms." The mere notion of rabbits, grapes, or even

For the source of this selection, please refer to the Acknowledgments, page ii.

boats at sunset is not the "idea" that inspires a painting. The artistic idea is always a "deeper" conception.

Several psychologists have ventured to unmask this "deeper" significance by interpreting pictures, poems, and even musical compositions as symbols of loved objects, mainly, of course, of a forbidden nature. Artistic activity, according to the psychoanalysts who have given it their attention, is an expression of primitive dynamisms, of unconscious wishes, and uses the objects or scenes represented to embody the secret fantasies of the artist.

This explanation has much to recommend it. It accounts for the fact that we are inclined to credit works of art with *significance,* although (by reason of the moral censorship which distorts the appearance of basic desires) we can never say what they signify. It does justice to the emotional interest, the seriousness with which we receive artistic experience. Above all, it brings this baffling department of human activity into the compass of a general psychological system—the so-called "dynamic psychology," based on the recognition of certain fundamental human needs, of the conflicts resulting from their mutual interference, and of the mechanism whereby they assert, disguise, and finally realize themselves. The starting-point of this psychology is the discovery of a previously unrecognized *symbolic mode,* typified in dream, and perfectly traceable in all works of fantasy. To assimilate art to the imaginative life in general is surely not a forced procedure. It seems, moreover, to bring the problem of aesthetic experience into the symbol-centered philosophy that constitutes the theme of this book.

These are strong recommendations for the psychoanalytic theory of aesthetics. But despite them all, I do not think this theory (though probably valid) throws any real light on those issues which confront artists and critics and constitute the philosophical problem of art. For the Freudian interpretation, no matter how far it be carried, never offers even the rudest criterion of *artistic* excellence. It may explain why a poem was written, why it is popular, what human features it hides under its fanciful imagery; what secret ideas a picture combines, and why Leonardo's women smile mysteriously. But *it makes no distinction between good and bad art.* The features to which it attributes the importance and significance of a great masterpiece may all be found just as well in an obscure work of some quite incompetent painter or poet. Wilhelm Stekel, one of the leading Freudian psychologists interested in artistic productions as a field for analysis, has stated this fact explicitly: "I want to point out at once," he says, "that it is irrelevant to our purpose whether the poet in question is a great, universally acknowledged poet, or whether we are dealing with a little poetaster. For, after all, we are investigating only the impulse which drives people to create."

An analysis to which the artistic merit of a work is irrelevant can hardly be regarded as a promising technique of art-criticism, for it can look only to a hidden *content* of the work, and not to what every artist knows as the real problem—the *perfection of form,* which makes this form "significant" in the artistic sense. We cannot evaluate this perfection by finding more and more obscure objects represented or suggested by the form.

Interest in represented objects and interest in the visual or verbal structures that depict them are always getting hopelessly entangled. Yet I believe "artistic meaning" belongs to the sensuous construct as such; this alone is beautiful, and contains all that contributes to its beauty.

W. J. H. B. SANDBERG

Picasso's "Guernica"

Look: where round the wide horizon
Many a million-peopled city
Vomits smoke in the bright air
Mark that outcry of despair! . . .

Look again, the flames almost
To a glow-worm's lamp have dwindled:
The survivors round the embers
Gather in dread.

Shelley, "Prometheus Unbound" (1818)

GREAT ARTISTS by some hidden direction assemble where life is most intense, where a new world is about to be born:

In the fifteenth century: Florence and Flanders.
In the sixteenth: Venice.
In the seventeenth: Amsterdam.
Afterward: Paris.
From 1910 to 1920: Moscow (Chagall, Gabo, Kandinsky, Malewitch, Pevsner, Tatlin).

They come together to shape a new world. With the technique taken from their predecessors they create a new form.

More modest talents also are often attracted; they are inspired not by the turbulent life around, but by the work of greater artists, forerunners and contemporaries. They adapt to the taste of the public what in the creations of genius seems strange and abhorrent; they form a school.

Genius is inspired by life—talent, by art. Genius shocks—talent smooths.

In the beginning of the century Picasso and Braque come to Paris. In 1907 they meet. During a few years of daily contact they transform reality, give it a new shape—not the reality they see with the eye but the reality of the mind.

249

We see a rectangular table in perspective—that is, as a trapezium; our side of the table looks more important than the other side. But we know the table to be a pure rectangle.

The camera sees only one side of our face, but we know it to be in profile and *en face* at the same time.

Picasso and Braque quit visual reality and start to paint the environing objects as they know they are. The table top becomes a rectangle again, and the human face is rendered from the side and the front at the same time. This decisive act we call Cubism.

About 1500 the artists of the Renaissance invented the perspective we are still accustomed to: the artist sat down on his chair, looked at the scene from one definite angle, and tried to fix it on his panel accordingly.

Now after four hundred years the painter rises from his chair, starts moving around his object, and tries to render the totality. He changes his point of view. Cubism is: *Welt-an-Schauung.* Cubism concerns our intellect, not our heart—that is left to Expressionism.

For three decades Picasso investigates the field of form. His researches are laid down in a long series of masterpieces. Again and again he startles us with new discoveries.

Paris 1937: Every nation prepares its contribution to the world fair. The Spanish Government, assailed by Franco and his blood-stained friends, decides to demonstrate its love for freedom and humanity in a pure and simple building. It commissions a few great artists to express their ideas. It is to be not a commercial *pavillon*, but a home for democracy.

Sert becomes the architect, Miró and Picasso are invited to paint great frescoes, Calder creates his famous fountain of Mercury. Gonzales forges "La Montserrat." The long wall near the entrance is given to Picasso. In January the artist starts making sketches, but inspiration fails. Months pass by. The battle for freedom goes on. Picasso hesitates. The Civil War had only inspired him to a few sarcastic etchings, of which "Songes et Mensonges de Franco" are the most widely known.

Then, on 28 April, Guernica, the holy city of the Basques, is destroyed in an air raid. Men, women, children, and cattle die miserably amid smoking ruins. An outcry of indignation shakes the world, but only a few realize that Guernica is merely the prelude to slaughter on a much larger scale.

On 1 May, Picasso begins with four sketches for the composition and two studies for the horse. On 2 May: only three sketches. For five days: nothing. He knows what he is going to make and does not yet want to fix his ideas: "In the beginning one should have an idea, but a vague one," he confides to Kahnweiler. He wants to remain free as long as possible.

Evidently during these days the big canvas, 11 feet 6 inches by 25 feet 8 inches, is being prepared. Then, from 8 May, the work goes on without interruption: compositional sketches, and studies for the bull, the horse, and the weeping woman.

On 11 May the canvas is ready, and immediately the composition is laid down as a linear structure that covers the whole surface. Work on the mural is accompanied by more than thirty studies for the details. The rough plan exists from the beginning, but it takes three weeks before the picture receives its final form.

The bull's head remains where it was first put, but the body is turned around to the left. On 20 May the horse lifts its head. The body of the soldier stretched on the floor from left to right changes position on 4 June, then head and hand take on their finished shape.

At the last moment the artist makes one decisive adjustment: the drama first took place on a street with burning houses in the background. Now, suddenly, the diagonals are accentuated, and thereby space becomes ambiguous, unreal, inside and outside at the same time. The lamp is hung over the horse's head, looking on the dreadful scene like a wide-open eye. The construction is strengthened, the mural more strongly integrated in Sert's architecture. Into the hand of the dying soldier, next to the broken sword, Picasso puts the little flower of hope.

The picture was finished about mid-June. Hundreds of thousands of exhibition-goers wandered by, looking on it as a wall decoration, just as Europe wandered by the human drama of the Spanish Civil War—as if it were a matter concerning only the inhabitants of the peninsula. They disregarded the warning, did not understand that democracy on the whole continent was at stake.

Only a few in 1937 understood Picasso's dramatic appeal as we might understand it now.

Today "Guernica" has become a part of the pattern of our own experiences. It is the pathetic symbol of the recent past and a warning for the future.

When seen in the light of "Guernica," all Picasso's earlier works look like preliminary stages, studies for the creation of a new language. This new language stands at the artist's disposal when, stirred by the weight of human fate, he is driven to take part with his own weapons in the great battle for freedom. Thus "Guernica" is an expressionistic message, written in the language of Cubism.

Picasso's great achievements are on two totally different levels: through the creation of Cubism (1907) he gives us a new vision of reality; by painting "Guernica" he transforms a stark act of war into an eloquent warning to humanity (1937).

PABLO PICASSO

Composition Study, 9 May 1937.
Collection Museum of Modern Art, New York.

Sketch for "Guernica," 11 May 1937.

Final State, "Guernica."
Collection Museum of Modern Art, New York.
On extended loan from the artist.

JAMES S. ACKERMAN

Art History and the Problems of Criticism

A RECENT editorial in one of our popular art journals took art
historians to task for not contributing to the criticism of contemporary painting and sculpture, and it genially encouraged
us to mend our ways. As the editor of an historical quarterly,
I read it with sympathy, since the critics in turn no longer
bother with the past. We agree that the alienation of history
from criticism is unnatural, yet the prospect of negotiating an
exchange of subject matter is not promising. There is no evidence that the critical principles of the scholars are firm enough
to stand without that support which the test of time gives to the
judgment of old masters, or that the limited techniques developed by the critics for the defense of abstract art can effectively cope with the images of the past.

In recognizing the limitations of specialization, I do not
propose to accept them passively; if the critic's job is to communicate the qualities of works of art, and the historian's is to
understand the arts of the past, then neither can perform properly without the accomplishments of both. The dry history and
wet criticism so common nowadays are penalties paid for over-
doing the division of labor. This industrial term is brought to
mind by our fundamentally mechanistic treatment of the arts.
Having no firm principles or even convictions in common, we
are bound to regard criticism and scholarship purely as techniques; and, as the techniques are, and should be, different, we
find no common ground. The typical critic is a specialist in
expressionistic prose, and the typical historian, in esoteric facts.
I believe we shall restore some unity of purpose only when we
recognize that writing about art is itself an art; one that may be
practiced in diverse techniques, but in which, as in all art, the
imaginative formulation must give meaning to the technical
apparatus.

Criticism becomes art when it communicates experiences and
stimulates sensations that the reader cannot get by himself, just

Based on a paper read at the Wellesley College Symposium on the Arts,
25 February 1959.

257

as a still-life painting becomes art when it transforms a certain number of apples and bottles into a meaningful formulation of the painter's imagination. The art in history is less obvious; indeed, we are so unaccustomed to seeking it out that we commonly slip into the shocking misconception that history is a science—that historians "find out what happened," without really intervening. But the historian, like the artist, exercises his taste and applies his acquired schemata in selecting his subject, in choosing certain facts from an infinitely large pool, and in formulating them into what we significantly call a "picture" of the past. This picture, like its counterpart in the museum, has a definite style, and may be identified as characteristic of a certain time, place, and author. Yet, unlike the artist, the historian is often unconscious of his formulative role, so that sheer prejudice or mere fashion may control his selection and arrangement. In posing as a technician without an art, he can only stuff his facts into forms created by one of his more profound predecessors. His picture of the past is like an illustration in a popular magazine, which communicates information in formulas purloined from fashionable masters.

The technique in most art history published today is impeccable; new facts, and new ways of finding them, appear faster than anyone can absorb them. We have developed a sturdy scientific method of an archaeological sort that uncovers works of art and reveals how, where, when, why, and by whom they were done. But our theories have hardly been molested for half a century, and in the course of time we have almost come to accept them as dogma. If artists had become satisfied with their forms over a generation ago and settled down to improve their studio methods, we would be sounding vociferous alarms, but apparently academic immunity protects historians from public criticism. Of course, historical or artistic forms are not necessarily invalid once they have aged; but they must be constantly challenged if we expect to control them rather than submit to their authority. It is a distressing symptom of weakness in our culture when intellectual leaders, particularly those concerned with the arts, put faith in technique alone. And it is hypocrisy for specialists to speak of conformism in the masses so long as they neglect to question their own patterns of thought.

I hope that the questions raised here will penetrate to some of the sources of the alienation of history and criticism. They are historical questions because criticism is bound to be based on the premises, if not the methods, of history. It is difficult to define these premises, because so many different media have developed in the course of a century of modern art history that the field has spawned a number of specialized schools: connoisseurship, or the detection of authorship through traits of style; iconography, or the study of symbols or concrete meanings communicated by works of art; social history, which approaches art as a guide to the economic and intellectual character of past times, and so on. But in varying degrees the several methods are committed to a basic philosophy of the history of art as a study of the development of styles, that is, the continuous unfolding of modes of artistic expression—and it is to this philosophy that I direct my questions.

Our concept of stylistic development is so basic to our thought and vocabulary that we proceed as if it were self-evident and understood alike by everyone. And yet a simple analysis of the phrase itself is sufficient to reveal a complicated and possibly illogical mating of ideas. Style is the mode or character of a work of art—its personality, in short; but it may also be the complex of traits of personality which a number of works of art exhibit in common. We speak of the style of Michelangelo's Sistine ceiling, or of Michelangelo's style as revealed by all his known works; we may also describe the style of an era—as the Renaissance—or of a country, or even a whole civilization—as when we compare East and West. So the term serves two purposes, defining in one case the special character of a single object, and in another the characteristics it shares with others. It is economical to make one word do two jobs, but misleading, because the two are uncongenial; the traits of style that give individuality to a single work of art are not those that associate it with other works. So there are two kinds of style, for example, in the Sistine ceiling: the singular style that differentiates it from everything else, and the communal style that identifies it as a work of Michelangelo or of the Italian Renaissance. A thorough critical or historical evaluation of the Sistine ceiling requires an understanding of both the singular and the communal.

But the concept of the development of style necessarily favors the communal kind. The word "development" evokes an image of growth or evolution, suggesting that the gross mass of historical monuments may be ordered by imposing on it some pattern implying process. Notice that the duality in the definition of style disappears in this pattern, for *development* cannot be illustrated by the singular traits of individual objects, but only by observing *changes* in the common traits of a *group* of objects.

Even this inept definition of words may suggest that the premise of style development, which we accept without challenge as a kind of basic natural law, is in reality a theoretical abstraction channeling our observation within arbitrarily defined limits. It dictates a commitment to process, and in con-

259

sequence submerges what is most individual and exceptional. Furthermore, this process must somehow be purposeful and orderly: styles cannot be said to develop unless, as in an organism, each observable change can be related to the preceding and succeeding states. The organic or evolutionary metaphor has insinuated itself into our whole vocabulary: we must speak of "renaissance," or "rebirth," which evolves in its Darwinian orthodoxy from the Italian or Flemish "primitives" to the "High Renaissance," and having reached the summit declines into the "Baroque" or "bizarre." The "Middle Ages" get their name from their hypothetical position in an evolution from antiquity to the rebirth of antiquity.

The adaptation of evolutionary theory to history was firmly established by the greatest minds of the nineteenth century; Darwin, as I suggested, gave it scientific justification, and Hegel and Marx gave it a dialectical inevitability. Art history, which appeared as an independent discipline in the middle of that century, absorbed its dialectic from this atmosphere. Evolutionary theory in political thought sanctified process, made it purposeful and controllable, and had the same implications for the individual man as it had for the individual work of art. The submersion of the individual in the process of history relieves us of the burden of free will, and this contributes to the revival of the totalitarian state, which can exact the penalty of present submission on the promise of liberation in the vague future. I do not mean by this observation to discredit the contributions of dialectical art history; Marxist criticism and Woelfflin's system have greatly enriched modern scholarship. But I want to emphasize that the scheme of historical process commits us to a certain philosophical position which some of us might wish to reaffirm, but which none of us should accept unconsciously.

I am convinced that there are serious *methodological* drawbacks to this historicism in the study of art, quite aside from any philosophical implications. When evolutionary history was borrowed from the political theorists, certain fundamental differences between the behavior of politics and of art were obscured. In examining these differences I find that the political act is much better suited to the metaphor of process than the creative act.

The primary difference is one of value. A political act must be evaluated in terms of its effects. The Battle of Waterloo was important because it changed the balance of power in Europe. This was good or bad depending on whether one was English or French, and the battle had no intrinsic value apart from its effects. But the value of the creative act depends on its intrinsic quality, and need not be judged by its effect upon succeeding creative acts. The Egyptian tomb painting immured with a dead monarch could not affect the balance of power in Egyptian painting, but this did not diminish its quality. The effects of the tomb painting were of course merely delayed until its discovery in modern times, which reveals a further contrast to the political act, the effects of which must be immediate. Being action, it cannot be preserved for later reference. An unnoticed action cannot affect history.

So political action is, indeed, process: it belongs to the endless flux of history. Whether intentionally or not, the political act makes a transition between the past and the future, altering one condition and promoting another. A revolution is not made for itself, but to change a known undesirable situation into an expected improved one. Political action cannot produce a stable or lasting condition, but only a new mode of flux; in this sense it can never be completed.

The chief purpose of the creative act, however, is neither to alter the present nor to affect the future, but to produce a thing of value. There have been, of course, so-called "revolutions" in art, but they differ fundamentally from political revolutions: they cannot erase or even alter the style against which they revolt, but can only add something different. This is because the artist may not properly be said to make a negative statement: his work is an affirmation. But its chief distinction from the political act is that it is not process; it culminates in a stable and lasting object unchanged by the ensuing flux of culture.

While the goal of the political act, then, is to initiate an evolution, the goal of the creative act is to complete something stable. While creation itself is a process, one that may be affected by any event or any work of art experienced by the creator, its goal is to consummate and to fix the process in an integrated object. This means that the final product is not definable in terms implying process: it cannot rightly be called "transitional" or "forward looking" because there is nothing in it that can be assured of affecting future events. It may happen to influence the future, but this is not an intrinsic characteristic; it depends first on its being seen, which is a matter of chance, and second on the receptivity of the seer, which it cannot control, regardless of how potentially compelling is its power.

Now it appears that the meaning of past and present is quite different for political and creative activity. In political action the past is literally passed, and the actor can only immediately experience what goes on around him. But the creative acts of the past are literally and bodily *present;* there is no art of the past in the sense of the word as employed by the political historian, except what has been destroyed. Since what we call the art of the past really exists in the present, the chronological sequence of its production is irrelevant to its potential for communicating quality or for influencing the present and future. So in the history of art there is no necessary relationship between chronology and cause-and-effect. Today's creative act may be inspired as readily by a work produced two millennia ago as by yesterday's production, and similarly what is created today is no more assured of affecting tomorrow's art than is the statue some archaeologist may be exhuming at the moment in Turkey. In 1420 the art of Ancient Rome was more influential in Italy than the lively and new Gothic naturalism of the International style, and fifty years ago primitive art played a more formative role in Europe than Impressionism did.

Let me characterize the differences in the two kinds of history by suggesting that the political may be seen as a stream, constantly flowing, whose course may be changed by a successful action, while the creative is a reservoir, constantly being filled. I must add, however, that historians are gradually abandoning the purely political, battle-and-reign kind of history, because they have seen that political, social, and economic ideas and institutions, like creative acts, have intrinsic and lasting qualities apart from their immediate effects. This new kind of history gives greater emphasis to human imagination than to relentless evolution, and provides the individual with some defense against being swept along with the mass. The stream remains, but here and there it has been dammed so that one may swim freely in it despite the current.

In short, while the evolutionary theory in pure political history is methodologically defensible (the fact that I find it philosophically distasteful is irrelevant at the moment), it is sheer mysticism in the history of the arts. Our concept of style is an abstraction, constructed from one or more stable and self-sufficient works which exist today and are available for our inspection. To impute to this abstraction functions of growth, expansion, or decline is to endow static objects with the potential of action. The action is not in the objects but in our minds: it is a chimera.

But allowing, for the sake of discussion, that the chronological sequence established by archaeological method justifies a metaphor of process, we observe that it is also necessary to suppose that the process obeys some purposeful and orderly pattern. If it were meaningless flux and change, we could not pretend to make sense of it. That the pattern of so-called development is purely metaphorical is demonstrated by our inability to project it into the future. An economist can predict with some confidence the effects of a change in the monetary structure, but we have no idea where Abstract Expressionism is "going." We can only construct chronological charts and assess the art of the past by hindsight. This method provides us with an index showing

262

which works of art were most influential. If it stopped there it would be unassailable, but inevitably the influential becomes the important. Because hindsight permits the standards of a later work to be applied to those of an earlier, the history of art can become a great success story. The work that was overlooked by subsequent generations becomes eccentric, while the work that won a following appears to be "in the mainstream."

Fortunately, the most influential art is usually of the highest quality; but there is no necessary relationship between influence and quality; bad art is sometimes a smashing success, and excellent art may be totally ignored. So it appears that the patterns of development that we construct are unrelated, and may even be antagonistic, to the distinction of quality. In practice it often happens that influence and quality get confused by the system, and I believe this may explain why eight large books about Caravaggio, a particularly influential painter, have been produced during a period when virtually nothing has appeared on Duccio, Titian, or Borromini. In the same spirit, any metal contraption of the nineteenth century may be resurrected as a significant precursor of modern architecture.

What saves the historian's perception is inconsistency. Most of us are willing to abandon the historical system when we see something we like that happens not to have been in the mainstream. Artists encourage this inconsistency because their new ways of seeing help us to perceive things we have overlooked. Expressionism stimulated a reassessment of El Greco, Cubism of Piero della Francesca, and so on. Whether artists will continue to support us in this way is uncertain; at the moment they appear to be victimized by dogmas, just as we are.

My suggestion that criticism is committed to the historical precepts of its time is borne out by the weaknesses of contemporary critical writing. Process, even progress, has become the measure of significance in the evaluation of modern art to the extent that whatever is, or appears to be, a forward step, is particularly recommended to our attention. The word "progressive" has become a term of praise, because future effects are more highly regarded than present qualities. A premium is placed on any sort of change in art, as it is in the design of automobiles and refrigerators.

I call this the fallacy of the *avant-garde. Avant-garde* is a military phrase used to designate the troops nearest to the objective. Yet the objective of creative activity is the work of art itself, and not any distant goal; we look to it for experience, not for prophecy. The artist who is primarily occupied in anticipating the future can at best hope to be a good prophet or propagandist because his mind is only partly on his work. It is not by chance that the Futurist movement produced so few

263

major works. Museums and art dealers are vigorous promoters of the *avant-garde* fallacy; both were caught napping by Cézanne and van Gogh, and for fear that this may happen again, they assume that quality and novelty will remain equivalents throughout time.

This observation is not meant as a plea for conservatism. If it is fruitless to attempt to anticipate the future, the alternative need not be to perpetuate the past; what matters most to us is the present. We have been living in a rapidly changing culture and have come to expect a rapidly changing art, but the critic must realize that there is no essential value in change, any more than there is value in stability. A work of art will not be either good or bad because it has novel features. Its quality does not depend on what forms and techniques it uses, but on how they are used, and to what effect.

The irony of contemporary criticism, and of much contemporary art, is that the novelty it earnestly seeks it seldom discovers. In painting during the last few years the Abstract Expressionists have passed as the *avant-garde*. But only the originators of this style were original, and today it is being manufactured internationally by the dead hand of academicism. Surely it is no more advanced to repeat Pollock than to repeat Rembrandt; their works stand side by side in museums, belonging at once to past and present. Conservatism is conservatism, whether it is the art of 1648 or of 1948 that is being conserved.

A few years ago the presentness of all past art was pointed out by André Malraux, whose observations led him to the abandonment of historical consciousness and to a philosophy of pure sensation. Malraux saw the weakness in history without criticism, and found an answer in criticism without history. This had the effect of turning isolation into antagonism, of tempting historians and critics into two camps battling to protect vested interests. There could be no more effective way to discourage a stimulating interchange of ideas. This situation is a microcosm of the failings of contemporary culture, which has estranged science from the humanities and the humanities from one another. We must find ways of communicating if we expect to regain any kind of synthesis, and this means that no one discipline or person will succeed alone. But we cannot wait for the other fellow to begin. There would be no point to my criticisms if they did not lead to some positive attempt to cut through the fences that isolate our fields.

I have referred to two kinds of process, historical and creative. While the first is a metaphor that simplifies generalizations about style, the second really goes on, whether or not historians and critics are at hand to observe it. This is the process

we ought to study if we want to find a way to evaluate the
uniqueness of works of art.

Starting with the premise of the autonomy of the individual
work, we would seek out the intention and the experiences of
the artist as he produced it. By autonomy I do not mean isolation, because the experiences of the artist inevitably bring him
into contact with his environment and traditions; he cannot
work in a historical vacuum. So we would need to know what
the artist had seen and done before, what he sees and does now
for the first time, what he or his patron wishes to accomplish,
how his intentions and solutions mature in the course of production. Every tool of history must be at hand to understand all
this, and some new ones, too, such as those of psychology and
other social sciences. In short, we would formulate the history
of art primarily in terms of contexts rather than developments.
Since knowledge of the context in which a single work is produced involves an awareness of the total environment of the
artist, our capacity to generalize about styles would not be
impaired but heightened by a constant awareness of the tension
between the uniqueness of the individual and the pressures
of prevailing modes of expression.

History in terms of contexts should foster a broader definition
of style by its awareness of the *intentions* of the artist. It should
draw attention to the fact that artists want to communicate
primarily with their contemporaries, and this means that their
relationship to the consumer may be a major factor in forming
their mode of expression. We cannot properly explain the differences between Renaissance and modern painting or sculpture without considering that in the one case the patron appears
before execution and in the other case after, if at all; the aspiration to have one's work hung in a chapel is quite different from
the hope that it may be bought by a museum. To speak of
architecture without knowing something of the patron's life as
well as the artist's is to regard it as a sort of habitable piece of
sculpture.

In recognizing that the purpose of a work of art is a component of style, we would remove the barriers that now separate art history into two hostile camps: the analysts of form,
who like to speak only in terms of plastic expression, and the
social historians, who employ art to document the cultural
milieu. Purely formal analysis, by isolating the object, must
overlook qualities that would be revealed if it were seen in its
physical and cultural setting. Social analysis, on the other hand,
normally associates the work of art with the occurrences in its
environment that for some arbitrary reason appear to be the
most significant. But when we start from the genesis of the
work we observe that the artist's experiences are selective; they

265

are exclusive as well as inclusive. An artist may not be aware of, or interested in, many aspects of his environment, or he may get his stimulus from exotic or eccentric sources. We cannot affirm *a priori* that Titian was affected by the Reformation or Picasso by the Theory of Relativity; conversely, insignificant events or discoveries may be more important for a given artist than for his contemporaries at large.

One reason for confidence in the method I propose is that, while it has not been specifically formulated, it has been anticipated in practice in a small number of works recently published in this country: Millard Meiss, in *Painting in Florence and Siena after the Black Death,* chose one generation of Tuscan painting as his context; Walter F. Friedlaender in his *Caravaggio Studies* and Richard and Trude Krautheimer in their *Lorenzo Ghiberti* expanded the traditional monographic study to a panorama of the artist in his milieu. They are distinguished for having liberated the artists from a relentless progression of their own production by showing that each successive work may be directed by the impulse of external stimulus as well as by an internal continuity of style. These are large books of formidable scholarship, which suggest that the kind of penetration I am seeking cannot be gained with facility. Probably it will be hard to write sweeping handbooks without the benefit of grand generalizations on style. But here, too, a pioneer work, though in another field, suggests a solution. Erich Auerbach's *Mimesis* embraces the whole history of literature in terms of selected contexts intensively examined and, I believe, with more success than any developmental treatment.

Mimesis is both history and criticism, and this fusion is exactly what I anticipate in the study of art. If we allow autonomy to the works of art we study, then nothing remains in the historical method that is uncongenial to critical activity.

Criticism would naturally continue to give more attention to contemporary art and to whatever past art was especially accessible to the modern eye, and historians would continue with documentary research and the pursuit of objects not at the moment of general interest. But while the subject matter and the emphasis might, and should, differ, the philosophy and method might be closely allied.

Perhaps a new focus will produce no better history and criticism; there is certainly a great difference between studying the genesis of a work of art and understanding it. We cannot hope to do more than remove certain obstacles to understanding raised by dialectical history. The detection of quality cannot be assured by this or any other conceivable approach: it is the issue of a dialog between the work of art and the observer. When the observer is a critic or a historian he will succeed in detecting and conveying the essence of quality only if his receptive sensibilities and gifts of communication are especially keen.

Fortunately, the dialog changes character at every encounter, so that there is no end in prospect to fresh discoveries in familiar as well as in unfamiliar places. For this reason we should be suspicious of any effort to specify absolute standards of value, since it would be as unhealthy for critics as for artists to accept a common standard.

But if specific value standards may be ruled out, there is a general standard imbedded in the philosophy of history that I am suggesting. If the goal of our studies is the discovery of the uniqueness of the work of art, this is because we are committed to a conviction as to the positive value of individuality. In opposing any philosophy that submerges the individual being or act in the stream of history, we are bound to turn away from works of art that are submerged in a prevailing style. This stricture, of course, does not indiscriminately cover the anonymous monuments of Gothic, Egyptian, or primitive art, the power of which comes from the tension between individual expression and the prevailing style.

Nearly everyone believes in individuality, but one should remember how easily we mistake the gesture for the real thing. In the art of the past we have confused it with the capacity to influence; in contemporary art we identify it with an easily affected novelty of technique or materials. This is the bogus "individualism" of the bohemians who all wear the same long hair and beards, the same dirty jackets, and drink the same *espresso*. The individuality of which I speak is the hardest won of all goals—difficult to achieve, difficult to understand, and impossible to imitate.

Notes on Contributors

JAMES S. ACKERMAN, born in 1919, San Francisco, is at present professor of architecture and art at the University of California, Berkeley. He is the author of *The Cortile del Belvedere,* and is the editor of *The Art Bulletin.*

JOSEF ALBERS, born in 1888, Bottrop, Germany, painter and graphic designer, taught first at the Bauhaus (Weimar), later at Black Mountain College (North Carolina). Since 1950 he has been at Yale University.

GEORGE AMBERG, Associate Professor in the Humanities Program at the University of Minnesota, received his doctorate at the University of Cologne in 1929 and was subsequently a lecturer at New York University and a staff member of the Museum of Modern Art in New York. He is a contributor to *Dictionary of the Arts, Encyclopedia of the Dance,* and *Dance Index;* his books include *Art in Modern Ballet* and *The Theatre of Eugene Berman.*

JEAN ARP, born in 1887, Strasbourg, sculptor, painter, wood engraver, was early associated with the Blue Rider group, dadaism, and surrealism. His sculptures aim at expressing the growth patterns in nature. His murals may be seen in several edifices, such as the UNESCO building in Paris.

PIETRO BELLUSCHI, born in 1899, Ancona, Italy, has been dean of the school of architecture and planning at the Massachusetts Institute of Technology since 1926. His architectural work includes residential, religious, and commercial buildings.

HARRY BERTOIA, born in 1915, San Lorenzo, Italy, is a sculptor and designer, particularly of chairs and architectural screens.

JOHN ELY BURCHARD, born in 1898, Marshall, Minnesota, is dean of the School of Humanities and Social Science at the Massachusetts Institute of Technology. He is both administrator and adviser in educational affairs and also a historian and critic of architecture. He is past president of the American Academy of Arts and Sciences.

REG. BUTLER, born in 1913, Huntingford, England, is a sculptor, editor, and lecturer on architecture. He won first prize in the international competition of the Institute of Contemporary Arts in 1953 for his model of "The Unknown Political Prisoner."

ALBERT CAMUS, born in 1913, Algeria, died in 1960, France, awarded the Nobel Prize for literature, 1957, wrote numerous essays, novels, and plays, the most recent a dramatization of Dostoevsky's *The Demons.*

EDUARDO CHILLIDA, born in 1921, San Sebastian, Spain, sculptor in metals, studied architecture in Madrid. At present he is living in Hernani, Spain.

STUART DAVIS, born in 1894, Philadelphia, painter, lithographer, illustrator, exhibited in the Armory Show in New York in 1913. For a time he taught at the New School for Social Research in New York City, where he lives now.

MAYA DEREN, born in Kiev, Russia, is an independent film-maker whose avant-garde work includes "Meshes of the Afternoon"; "A Study in Choreography for Camera"; and "The Very Eye of Night." Her writings include *An Anagram of Ideas on Art, Form, and Film;* and *Divine Horsemen: The Living Gods of Haiti.* She lives in New York.

FELIX DEUTSCH, born in 1884, Vienna, now consultant in psychiatry in several leading hospitals in the Boston area, was early an associate of Freud, and long served as clinical professor at the University of Vienna Medical School before coming to the United States in 1935.

JEAN DUBUFFET, born in 1901, in France, is a painter whose work combines rich textural surfaces with the brutal strength of primitive imagery. Since 1955 he has lived in Vence.

MARCEL DUCHAMP, born in 1887, Blainville, France, was one of the originators of dadaism and exhibited at the Armory Show in 1913. A free experimenter in "ready-made" objects, he has long resided in New York City.

JIMMY ERNST, born in 1920, Cologne, painter and son of Max Ernst, has taught at Brooklyn College since 1951. He uses a clear plastic language in which forms and lines are explicit.

NAUM GABO (PEVSNER), born in 1890, Bryansk, Russia, after studying mathematics and physics at the Technische Hochschule in Munich, lived in Oslo, Moscow, Berlin, London, and (since 1946) in the United States. One of the originators of the constructivist movement, both his sculpture and his writings have exerted wide influence. "Anything of action which enhances life, propels it and adds to it something in the direction of growth, expansion, and development, is Constructive."

ROBERT GARDNER, born in 1915, Brookline, Massachusetts, is director of the Film Study Center at the Peabody Museum, Harvard University. In 1959 he was a member of the Peabody Museum Expedition to the Kalahari Desert in Southwest Africa, described in this issue.

JAMES J. GIBSON, born in 1904, McConnelsville, Ohio, is professor of psychology at Cornell University. His writings include *The Perception of the Visual World* and a study (in progress) of the senses considered as avenues of knowledge.

SIGFRIED GIEDION, born in 1894, Switzerland, has taught at the Swiss Federal Institute of Technology (Zurich) and is currently professor in the School of Design at Harvard University. His writings include *Space, Time and Architecture* and *Mechanization Takes Command.*

E. H. GOMBRICH, born in 1909, Vienna, is director of the Warburg Institute at the University of London. His many publications on the history and psychology of art include *The Story of Art* and *Art and Illusion.*

Juan Gris, born in 1887, Madrid, died in 1927, Boulogne-sur-Seine, was a painter and lithographer as well as designer of décors and costumes for Diaghilev. He is regarded as the clearest and most consistent of the cubists, whose work is at the same time lyrical.

Walter Gropius, born in 1883, Berlin, architect and founder of the Bauhaus School at Dessau. A voluntary exile from Germany (1934), he came to the School of Architecture at Harvard University in 1938, and is now professor emeritus. He has exerted wide influence through his achievements in architecture as well as in his many writings, such as *The Bauhaus* and *Rebuilding Our Communities*.

Jean Hélion, born in 1904, Couterne, France, painter and lithographer, was early a member of the "Abstraction-Création" group, but in recent years has returned to figurative painting. He now lives in Paris.

Wassily Kandinsky, born in 1886, Moscow, died in 1944, Neuilly-sur-Seine, a founder of the Blue Rider group, taught at the Bauhaus (1922-1933). He has had a major influence in developing the idioms of modern art, both through his painting and his writings, such as *The Art of Spiritual Harmony; Point and Line to Plane;* and *Essays über Kunst und Künstler*.

Boris Kaufman, born in Russia, entered cinematography in France in 1928. Since 1942 he has lived in New York. He did the camera work on such films as "Seine"; "A propos de Nice"; Zéro de Conduite"; "L'Atalante"; "On the Waterfront"; "Crowded Paradise"; "Patterns"; "Baby Doll"; "Twelve Angry Men"; and "That Kind of Woman."

Gyorgy Kepes, born in 1906, Selyp, Hungary, painter and designer, worked in Berlin and London on film, stage, and exhibition design (1930-1936). In 1937 he came to the United States to head the Light and Color Department at the Institute of Design in Chicago. Since 1946 he has been professor of visual design at the Massachussetts Institute of Technology. His writings include: *Language in Vision* and *The New Landscape in Art and Science*.

Paul Klee, born in 1879, Berne, died in 1940, Muralto, Switzerland, a founder of the Blue Rider group of artists and a teacher at the Bauhaus, wrote in his journal what became his epitaph, "I cannot be understood in purely earthly terms. For I can live as happily with the dead as with the unborn. Somewhat nearer to the heart of creation than is usual. But still far from being enough."

Oskar Kokoschka, born in 1886, Pöchlarn, Austria, painter, graphic artist, sculptor, and poet, was an early pioneer in the expressionist movement. Always a major innovator, he is known for his portraits as well as for his landscapes. He resides in Villeneuve, Switzerland.

Suzanne K. Langer, born in 1895, New York City, is professor of philosophy at Connecticut College. Among her books are: *The Practice of Philosophy; Introduction to Symbolic Logic; Philosophy in a New Key; Feeling and Form;* and *Problems in Art*.

Charles-Edouard Le Corbusier, born in 1887, Chaux-de-Fonds, Switzerland, architect, painter, and writer, has pioneered in finding contemporary forms of architecture. His books include: *Vers une architecture; Quand les cathédrales étaient blanches; Le Modulor.*

FERNAND LÉGER, born in 1881, Argentau, France, died in 1955, near Paris, gave a robust expression of the mechanized environment of the twentieth century not only in his paintings, but also in ceramics, mosaics, tapestries, murals, film, décors, and costumes for the ballet.

RICHARD LIPPOLD, born in 1915, Milwaukee, sculptor of the younger generation, has taught at Hunter College since 1952. His work is often used in architectural ensembles.

MARGARET MEAD, born in 1912, Philadelphia, has been associate curator of the American Museum of Natural History since 1942, and professor of anthropology at Columbia University since 1954. Her books include: *Coming of Age in Samoa; Male and Female;* and *New Lives for Old.*

JOAN MIRÓ, born in 1893, Montroig, Catalonia, Spain, is a painter, engraver, designer, and sculptor. Though he was associated with the surrealist, cubist, and dadaist movements, he remains unclassifiable and inimitable.

PIET MONDRIAN, born in 1872, Amersfoort, Holland, died in 1944, New York City, has served through his painting and his writings as a main catalyst in the modern scene. With Theo van Doesburg he founded *De Stijl* (1917), and in his *Neo-plasticism* (1920) he set forth his theory of "relationship" in art.

WALTER NETSCH, born in 1920, Chicago, one of the younger generation of architects, has been codesigner of several important contemporary structures in the United States and the Far East.

JOSÉ ORTEGA Y GASSET, born in 1883, Madrid, died in 1955, Madrid, philosopher, writer, statesman, is perhaps best known for his *Revolt of the Masses.* Founder of the *Revista del Occidente* and the liberal newspaper *El Sol,* he went into voluntary exile after the Spanish Civil War until the end of World War II.

PAUL RAND, born in 1914, New York City, typographer and designer, is the author of *Thoughts on Design* and *Typography in the United States,* as well as other contributions to technical literature.

IRENE RICE PEREIRA, born in 1907, Boston, is an artist interested in transparency and light effects. Her many publications include *Light and the New Reality* (1952).

THEODORE ROSZAK, born in 1907, Poland, sculptor in welded and hammered steel, has exhibited regularly in the United States and abroad. Since 1941 he has taught at Sarah Lawrence College.

W. J. H. B. SANDBERG, born in 1897, Amersfoort, Holland, has been director of the Stedelijk Museum in Amsterdam since 1947. Early a painter and designer, he has held many consultative and directorial posts.

EDUARD F. SEKLER, born in 1920, Vienna, architect, teaches the history and theory of architecture at Harvard University. He is especially concerned with problems of historic cities in transition and with the concept of urbanism. His publications include a book on Sir Christopher Wren (1956).

JOSÉ LUIS SERT, born in 1902, Barcelona, is professor of architecture and dean of the Faculty of Design at Harvard University. The designer of many buildings in Europe as well as in North and South America, he is also the author of *Can Our Cities Survive?*; *The Heart of the City*; *The Shape of the City* (the latter two with J. Tyrwhitt); and a study of Antoni Gaudí y Cornet (in progress).

BEN SHAHN, born in 1898, Kovno, Lithuania, painter, muralist, designer, illustrator, and teacher of art, is also author of *The Shape of Content*, the Charles Eliot Norton lectures at Harvard University, 1956-1957.

PIERRE SOULAGES, born in 1919, Rodez, France, is one of the early exponents of the *tachiste* movement in painting. He has also done the décors and costumes for several theatrical productions. Since 1946 he has lived in Paris.

ANDREAS SPEISER, born in 1885, Basel, was for many years professor of mathematics, first at the University of Zurich, then at the University of Basel. Among his publications are: *Theorie der Gruppen*; *Ein Parmenides-Kommentar*; *Die mathematische Denkweise*; *Elemente der Philosophie und der Mathematik*.

EDWARD STEICHEN, born in 1879, Luxembourg, photographer, artist, plant breeder, has been a major force in the development of American photography. His *Family of Man* has been recently shown in Russia. He is director of photography at the Museum of Modern Art.

SAUL STEINBERG, born in 1914, Ramnic-Sarat, Rumania, once a practicing architect, is a satirist of the present-day scene. Collections of his drawings have been published in *All in Line*; *The Art of Living*; and *The Passport*.

VINCENT VAN GOGH, born in 1853, Groot-Zundert, Brabant, Holland, died in 1890, Auvers-sur-Oise, France, wrote to his brother Theo in July 1880 a letter in which he turned his back on repeated failures, to devote himself to painting. The passage quoted in this issue is from that letter.

PAUL WEISS, born in 1898, Vienna, head of the laboratory for developmental biology of the Rockefeller Institute for Medical Research, has held important posts in research organizations and on the faculties of American universities.

RUDOLF WITTKOWER, born in 1901, Berlin, is professor of fine arts at Columbia University. Earlier he was a member of the Warburg Institute and professor of the history of art at University College. His publications include *Art and Architecture in Italy, 1600 to 1750*.

Date Due